HOW TO ACHIEVE YOUR QTS

A GUIDE FOR STUDENTS

Edited by

NEIL DENBY

SAGE

Los Angeles • London • New Delhi • Singapore

First published 2008

SAGE Publications Ltd
1 Oliver's Yard
55 City Road
London EC1Y 1SP

SAGE Publications Inc.
2455 Teller Road
Thousand Oaks, California 91320

SAGE Publications India Pvt Ltd
B1/11 Mohan Cooperative Industrial Area
Mathura Road
New Delhi 110 044

SAGE Publications Asia-Pacific Pvt Ltd
33 Pekin Street #02-01
Far East Square
Singapore 048763

Library of Congress Control Number: 2008920790

British Library Cataloguing in Publication data

A catalogue record for this book is available from the British Library

ISBN 978–1–84787–284–5
ISBN 978–1–84787–285–2 (pbk)

Typeset by C&M Digitals (P) Ltd., Chennai, India
Printed in Great Britain by TJ International, Padstow
Printed on paper from sustainable resources

CONTENTS

The companion website for this book includes:

- *Instructor's manual*
- *Support by chapter*
- *Exam resources*
- *Additional resources*
- *Online readings*

NOTES ON CONTRIBUTORS

Robert Butroyd is a Teacher Educator with 16 years' experience. Prior to this he taught Economics and Business Education in secondary schools for 14 years, including schools in the West Midlands, Yorkshire and Galloway. His current research interests include teachers' occupational experiences and pupil disengagement.

Roger Crawford is a Senior Lecturer in Education and a member of the Institute of Educational Assessors. His background is as a systems analyst/computer programmer in commercial companies in London and New Zealand. He has been a Chief Examiner for GCSE for over 18 years and also an Ofsted inspector. He has considerable experience as a teacher in multicultural, urban secondary schools in the UK, New Zealand and Australia. Publications include textbooks and resources for teaching and learning covering GCSE and Functional Skills along with academic articles in practitioner publications and journals. He has also written on the management of ICT in secondary schools. For more information see http://www.hud.ac.uk/ITsec/rac1.htm.

Matthew Crowther is Key Stage 3 Manager and teacher of Business and ICT at Rastrick High School, a large comprehensive school in Brighouse, West Yorkshire, in the North of England. He has a background in industry and is currently in his fourth year of teaching. He also has responsibility as a teacher training subject mentor in Business Studies.

Neil Denby has been involved in teacher education for over 10 years. An experienced and successful author, he has written over two dozen texts at various levels from GCSE to post-graduate. He is a Senior Lecturer in Education at the University of Huddersfield and Partnership Co-ordinator for PGCE Schools. Research interests include using the abilities of gifted and talented students to enhance the learning experience and the training and certification of teachers in Citizenship at Masters Level.

Jonathan Glazzard is a Senior Lecturer in Education at the University of Huddersfield. He has worked in primary schools and has experience of teaching across the Foundation Stage and Key Stages 1 and 2. He now coordinates the primary education provision at the university and is actively involved in research in special and inclusive education.

John McComish has worked in education for 30 years and has taught Science subjects and Information Technology (under a number of subject titles) since early in his career. He has taught at the University of Huddersfield on the PGCE, BEd and Masters courses in Education since 1999. He currently carries out research into ICT issues in education and supervises doctoral students working in this area.

Joanne Pearson is a Senior Lecturer in History Education and lectures on the professional development programme and the primary education course. She is currently the Yorkshire and Lincolnshire advisor for the new History National Curriculum at Key Stage 3 and has worked in a range of secondary schools in the North of England.

Lesley-Anne Pearson is Course Leader PGCE/BEd for the Secondary Initial Teacher Education course and a Music Education tutor at the University of Huddersfield. Her main research interests include the transition between Key Stage 2 and Key Stage 3 in music – issues of provision, resourcing and teaching; the assessment and mentoring of students; the use of ICT in music at Key Stage 3; music and the deaf. She is on the Board of Directors for 'Music and the Deaf'.

Jayne Price taught for 15 years and was Head of Music and Continuing Professional Development Manager in an inner-city secondary school in Leeds before becoming involved in teacher training at Huddersfield in 2003. She is now Subject Coordinator for the PGCE Music course.

Ian Quigley is Assistant Headteacher at Sowerby Bridge High School in West Yorkshire, where he is responsible for Curriculum and Assessment. He has been the Professional Mentor to ITE students for many years. His enthusiasm for statistical data and support of Burnley FC should not be held against him.

Rod Robertson is a Senior Lecturer in the School of Education at the University of Huddersfield. He worked for 16 years in secondary schools as a head of department and head of faculty. His main interest is leadership/management in secondary schools, in particular the relationship between middle teacher/leaders and teachers.

Helen Swift is the Head of Continuing Professional Development and Course Leader for the MA in Professional Development in the School of Education at the University of

Huddersfield. Previously she taught in a variety of school and college settings. Her research interest is in the impact of continuing professional development (MA) on institutions, teachers and pupils.

John Trafford is Head of the Department of Initial Teacher Education and Continuing Professional Development at the University of Huddersfield. Prior to this he was a secondary school French and German teacher, then languages tutor and PGCE course director at the University of Sheffield. He is a former president of the Association for Language Learning.

Fiona Woodhouse is presently the Science and Admissions Tutor for the PGCE course at Huddersfield University. She has taught predominately Science in schools for 15 years and had a variety of responsibilities before moving into initial teacher education. Her main interests are the selection of candidates for PGCE courses and the science subject pedagogy.

Mick Woodhouse is the Head of Sixth Form at Rhodesway School in Bradford. He has been teaching for nearly 30 years in which time he has taught several subjects, predominately PE and Business Studies. He has held several management roles from head of careers to senior management. His main interest is in educational management.

FOREWORD

Everyone has a view on education; we've all been to school, so we are a nation of self-styled experts, always ready with advice and criticism. In reality teaching is a tough, challenging, complicated job and society demands more from its teachers than ever before. The environment has changed: we aim to send fifty 50 per cent of young people into higher education, demand better and better examination results and yet teachers are now responsible for so much more than the delivery of subject-specialist teaching. They have to be multi-skilled and must fulfil many roles at once. They must be expert in their subjects, but also in their understanding of current legislation, information technology, relationship building and partnership working with other professionals. They have to be managers of the media, learning innovators and experts in tailoring learning to the needs of each and every individual. This is all happening in a society that is less deferential, and more questioning and demanding, where children and parents may resist as well as cooperate and the management of out-of-school relationships is vital.

Teachers need training that reflects all of this and the authors of this book have shown how the new standards in teacher training ensure that the next generation of teachers can meet the challenge. Each chapter addresses aspects of the new standards, and in doing so the book sets out all of the elements which contribute towards being a good teacher and shows the novice what each of these elements means and how they fit together in practice.

In Part 1, Professional Attributes, the authors discuss the all important question of relationships with children and young people, but also focus on partnerships. The importance of partnership working both within the school setting and with the wider professional network involved in supporting children and families is emphasised. Promoting health and well-being for all children in a school community cannot be achieved even by the best co-ordination of effort solely within the confines of the school. It is important that teachers take the trouble to understand the contributions of different professionals within the childcare field and develop their own skills of collaboration. Increasingly, virtual teams of people are involved in working together to support children. This responsibility does not rest solely with special educational needs coordinators and named professionals in child protection but is the shared responsibility of all teachers and staff in schools.

In Part 2, the focus is on the classroom and the organisation of learning, and the book incorporates valuable information about the way young people learn, behaviour management, planning for learning and assessment. This is the essential knowledge needed to succeed in the day-to-day management of the classroom, ensuring good quality learning for all the young people for whom you have been given responsibility. There is an emphasis on inclusivity and personalised learning and this of course links back to the importance of partnerships. Satisfying the particular needs of vulnerable children, children with special needs and children with additional needs relies heavily upon collaboration. Schools are now able to support children in mainstream education with a wide variety of complex needs. This requires a sophisticated understanding of not only the needs of those children but the types of support that are available to them. We have seen in recent years an increasing ability for mainstream schools to include children of all abilities. With the right support we see such children thriving and also benefiting from the lessening of stigma associated with disability or special needs. We also see all children in the school gaining an understanding and tolerance of difference which equips them to be more thoughtful and compassionate adults in society.

In Part 3, the authors outline a range of essential information about current policy and legislation and important initiatives. From the beginning the new teacher needs to understand the examination system, major curricular issues and the importance of evaluation and ICT. This section outlines the implications of wider policy for day-to-day practice. Good teachers and good schools have always seen the child in the context of their family and wider community and used that understanding to tailor their teaching to how that individual child can best learn. So in a sense there is nothing new in some of today's ideas arising from the Every Child Matters agenda and the personalisation of learning. But never before have the frameworks and expectations been so clear. Never before have teachers been so held to account to deliver attainment and achievement for children but also to promote their social and emotional well-being. The focus in this section on the Every Child Matters agenda is important for this reason, but also permeates the book as a whole.

While it is the case that teaching has become technically demanding with more measurement and evaluation than ever before, at the heart of being a good teacher is a fundamental enjoyment of children and a liking for them. The personal qualities of empathy and valuing and respecting children and young people underpin the profession. To be a good teacher you give a lot of yourself. This requires a well developed sense of who you are and what drives you and a sophisticated understanding of your own personal values and behaviours. A good teacher knows how others see them and has a wide repertoire of communication and engagement skills which enable them to inspire others.

Teaching is undoubtedly most challenging work but also carries great rewards. Sometimes this may be recognised and appreciated, as it is by the many who acknowledge the teacher who motivated or inspired them in some way. But good teachers often work very subtly, helping others to achieve for themselves, so that they are hardly aware of the role the teacher has played in their success. The emphasis on planning, partnership and individual learning set out in this book will help the next generation of teachers ensure that the next generation of children experience that sense of achievement and success that will enable them to go on to make the most of life's opportunities.

Alison O' Sullivan and Christine Jarvis

CHAPTER 1

QUALIFYING TO TEACH : AN INTRODUCTION

Neil Denby

Welcome to the teaching profession and the start of your journey to gain your Qualified Teacher Status (usually just referred to as QTS). By now you have probably chosen to teach either primary or secondary, probably intend to teach in England or Wales, and already know in what subject you will specialise. You may already have a degree and be intending to use this to teach a specialist subject; alternatively, you may be taking an undergraduate degree in Education.

You have recognised that the rewards of teaching far outweigh the hard work and effort that goes into training and into becoming an effective classroom practitioner. More than that, though, you have also accepted that you are about to set out on a life-long journey of learning and discovery. You will have recognised that, as individuals, we never stop learning, but that as young people, we need to be equipped with the skills and competencies to enable learning to take place. You should also know that you will be entering one of the most hard-working, dedicated and rewarding professions.

There are over 40,000 teacher trainees per year, spread over higher education institutions (HEIs) such as universities and teacher training colleges, employment-based routes, 'SCiTTs' (School-based Initial Teacher Training) and Teach First (based in challenging schools in London and Manchester), and GTPs (Graduate Teacher Programmes) and RTPs (Registered Teacher Programmes). Intending teachers can choose the route that is most appropriate to their own needs, circumstances and experience.

This book is designed to be of use to anyone either contemplating teaching or who has already joined a teacher training course. It will also be of value to those on post-compulsory (16+) courses. It is designed and written to give you an overview of requirements for each standard, and to point you towards specific further reading, reflection, study and practice. Appropriate reference is made to underpinning theory, and features are used to link this to practical applications in the classroom and generic areas of professional studies.

Features

Each chapter is linked directly to one or more of the new standards. However, this does not stop any appropriate standard being referred to in any chapter, or the information in any chapter being used to support an appropriate standard. The standards flagged refer merely to the focus of that chapter. You will find that some concepts, ideas and policies are so important that they are mentioned in many different contexts. Every Child Matters, for example, has its own chapter, but cannot be avoided in several other important areas. Each of the boxed features you will find in every chapter has a specific function or purpose. At the end of the chapter, there is a bullet-pointed summary to help you remember and apply what you have learned. The group exercise is an idea for an activity or discussion that can take place during university or college-based learning sessions or can be adapted for use by those of you who are on non-HEI-based training routes. The individual reflection is a prompt for you to think about your own practice and progress, and how you can improve. There is a short list of focused, key reading – in general reduced to particular articles, webpages or chapters of books to make it manageable, but a full list of references is also provided. The application to teaching is a suggestion for a lesson plan or technique that will help you to underpin the particular standard or standards that are the focus of the chapter. In each chapter there are also several 'thoughts'. These are tips, ideas or thought-provokers to encourage thought and reflection on your part.

What is QTS?

Qualified teacher status is the accreditation that enables you to teach in state-maintained and special schools in England and Wales. Your initial teacher training (ITT) provider recommends you for this status; the Training and Development Agency (TDA) awards it. To gain accreditation you must follow a course of initial teacher training and meet all of the standards as set out by the TDA. These standards are a set of statements that set out, in a formal way, the knowledge, understanding, skills and experiences that you must demonstrate. The QTS Standards have been rewritten to provide the first stage in a continuum of teacher development from trainee to qualified teacher status (on successful completion of the induction year) through to excellent and advanced skills teachers. They are published under three headings:

- **Professional values and practice**. These outline the attitudes and commitment expected of anyone qualifying to be a teacher. Fairness, honesty, integrity and mutual respect feature highly.
- **Knowledge and understanding**. These detail required levels of subject knowledge from the teacher, along with expectations of what pupils should achieve.
- **Teaching**. These relate to the skill set needed to deliver effective lessons such as managing a class, assessment and monitoring progress. QTS standards in Wales are similar but cover some issues specific to Wales. In addition, in order to teach in England, you must pass the QTS skills tests in numeracy, literacy and information and communications technology (ICT).

You will also become a member of the General Teaching Council for England (GTCE), the independent professional and regulatory body for teaching in England. From September 2008, provisional registration with this body will be automatic, via your ITT provider.

Primary or secondary?

Compulsory schooling in England and Wales is divided into four key stages, sandwiched between pre-school learning and post-16. You will train to teach at least two key stages. The stages are:

- Age 0–3: Pre-school
- Age 3–6 – Years 1, 2, 3: Key Stage 1
- Age 6–11 – Years 3, 4, 5, 6: Key Stage 2
- Age 11–14 – Years 7, 8, 9: Key Stage 3
- Age 14–16 – Years 10 and 11: Key Stage 4
- Age 16–19 – Post-16: Years 12 and 13: sixth form or post-compulsory education.

The role and importance of your subject specialism is greater at secondary level than at primary. At primary your 'specialism' is the core curriculum.

To teach primary at Key Stage 1 or 2 you will train to teach all the national curriculum subjects – the core of English, mathematics and science, plus the eight foundation subjects. You are expected to have a good knowledge of all subjects. (The only exception to this 'general' rule is modern foreign languages. Because every Key Stage 2 pupil in England is entitled to study a foreign language it is possible to train as a primary teacher specialising in languages.) The teaching and learning emphasis is therefore on a range of subjects, but to a level appropriate for children of this age group.

At secondary (Key Stage 3, 4 and Post-16) you will be expected to be a subject specialist, in a national curriculum subject or an accepted non-national curriculum subject such as Business Education, in which you have an appropriate and relevant degree. In some subjects, where there are shortages of teachers, you can undertake an enhancement course to improve your subject knowledge to the required level. These are currently available in physics, mathematics and chemistry. Details of all courses, requirements and training routes can be found on the TDA website at www.tda.gov.uk/.

A thought

If you are teaching secondary, go and watch a primary teacher at work. You will be amazed at their energy, ingenuity and enthusiasm. Of course, the opposite case holds if you are training at primary level!

Application to teaching

When introducing yourself to a new class it is essential that you learn names. Children and young people respond much more readily when spoken to by name. You could make this part of a game or exercise, supply labels, or make learners state their name before answering a question. A seating plan will also help you to remember.

The reflective practitioner

You are entering a profession where lifelong learning is an expectation. Innovation and experimentation will always be a part of your working life. This is just one reason why the skills you will gain in the classroom and through your study should be augmented by further professional development. You will find that you go through a number of stages on your way to becoming a confident classroom practitioner. Fuller (1969) suggests a three-stage model of teacher training. Initially, the trainee has a concern about 'self' – how am I doing? how will I cope? what will the kids think of me? Secondly, a concern about tasks is developed – how are my lesson plans? have I prepared enough material? what about my marking? Finally, the focus turns to the learners, first as a class, then as individual learners – how well is so-and-so doing?

what extra materials might help? how can I explain this more clearly? Each stage of this development requires you to reflect on your progress, i.e. to think about the journey, where you are, where you want to be and what is going to take you to the next stage. As one who delivers education, you are a practitioner; as one who considers how they can improve and move forward, how they can learn from their own and others' experience, you are reflective. Your goal is therefore to be a reflective practitioner.

G R O U P   E X E R C I S E

Consider Fuller's three stages of trainee teacher development. Talk about these with a qualified teacher in post and see if they agree with the stages. Discuss the intermediate stages that might also take place and how you could manage them.

Reading and writing

In order to progress and reflect, you must read extensively. While each chapter will introduce you to some key texts, you will need to find others for yourself. Should you find an area particularly useful or interesting, use your library service to find out more about it. A good starting point is often the list of references that the writer of a chapter, article or book has themselves cited. As with any 'social science' education has its different theorists who may not agree with one another. You need to consider what each is saying and how it applies to your own set of circumstances before making your own judgement as to which theorist you feel is correct. In time you will develop your own theories and methods that are particular to your, and your learners', needs.

You will be expected to write at a reasonably high level. On many teacher training routes you will not only have the opportunity but be positively encouraged to write at Masters level. You will find this (and subsequent professional development) easier if you are used to reading widely. More detail on this is in Chapter 7.

Some things of which you should be aware!

There are several features which single out education and training from other professions. You will encounter many of these within the pages of this book. Three key areas are particularly apposite to education: external factors, change as the norm and the use of specialised terminology and acronyms.

External factors

Unlike other professions where the professional can often take the lofty position that s/he is the expert, in education everyone is an expert. All have been to school and therefore all have an opinion on some aspect or other of education. You must learn to take this in your stride and not be put off by the many times a parent, governor or friend will tell you that 'this is how it should be done' or 'this is what really works' or the even more traditional 'in my day'. Ignore them. You are doing the best possible job for these young people, in this situation, here and now.

Your effectiveness will also increase or decrease in relation to the circumstances in which you are teaching. Social and economic circumstances, for example, may have a huge effect on a child's ability to learn and their ultimate attainment. Recently published research (Blanden and Machin 2007) suggests that social class is still the most powerful influence on educational attainment, even to degree level. Forty-four per cent of the richest fifth of the population have degrees, compared with just 10 per cent of the poorest fifth. The authors of this Sutton Trust report state that both attainment and behaviour are affected by social class, and movement from one class to another has slowed to a standstill since 1970.

A thought

How important do you think social and economic circumstances are to educational attainment? What other external factors do you think might be important? How could you mitigate their effects?

Change as the norm

There is never a moment when there is not some change being proposed, implemented, monitored, measured or assessed. As this book was being written, the Secretary of State Ed Balls contacted all state schools to tell them of the current bout of changes. These include:

- the new Secondary National Curriculum published in July 2007 for implementation in September 2008, with new programmes of study designed to give teachers a less prescriptive, more flexible framework for teaching, creating more scope to tailor the curriculum to meet the needs of individual learners;
- the new A Levels produced for 2008 with a reduction in the number of units of assessment from six to four to encourage greater depth of understanding and to reduce the assessment burden;
- an A* grade introduced to the grading of A Level for those who score 90 per cent or more on the uniform mark scale across their A2 units;

- the new A Level extended project being introduced as a separate qualification that students may add to their programme. Projects will involve planning, research and evaluation, and their outcome may be a dissertation, the findings of an investigation or field study, a performance or an artefact. This is designed to develop research skills and independent learning skills.

INDIVIDUAL REFLECTION

Which of the three sets of changes described here is likely to have the most effect on your teaching? Think about how you can alter your teaching to take this into account.

As the book goes to press there will be new diploma courses at 14–19, there will be new GCSE courses, written to new subject criteria, economic well-being (personal finance) will have become part of PSHE and a cross-curricular theme (again), coursework for 16–19 year olds will be either on or off the menu. The 'Children's Plan', in whatever form it ends up, will have been launched. This is a long-term vision to improve schools and produce a step-change in the way parents and families are supported to deal with the new challenges faced by young people in the twenty-first century. It encourages the development of 'world-class' schools, the greater involvement of parents and a greater emphasis on activities for children, including sport and play.

It proposes 'a root and branch review of the primary level curriculum to ease the transition from early years into school, to create an even sharper focus on mathematics and English ... Sir Jim Rose, whose groundbreaking review placed the teaching of synthetic phonics as the key to literacy, will lead the review' (DFCF Press Release, December 2007).

Even the fabric of education changes. For example, it is proposed that new (and existing) schools will combine child health services, social care, advice, welfare services and police where possible on the same site. Specifically with regard to educational attainment, 90 per cent of children will be expected to develop well across all areas of the Early Years Foundation Stage profile by age 5, 90 per cent of children should reach or exceed expected levels in English and mathematics by age 11, 90 per cent should achieve the equivalent of five higher level GCSEs by age 19 (with 70 per cent achieving at least two A levels or equivalent) while every young person will have the skills for adult life and further study.

Terminology

'Children and young people' is now the preferred nomenclature for pupils or any young person in an educational setting. In this book, to save using the entire 'children and young people' phrase at every turn, we tend to use it sometimes, but at others to refer to 'pupils', 'children', 'young people', 'students' or even 'learners'. You can presume that these terms are interchangeable. Trainee teachers are generally referred to as 'trainees', although the book addresses the reader directly whenever possible. Teachers are also referred to as 'practitioners'.

You will find that education is rife with 'TLAs' – no, not teaching and learning assistants (although they are, of course, TLAs), but Three Letter Acronyms. Examples include AQA, HMI, CPD, QTS, QCA, ICT and ZPD along with other codes such as 'Key Stage 3', 'Key Stage 4' and 'Early Years'. If someone uses one of these, whether it is at a meeting, on your placement or during taught sessions, they will be using it in the expectation that everyone in the audience recognises and understands it. This is seldom the case. If you are the one that doesn't know what the acronym stands for, don't be afraid to ask. Often you will find that you are one of many who did not know, as new terms are coined almost on a daily basis. There is a list of some of the terms in most widespread use in the appendix at the back of the book, along with space for you to add others as they are invented.

And the reason you are taking up teaching?

You will remember what it was all about when Shawn (*sic*), Kylii (*sic*) or Leeza (*sic*) (for it will be they) come up to you on the last day of term and say 'Thanks, Sir', 'Thanks, Miss'; when you have sweated over a trip, through the minefield of health and safety, travel sickness and the emotional trauma of being more than five miles from home and the last kid off the bus, in the dark, says 'That was great, Miss, I've never seen anything like that before, can we go again?'; when the examination results are published and your quiet pleasure is greater in the D grade that your 'failing' student achieved rather than the A grade that your top student gained. As teachers, we all have the potential to have a huge influence on the lives and outlooks of all of those that we teach. If we have been effective, we will loom large in their memories; if we've been fair, we'll be remembered with respect, if we've been kind, or humorous, we'll be remembered with affection.

Pupils will come up to you years later and say 'Hi Sir, remember me?'

Summary

- Qualified teacher status is the accreditation that enables you to teach in state-maintained and special schools in England and Wales.
- The QTS Standards are a set of statements that set out, in a formal way, the knowledge, understanding, skills and experiences that you must demonstrate to become a qualified teacher.

- The QTS Standards are published under the three headings of professional values and practice, knowledge and understanding and teaching.

- You will train to teach at least two key stages.

- You will aim to become a reflective practitioner and a lifelong learner.

- You are entering a profession where, in spite of numerous external factors, you have the power to change young people's lives.

Key reading

www.tda.gov.uk/ The Standards for Qualified Teacher Status

References and bibliography

Blanden, J. and Machin, S. (2007) *Recent changes in intergenerational mobility in Britain*. London: Sutton Trust.

Fuller, F. (1969). 'Concerns of teachers: a developmental conceptualization.' *American Educational Research Journal*, 6, 207–226

www.tda.gov.uk/ The Standards for Qualified Teacher Status

Part 1
PROFESSIONAL ATTRIBUTES

CHAPTER 2

RELATIONSHIPS WITH CHILDREN AND YOUNG PEOPLE

Robert Butroyd

Standards addressed

Q1 Have high expectations of children and young people including a commitment to ensuring that they can achieve their full educational potential and to establishing fair, respectful, trusting, supportive and constructive relationships with them

Q2 Demonstrate the positive values, attitudes and behaviour they expect from children and young people

Introduction

Pupils observe teachers, even when they are off guard. Whether they like it or not pupils learn from the ways in which teachers carry out their role, how they behave towards them and towards other adults. This does not necessarily mean that teachers have to conform to a model. New teachers may struggle with the idea of being a role model and can still be successful. Others, with the confidence of experience, are more relaxed about their role and are nonetheless successful for it. Teachers need not lead the lives of saints – indeed if they imply that they do then many pupils are lost to them. Pupils and teachers need to develop an awareness of 'audience' and 'appropriate' behaviour. This chapter will start you on your way to developing the values, attitudes and behaviour that will encourage children to achieve their full educational potential.

Context

The Education and Inspections Act 2006 requires schools to promote children's well-being. The notion of well-being is underpinned by an exploration of values: being healthy; staying safe; enjoying and achieving; making a positive contribution; achieving economic well-being. These values form the outcomes for Every Child Matters. Values infuse schooling. They are evident in the curriculum, the organisation of the school day, the selection of teaching materials, methods and lesson content. This might be termed the hidden curriculum. This chapter focuses upon another aspect of this curriculum: teachers and their relationships. These relationships can on occasions be difficult, particularly with pupils. Pupils are perhaps wise to be wary of teachers who are felt to 'pry' too much into what they really think, if those teachers are responsible for assessment and discipline and can compel pupils to work in groups, speak in public or conform to other forms of social behaviour. While pupils view teacher motives with a certain degree of scepticism, they want relationships of integrity, relationships where teachers listen and respond to pupil interests and motivations.

Communities

Teachers do not operate in a vacuum. Many schools can draw upon communities that are sympathetic to education. Others draw upon communities that do not appear particularly sympathetic to the aims of education. In these circumstances where those little things which attempt to create a unity of identity – specific rules of personal appearance, restricted access to parts of the building, pronouncements in assembly – can become negative influences on the experiences of those pupils who are not acknowledged as academically successful, and these pupils can become resentful of school and the teacher.

As teachers, you should strive to maintain your own approach, to maintain your integrity, but it can be a struggle. It is not intolerance to difference; it is more self-censorship. Ofsted, parental views, management teams, colleagues, syllabus constraints and poor resources are often cited as reasons for an inability to explore different pedagogies and different approaches to relationships.

Intellectual challenge

Pupils, like teachers, wish for relationships that are comfortable in an environment that is positive. An exploration of values in education raises fundamental questions about the curriculum, pedagogy and relationships. This can be a cause of insecurity for teachers and pupils alike. Exploration of these issues needs to focus upon improvements to teaching and learning, and to take place in circumstances that are supportive and non-threatening.

Teaching is often about compromise, full of dilemmas created by the tension between the intentions of the teacher and the demands of the school. This is one of the things that makes teaching intellectually challenging, and rewarding. The concept of the teacher as role model, the nature of friendship and the impact of school rules on teaching are indicative of some of these dilemmas. These ideas are discussed below with examples from two secondary schools (Butroyd and Somekh 1999).

A thought

What about the teacher who sends out mixed messages? For example, the teacher who promotes safety but drives into the car park too fast, or who can be seen by the pupils as s/he takes a smoke outside the school gates? Is your life as a person (social or otherwise) more important than your professional role? In this context, think about the advantages and disadvantages of living within the school catchment area.

Teacher as role model?

Barry had just become head of English in Churchschool, after 30 years' experience. Barry saw himself as unconventional with strong opinions.

… role model is nonsense as far as I'm concerned. Do your job. Certainly don't think in those terms. Do the job. It is a presumption. If I'm an organ player and play the organ I don't come out and say well did you like that change from F sharp to G minor, and shall we do something different next week? You just play the organ.

His approach was to be his 'natural self' even to the extent of using language that some might consider inappropriate in a classroom. When asked about this he said that he had not considered it before, but that on reflection he felt that it created a type of 'intimacy' with the pupils and it prevented him sounding 'too pukka'. His pupils (whose names have been changed) had no difficulty with this and, indeed, were glad that Barry could be seen as a 'person'.

> **James**: … you feel he is more like you.
>
> **John**: I like him, he's a good teacher. Other teachers are more stuck up.
>
> **Mary**: He relates to you.
>
> **John**: He gets on the same level so that you can understand.

This approach contravenes all that young teachers are told about techniques that a teacher should employ, and Barry recognises this.

> I really cannot consider myself a proper teacher. I suppose that gets through. I mean that I am not credible myself as a proper teacher … somebody who has got the rhetoric and the solemnity that you expect. I can remember when I started teaching at school there were solemn rebukes that did the job. Nobody is frightened of me. I feel that you have got to have a few missiles to carry around to be a proper teacher and I haven't got any. I'm sort of naked in the conference chamber. (Laughter)

June, at Girlschool, was an English teacher of three years' experience who had a more conventional approach to the notion of the teacher as a role model.

> It is part of what you do. I also look at other teachers as role models. That is how people learn. I'm not sure that you always agree with them. You discard some bits and concentrate on the bits you like, and hopefully that is what the kids do as well. They get out what they like and discard what they don't.

June's pedagogical method was very different to the teacher-centred approach of Barry. In June's classroom the focus was upon the pupil. The class dealt with some very important ethical issues, mainly concerned with the nature of domestic violence. This required June to monitor effectively and to provide the appropriate framework and stimulus for learning. June's influence on her pupils was in terms of her organisation and the nature of her interventions.

> What sort of person do you think the teacher would like you to grow up to be?
>
> **Joanne**: A friendly and kind person because she is like that now.
>
> **Kate**:   Helpful, she likes to help you out when you are stuck with things.

Andy: She gets along with us all and she is nice, and she is supportive of people who do not understand the work as much. So, she would like us to be like, helpful.

According to June, pupils 'get out what they like and discard what they don't'. Pupils are active evaluators, not passive receivers of models. What are the implications for this in the way that, as teachers, you behave towards pupils and adults?

A thought

How do you think that you come across as a role model to your pupils? What sort of ethos do you think you are projecting? You could check this out with friends and colleagues to see if they agree with you!

Friendship?

Teachers often keep a deliberate distance between themselves and their pupils. However, an effective teacher needs to pursue quite deep and emotional issues. Colin, head of Science at Churchcomp, with 24 years of experience, looks back wistfully at the nature of the teacher–pupil relationship.

Q. What values underpin your lessons?

A. That might vary from group to group. I'm not quite sure, maybe friendship. Maybe friendship between children and adults is frowned on. … It should be friendly.

Relationships are complex, as in many walks of life. Colin talks tentatively about the nature of relationships and suggests that he hasn't really found an approach with which he is satisfied. Here, his pupils talk about teacher relationships in general and not specifically their relationship with Colin.

Q. When a teacher shouts at you what sort of effect does it have on you?

John: I think it's funny.

Q. Why?

John: I don't know, it's just funny when you see them lose their rag, and see them get right mad and uptight when it's over little things and you should have a laugh about it. But they get really mad and upset, and we don't understand why.

Q. Why is it funny?

John: Because we are only kids. When they were little they would have messed about as well, but they take it right serious if someone throws a rubber across [the] classroom or something like that. [I] just laugh.

Q.   Why do you think that teachers shout?

John: So we get on with our work and that we get good grades.

Kate: Because they think that it will teach us, but it doesn't. If they just said it politely and stuff like that.

John: Talked to us like friends.

Kate: Yeah.

Friendship implies a relationship of equals. Despite the best efforts of many teachers and pupils, their relationships are underpinned by the power of the teacher over the pupil. There are many disadvantages in this uneasy relationship. For example, it makes genuine exploration of the values of teachers, pupils, the school and the subject difficult. Is Colin unreasonable in wishing to have warmer relationships with his pupils? How does schooling intervene to make closer relationships more difficult?

> ### A thought
>
> As a person you will relate on various different levels depending on to whom you are relating. You will relate differently to friends, colleagues, family, peers, etc. Think about these different roles and their application to your teaching. Which of them can you safely take into the classroom? Which class? What sort of situation?

School rules

The intention of teachers to make pupils do things that they don't want to do can be a point of conflict. Barry, when asked if there was anything about school rules he did not like, had this to say:

A: Anything that gets in the way of getting the kids the best results, and most of them do. I know that they are not intended to, but the effects are, if you are going to give kids detention for chewing gum, for having their shirts out.

Q. For wearing the wrong coloured footwear?

A: Yes. It's an irrelevance to my concerns.

Barry expresses a controversial point of view. But it is also reflected by pupils, especially those in 'middle ability' groups, where a sense of frustration and grievance can be more apparent. Those for whom academic success was in the offing did not find school rules, and in particular school uniform, an issue. Pupils from another 'middle ability' group at Churchschool had strong views on school rules:

Q.   Some people think that they should be teaching you about right and wrong. Do you think that it is the place of the school to do that?

Marisa: Yeah, but we don't have rules like that, we just have 'don't carry coats in school, don't chew gum, don't wear earrings, don't wear make up.' It's totally irrelevant to the teaching.

Kerry: They're not positive things, they are negative things.

Q.   What do you mean by positive things?

Kerry: Well, they don't treat you level headedly. They look down on you.

Marisa: In assembly, like with one teacher it's all about what we are doing wrong, not about what we are doing right.

Jez: One teacher says, just like don't chew gum. They only have them so you like don't break bigger ones. They could say like 'don't take drugs,' but then you'll go out and do that and go onto bigger things. But if they have like stupid little ones like 'don't chew gum.' I know what I mean. (Laughter)

Q.   What sort of school rules would you like to see?

Kerry: A lot of encouragement.

For these pupils many of these smaller issues, such as dress, coats, gum, which some teachers argue can help in the smooth running of the school and create habits among pupils they think will help in later life, are viewed as negative intrusions that make little sense from the pupils' point of view other than to suggest the all powerful 'school'.

GROUP EXERCISE

In your group, or with colleagues, consider why those in the 'middle ability' groups may be more concerned with school uniform than other students. Do you think that Barry is right to talk of school uniform as an irrelevance? What do you think that pupils mean when they say they consider some school rules to be negative? What other examples can you list of 'negative' school rules (from your own experience or from your placement)? What examples can you give of positive school rules?

Theory

Intrinsic and instrumental values

Dewey (1966) offers some clarity in the area of values. He argues that educational values are often coincidental with educational aims. He makes a useful distinction between two types of educational value: intrinsic and instrumental values. This distinction between intrinsic values, which are ends in themselves, and instrumental values, which are means to ends, is an important one. Educational aims may have value, and may be revered for that reason. However, if they are instrumental values then the purpose of their inclusion in any curriculum, hidden or formal, may appear obscure and irrelevant if the end, the intrinsic value, is hidden behind an instrumental value. It is also important to recognise that a value is not inherently intrinsic or instrumental. As 'occasions present themselves' a value may move from one classification to another. For example, examination success may be an instrumental value, in that it enables a successful student to gain access through further study or employment to the work or lifestyle that offers (intrinsic) satisfaction. However, on achieving examination success that achievement may offer intrinsic value in itself. Whether a value is intrinsic or instrumental depends upon individual perception and the 'occasion'.

INDIVIDUAL REFLECTION

The bullet points below indicate a range of values teachers said they touched upon in a particular subject context. It is not possible to say that these values are explored in *all* classrooms, because this depends upon the relationship to pedagogy. For example, curiosity may remain an aim of the curriculum, but could remain untouched in the classroom. Equally, Science can be taught in a way that constantly helps pupils explore their own life circumstances, but this may not be in the syllabus. What is clear is that the potential for engagement with values in subject matter is enormous.

- **Illustrative values in science** – curiosity; exploration; cooperation; respect; learn about life; learn about the way things work; tolerance; reasoning; independence; questioning things that are taken for granted.
- **Illustrative values in English** – power of language; love of literature; pleasure in reading; tolerance; sympathy; understanding; anti-racism; discovery of the inner person; independence; developing potential; appreciation of different cultures; discussion of important issues; respect for individuals.

What do you think these values mean? Do you agree that they are likely to be evident in the teaching of Science and English? What values do you think are evident in the subject matter that you teach? Are they intrinsic to the subject? What role do you think you should have in exploring these values?

Multiple selves

Cairns (2000) points to the changing nature of values throughout a person's life. Context is therefore crucial to understanding values. An important question to consider is the relative importance of contexts, and whether the identity, or self, remains constant in each context. Life history research suggests that the context of other aspects of a teacher's life does impact upon the teacher's self-identity. So it is worth considering 'what else do I do?' and how this impacts on my role as a teacher. Layder (1994) refers to the work of Goffman and the way individuals distance themselves from their roles in order to reduce tension, and the way that individuals act out different roles in different aspects of their lives.

Substantial self – situational self

An understanding of the teacher's self-image is also an important factor in the knowledge and skills upon which teachers depend. Nias's (1989, 1996) work offers some insight into how teachers maintain and adapt their values. The substantial self 'comprises the most highly prized aspects of our self concept and the attitudes and values which are salient to them'. In new situations the values of the substantial self are protected through the development of the situational self, such as the individual's teacher identity or being in the teacher role.

Teacher's problematic

The theme of pupil resistance to what they see as unreasonable intrusions is evident in the writings of Woods (1979, 1980, 1990). He examines pupil behaviour and the strategies for coping that underpin it. He draws parallels between the behaviour of pupils and the behaviour of teachers. For example, he examines the use of laughter from the point of view of the teacher. Laughter can be used to control a situation, sometimes to subvert it and often to do both. He recognises that teachers can be drawn between two models of teacher: the bureaucrat and the person. Sachs and Smith (1988) refer to this as the teacher's problematic and recognise that the teacher is tempted to oscillate between both.

Summary

- Values permeate the curriculum, pedagogy, schooling and relationships.
- Values can be implicit or explicit, instrumental or intrinsic.
- As teachers we are not always aware of the values that we transmit.
- Pupils interpret values and are not simply passive receptors.
- We need to be aware of values and consider their impact.
- Values create dilemmas and these cannot always be resolved.
- Teachers have to make decisions taking into account tension between the demands of the school and their own intentions.

Key reading

Butroyd, R. (2007) 'Denial and distortion of instrumental and intrinsic value in the teaching of Science and English: its impact upon fifteen Year 10 teachers'. *Forum,* 49 (3), 313–329

Day, C., Kington, A., Stobart, G. and Sammons, P. (2006) 'The personal and professional lives of teachers: stable and unstable identities'. *British Educational Research Journal,* 32 (4), 601–616

Nias, J. (1996) 'Thinking about feeling: the emotions in teaching'. *Cambridge Journal of Education,* 26 (3), 293–306

Application to teaching

A useful exercise when first establishing yourself in a classroom is to have the pupils create a set of rules. In this way, you can generate discussion of what is positive and what is negative, have a good idea of what works and what doesn't, and allow the pupils to have ownership of the rules (a powerful tool). Small groups of pupils can devise five rules each. These are then shared with the rest of the class to form a master list. This list can then be put into order of priority and created as display material. You will be surprised at the amount of conformity and understanding of social norms even in quite young children. Older ones may take the opportunity to try to subvert school rules, but this can lead to a useful discussion. Beware (particularly with younger children) of their ideas of appropriate rewards and punishments. They can be particularly venal with rewards and vicious with punishments!

References and bibliography

Butroyd, R. and Somekh, B. (1999) *Research into values in secondary education,* Report to the Gordon Cook Foundation. University of Huddersfield

Cairns, J. (2000) 'Schools, community and the developing values of young adults: towards an ecology of education in values'. In Cairns, J., Gardiner, R. and Lawton, D. (eds) *Values and the curriculum.* London: Woburn Press, pp. 52–73

Cullingford, C. (1991) *The inner world of the school.* London: Cassell

Dewey, J. (1966) *Democracy in education.* New York: Free Press

Goodson, I.F. and Hargreaves, A. (1996) *Teachers' professional lives.* London: Falmer Press

Nias, J. (1989) *Primary teachers talking.* London: Routledge & Kegan Paul

Nias, J. (1996) 'Thinking about feeling: the emotions in teaching'. *Cambridge Journal of Education,* 26 (3), 293–306

Sachs, J. and Smith, R. (1988) 'Constructing teacher culture'. *British Journal of Sociology of Education,* 9 (4), 423–436

Woods, P. (1979) *The divided school.* London: Routledge & Kegan Paul

Woods, P. (ed.) (1980) 'Pupil strategies'. In *Explorations in the sociology of the school.* London: Croom Helm

Woods, P. (1990) *The happiest days? How pupils cope with school.* London: Falmer Press

CHAPTER 3

PROFESSIONALISM, THE PROFESSIONAL DUTIES OF TEACHERS AND LEGAL REQUIREMENTS

Mick Woodhouse and Fiona Woodhouse

Standards addressed

Q3   (a) Be aware of the professional duties of teachers and the statutory framework within which they work.

  (b) Be aware of the policies and practices of the workplace and share in collective responsibility for their implementation.

Q21   (a) Be aware of the current legal requirements, national policies and guidance on the safeguarding and promotion of the well-being of children and young people.

  (b) Know how to identify and support children and young people whose progress, development or well-being is affected by changes or difficulties in their personal circumstances, and when to refer them to colleagues for specialist support.

Introduction

Teaching consists of a lot more than many practitioners at first realise. It is a professional activity and as such it is underpinned by a professional code of practice for which the General Teaching Council of England (GTCE) has responsibility. Teachers also have to work within the statutory and non-statutory frameworks that inform practice in schools. It is essential that, as teachers, you have an understanding of your own professional role within the context of these frameworks. This chapter will give you an overview of the professional nature of a teacher and of the various frameworks currently of importance to teachers and within which you will have to work.

The Teacher as a Professional

A thought

Is teaching a profession? Does it require thinking about at a deeper level or is it a function anyone can do? In a recent conversation an NQT said that their course was much better than others as it was more practically based. They could now manage the class better than the other NQTs and didn't see the need for having to understand all the theory such as why children learn. Is teaching just about managing a class?

Teaching: a job of many parts

'The new professionalism' of teachers as explored by commentators such as Hargreaves (1994) and Caldwell and Spinks (1998) focuses on the teacher as a provider of quality service rather than on the status of the profession. However, it is also agreed that the status of teachers is enhanced through improved service delivery (Hoyle 2001). First and foremost, therefore, teachers should be skilled practitioners if they are to deliver both a quality of service and have professional status.

As a teacher, you need to be able to apply your knowledge of content and knowledge of transmission effectively to develop your pupils fully (Hoyle 2001). Good teachers have professional insight, which is based on knowledge of theory and experience of practice. Good teachers can deliver effective teaching strategies and interventions using their knowledge, skills and experience. A 'professional' teacher uses the skills of a theorist, an artist, a technician and a performer to deliver a complex service. The teacher's role also combines the work of a communicator, a manager and a critical researcher. As if that was not enough the terms planner, disciplinarian, moral leader and team member also arise – and so the list goes on. The skilled practitioner also displays professional accountability or what Hoyle and John (1995) call 'professional responsibility'. This means, as a teacher, being not only part of the formal quality assurance structure but also taking responsibility for your own quality as a professional.

Hegarty (2000) points to the teaching *moment* being core to the work of the skilled practitioner. This moment occurs when a teacher interacts with learners to stimulate and direct learning. It is what Yarker (2005: 171) labels 'the moment-by-moment interchange in the classroom'.

The Hegarty model uses a teacher's 'insight' to deliver knowledge, skills, experience and teacher research into the teaching moment. He argues that:

> What is essential is that the teacher relates the knowledge that is used in that particular situation and does so by generating a new insight specific to the situation. (Hegarty 2000: 462)

The model is an idealised concept and all of its components and facets may not be present for every teaching situation, but it does provide a range of cognitive and skill-based components which as a practitioner you may draw upon in constructing your teaching behaviour.

Theory

The skilled practitioner takes theory, reflects upon it and turns it into applied theory or knowledge which can be used in learning. Theory sets the rules, which are applied to specific activities as opposed to the equally important practical knowledge generated by working alongside an experienced practitioner (Carr 2003).

Professional knowledge

The teacher therefore requires knowledge, which Winch (2004) calls 'professional knowledge'. This can only be acquired after a lengthy foundation period of study, usually at university or college. He identifies three areas of knowledge to make up this professional requirement.

1   **Appropriate subject knowledge, underpinned by systematic unified theory.** It is difficult to teach something which one has not fully mastered (as you have no doubt discovered already!). He warns against believing that elementary subject knowledge is required to teach pupils who have generally modest academic attainments and argues that actually the reverse may be the case.

2   **Pedagogic knowledge.** The skilled practitioner requires a wide range of pedagogic knowledge to enable her/him to apply or transmit subject knowledge. Hegarty calls this 'craft knowledge'; it encompasses knowledge of teaching. For instance, the teacher needs to have an understanding of the use of formal and informal assessment or the art of differentiation. The teacher requires knowledge of the structures of how people learn and how to motivate and manage individuals and classes.

3   **A mixed bag labelled 'other knowledge'.** It includes knowledge of individual pupils including their home background, knowledge of the curriculum and the skill to navigate around the often complex array of teaching materials, study programmes and guidance and information from the media.

Knowledge of self and a positive view of self-concept are important to the survival and professional growth of the teacher. The belief that you have in your subject is also important as it will impact, often subconsciously, on how that subject is taught.

Research

Good teachers continually seek out ways of improving practice. Stenhouse (1975) advocated that teachers should become research practitioners as a way of providing empirical knowledge and self-improvement. This action-research approach tends to make the full-time educational researcher more of a collaborator than a leader. Stenhouse even argues that it is the professional responsibility of the teacher to deliver research from the classroom. Others champion the teacher as a reviewer and practical sampler of other's research. According to some commentators, as a teacher you should review current theory proactively and where appropriate apply it in practice. (Cooper and Hedges (1994) provide interesting detail on this aspect.) Hegarty criticises the traditional top-down structure where educational research feeds downwards directly into a teacher's practice. He points out that this is a burden to both researcher and an affront to the teacher and advocates that:

> Teachers are professionals and teaching excellence is not a matter of accumulating tips from researchers. (Hegarty 2000: 464)

Experience

As a skilled practitioner you will use a wide range of learning experiences to improve the quality of your performance and generate new insights (see below). You will experience an accumulation of insights that not only draw from your knowledge and skills but also help to develop them. It will give a personal meaning to the learning situation which is strongly influenced by a teacher's own experiences and working environment (Helsby 1996). Critical reflection on learning outcomes is fed back into the model to enhance performance and development. The skilled practitioner starts to seek out new experiences from which to learn from day one and continues to do so throughout a career.

Skills

While a comprehensive knowledge base is important, skills are also vital. The skills required of a good teacher are both comprehensive and demanding. Even the 'best' practitioners are still acquiring skills late in their careers. Teaching skills range from the use of complex verbal and non-verbal communication strategies (Harrison 2007) to various methods of using knowledge. They encompass the skills of the technician in planning complex activity and the improvisation of the artist (Humphreys and Hyland 2002). They include diagnostic, problem-solving and decision-making skills, along with motivation and classroom control. All these and more make for an excellent practitioner.

Insight closes the circle and is a reflective process; it is the application of judgement, which makes sense out of the situation and leads to personal development. Insight in this context takes the process a stage further to what Lonergan (1957) called insightful common sense, which enables someone to learn from his or her experience.

Hegarty argues that teachers need to build a bank of insights from their experiences, which can be adapted to bring insight into new teaching moments. He states:

> Different situations need to be approached with different sets of insights, which in turn need to be completed in different ways. Intelligent practical behaviour, therefore, calls for a large repertoire of incomplete sets of insights, skill in selecting appropriately from them, and the ability to generate fresh insights which complete the set in an illuminating way. (Hegarty 2000: 461)

💭 A thought

In an article in the *Times Educational Supplement* on 5 October 2007, Keith Bartley, the chief executive of the General Teaching Council, talking about professionalism and registration to the GTCE, said: 'For teachers, professional values are often expressed through their personal commitment and relate directly to where they work and the pupils that they teach.' What do you think this means to you as a teacher?

Pupils' well-being

One of the most important professional duties is linked to the well-being of pupils. You are responsible for the well-being of the pupils that come into your care either as their subject teacher, form teacher or in any other context. The Every Child Matters (ECM) agenda now forms the basis for a school's approach to safeguarding children and for working with several agencies to ensure that all children are able to meet the key outcomes highlighted by ECM. All of the standards for gaining Qualified Teacher Status (QTS) are underpinned by the ECM agenda and it will inform much of your work in school over the next few years.

Central to ECM are the five outcomes that every child and young person, regardless of their background or personal circumstance, should meet. They are to:

- be healthy;
- stay safe;
- enjoy and achieve;
- make a positive contribution;
- achieve economic well-being.

(Further details and discussion of ECM is to be found in Chapter 15.)

These outcomes need to be considered in every context of your work with pupils. You need to be aware of the policies schools currently have for addressing issues that are linked to these outcomes. For example, what is the policy on bullying and what do you do if you are aware of it occurring? If you suspect a child is being abused what should you do and with whom should you share your concern? You also need to work more closely with other agencies such as the social services departments, police or medical practitioners to ensure that the well-being of each child is paramount. The implications of the Children Act 2004 and ECM are still being developed and worked through at both national and local levels and will result in teachers modifying and changing present practice.

Being a professional practitioner is multidimensional and requires a complex array of attributes. Teaching is a lifelong journey, along which, as you travel, you will continue to acquire and develop the skills and knowledge that help to maintain and develop good practice in the classroom.

What are the statutory frameworks under which you work?

There are many statutory frameworks that require certain responsibilities and activities as you teach. There is also non-statutory guidance that advises you further on how you should work within schools. These are regularly updated with amendments to Acts as further initiatives are introduced. Education is a continuingly evolving profession; change is the norm, so amendments and additions are varied and numerous. This section seeks to give an overview of some of the main frameworks.

The School Teachers' Pay and Conditions Document 1999 and 2001

One of the most important frameworks is that of School Teachers' Pay and Conditions. This sets out your responsibilities as a teacher. Classroom teachers should carry out their professional duties under the reasonable direction of the head teacher. Twelve professional duties are specifically included in the document, the first (and most important) of which is that of teaching (see Table 3.1).

> ### A thought
>
> The School Teachers' Pay and Conditions Document outlines twelve professional duties of a teacher. What do you think ought to be the duties of a teacher? Should they be the same regardless of the age group being taught? Who do you think should decide on what they are – our professional bodies, the government or employers?

Additionally this document gives details on your working time. You should be available for work for 195 days in any school year of which 190 are days on which you are required to teach pupils. Your commitment is to 1,265 hours as directed by the head teacher (often referred to as directed time). This time does not include time for preparation of teaching materials and similar work required to enable you to discharge the duties as outlined.

National Agreement on Raising Standards and Tackling Workload (2003)

Another key document, which has implications for your role as a teacher is the National Agreement. This sets out ways of realising the potential of our children in the twenty-first century. It looks to change the role of teachers so that you undertake fewer administrative and clerical tasks, these being devolved to support staff. This means that you need to work more closely with support staff in school.

Table 3.1 The teacher's professional duties

1. Teaching	In each case having regard to the curriculum for the school,
	• planning and preparing courses and lessons;
	• teaching, according to their educational needs, the pupils assigned to him, including the setting and marking of work to be carried out by the pupil in school and elsewhere;
	• assessing, recording and reporting on the development, progress and attainment of pupils.
2. Other activities	• promoting the general progress and well-being of individual pupils and of any class or group of pupils assigned to him;
	• providing guidance and advice to pupils on educational and social matters and on their further education and future careers, including information about sources of more expert advice on specific questions; making relevant records and reports;
	• making records of and reports on the personal and social needs of pupils;
	• communicating and consulting with the parents of pupils;
	• communicating and cooperating with persons or bodies outside the school;
	• participating in meetings arranged for any of the purposes described above.
3. Assessments and reports	• providing or contributing to oral and written assessments, reports and references relating to individual pupils and groups of pupils.
4. Appraisal	• participating in arrangements made in accordance with the Education (School Teacher Appraisal) Regulations 1991 for the appraisal of his performance and that of other teachers.
5. Review, induction, further training and development	• reviewing from time to time his methods of teaching and programmes of work;
	• participating in arrangements for his further training and professional development as a teacher;
	• in the case of a teacher serving an induction period pursuant to the Induction Regulations, participating in arrangements for his supervision and training.
6. Educational methods	• advising and cooperating with the head teacher and other teachers (or any one or more of them) on the preparation and development of courses of study, teaching materials, teaching programmes, methods of teaching and assessment and pastoral arrangements.
7. Discipline, health and safety	• maintaining good order and discipline among the pupils and safeguarding their health and safety both when they are authorised to be on the school premises and when they are engaged in authorised school activities elsewhere.
8. Staff meetings	• participating in meetings at the school which relate to the curriculum for the school or the administration or organisation of the school, including pastoral arrangements.
9. Cover	• subject to 1 below, supervising and so far as practicable teaching any pupils whose teacher is not available to teach them;
	• subject to the exceptions in 2 below, no teacher shall be required to provide such cover:
	(1) after the teacher who is absent or otherwise not available has been so for three or more consecutive working days; or
	(2) where the fact that the teacher would be absent or otherwise not available for a period exceeding three consecutive working days was known to the maintaining authority or, in the case of a school which has a delegated budget to the governing body, for two or more working days before the absence commenced;

(Continued)

Table 3.1 (continued)

	• the exceptions are:
	– he is a teacher employed wholly or mainly for the purpose of providing such cover ('a supply teacher'); or
	– the authority or the governing body (as the case may be) have exhausted all reasonable means of providing a supply teacher to provide cover without success; or
	– he is a full-time teacher at the school but has been assigned by the head teacher in the timetable to teach or carry out other specified duties (except cover) for less than 75 per cent of those hours in the week during which pupils are taught at the school.
10. Public examinations	• participating in arrangements for preparing pupils for public examinations and in assessing pupils for the purposes of such examinations; recording and reporting such assessments; and participating in arrangements for pupils' presentation for and supervision during such examinations.
11. Management	• contributing to the selection for appointment and professional development of other teachers and non-teaching staff, including the induction and assessment of new teachers and teachers serving induction periods pursuant to the Induction Regulation;
	• coordinating or managing the work of other teachers;
	• taking such part as may be required of him in the review, development and management of activities relating to the curriculum, organisation and pastoral functions of the school.
12. Administration	• participating in administrative and organisational tasks related to such duties as are described above, including the management or supervision of persons providing support for the teachers in the school and the ordering and allocation of equipment and materials;
	• attending assemblies, registering the attendance of pupils and supervising pupils, whether these duties are to be performed before, during or after school sessions.

Source: The School Teacher Pay and Conditions Document 1999.

INDIVIDUAL REFLECTION

As a teacher in the state sector in England you are a member of the GTCE, the professional body for teaching. Consider the statements below and reflect on how you carry these out in your classrooms.

First and foremost, teachers are skilled practitioners.

Teachers place the learning and well-being of young people at the centre of their professional practice.

Teachers respond sensitively to the differences in the home backgrounds and circumstances of young people, recognising the key role that parents and carers play in children's education.

Teachers see themselves as part of a team, in which fellow teachers, other professional colleagues and governors are partners in securing the learning and well-being of young people.

Teachers entering the teaching profession in England have met a common professional standard.

(GTCE 2006)

The Secondary National Strategy for school improvement (SNS)

This was first introduced into schools as the Key Stage 3 Strategy and aimed to raise standards across the curriculum. It was subsequently renamed the Schools National Strategy to encompass Key Stage 4. It aims to transform secondary education to enable children and young people to attend and enjoy school, achieve personal and social development and raise educational standards in line with the Every Child Matters agenda. It has had a huge impact in many areas of the curriculum since being introduced. It concentrated initially on the core areas of mathematics, English, science and ICT before being introduced into the foundation subjects and tackling whole-school issues such as behaviour and attendance and assessment. It considered generic aspects of teaching such as lesson design and starters and plenaries as well as producing core-specific subject guidance and yearly teaching targets for the teaching of particular topics. A lot of the material has been concentrated into short easy-to-read booklets covering some of the key aspects of teaching. These will give you a basic overview of some of the aspects you will need to consider as you develop your teaching skills (for example, DfES (2004) *Pedagogy and Practice: Teaching and Learning in Secondary Schools. Units 1 to 20*. London: HMSO, available in schools or on the DfES or DCSF standards website (www.standards.dfes.gov.uk/).

National legislation and guidance

As both a teacher and an employee there is a range of legislation and guidance of which you need to be aware and to which you must respond. Below are some of the key areas that you need to be aware of as you meet the professional standards. Details of many of these can be found via the Office of Public Sector Information website at www.opsi.gov.uk/acts or the Department for Children, Schools and Families website (www.dfes.gov.uk or www.dcsf.gov.uk) or via links on www.teachernet. gov.uk.

- **Education Act 2002 and 1996.** This is a broad-reaching Act that has many implications for teachers. Guidance on conforming to the Act is produced by the DCSF which includes information on a wide range of subjects including the School Teacher Review Body (STRB), SEN provision, maintained schools and the curriculum.
- **Children Act 2004 and 1989.** In all schools there will be policies that have been developed to address aspects of this Act, which deals with the well-being of children. It includes the requirement for teachers to be familiar with the procedures in school for dealing with issues such as suspected child abuse. Every Child Matters 2003 was published with the Children Act and there are many commonalities between them. This is currently a key driver behind much educational policy and change. Go to www.everychildmatters.gov.uk/ for more details, particularly regarding the Children's Workforce Strategy 2005 and Amendment 2007. Guidance on Safeguarding Children in Education is closely linked with Every Child Matters. Details and resources are available at: www.teachernet.gov.uk/wholeschool/family andcommunity/childprotection/guidance/.
- **Education and Inspections Act 2006.** Many of the requirements of this Act will have been built into school policies. For example, it gives advice about the detention of pupils. It also outlines the school's (and therefore your) obligations to Ofsted.
- **Race Relations Act 1976 and Amendment Act 2000; Sex Discrimination Act 1975.** It is unlawful to discriminate against a pupil on gender, sexuality, religious or racial grounds. The website www.cre.gov.uk is the home of the Commission for Racial Equality.
- **Disability Discrimination Acts 1995 and 2005; Disability Equality Duty 2006.** It is unlawful to discriminate against disabled pupils or for schools and colleges to treat disabled pupils less favourably than non-disabled pupils. For more information on the Disability Equality Duty you can look at the website of the Equality and Human Rights Commission at: www.equalityhumanrights.com.
- **SEN and Disability Act (SENDA) 2001 and the Special Education Code of Practice (DfES 2001).** Together these give the requirement for and guidance on the identification and assessment of pupils with special educational needs (SEN). Once a pupil has been identified as having SEN there needs to be intervention in the form of personalised provision (see Chapter 12). A good starting point for classroom teachers is the SEN toolkit found at: www.teachernet.gov.uk/wholeschool/sen/. Prior to these were the Green Papers *Excellence for All Children: Meeting Special Education Needs* (DfEE 1997) and *Meeting Special Education Needs: A Programme of Action* (DfEE 1998), details of which are given at: www.teachernet.gov.uk/ wholeschool/ sen/publications/excellencegp/.
- **Health and Safety at Work Act 1974.** Employers must take reasonable care for the health and safety of their employees, i.e. you, while you have a duty to take reasonable care of your own health and safety and that of those affected by this, i.e. your pupils. You need to be aware of LEA and school policies plus the additional regulations that may pertain to some areas such as PE, science and DT, for instance regarding first aid

or the storage of hazardous substances. Further details can be found at: www.hse. gov.uk/legislation/hswa.htm.

- **White Paper 14–19 *Education and Skills* (DfES 2005).** This is a current reform of the 14 to 19 provision which has three main elements:

  - raising attainment now;
  - designing new curriculum and qualifications;
  - delivering on the ground.

It is working in partnership with colleges, schools, work-related learning providers and the Learning and Skills Council. For details of the new qualifications and developments see the following websites: www.dfes.gov.uk/14-19/ and www.qca.org. uk/14-19/.

Application to teaching

Pupils have to work within frameworks in your classroom and one way of setting up routines and expectations (see Chapter 8) is to establish them through an initial lesson in which you point out that you, too, have to work within frameworks.

Ask pupils to list what they think are the 'duties' of teachers (you may want to limit this to, say, five). Ask them to then rank these in order of importance.

You should not be surprised to find that even pupils recognise that teaching is a primary duty, although younger pupils may think the duty of care is more important. You should be able to confirm your duties from those given on page 31. Then have the pupils turn their attention to the framework in which they will work (your classroom) and repeat the exercise, in this way effectively underpinning your own structure and routine and their responsibilities within it.

LEA/employer legislation

Most local education authorities (LEAs) will have policies which are individual to them and which you will need to comply with once you take up employment with them. With many schools being regulated by different bodies these will be varied and you will be made aware of them when you are issued a contract of employment.

School policies

All schools have to have clear policies on issues in school such as bullying, behaviour and child protection. These will have been developed in response to the Acts and guidance issued but designed specifically for the school. As a teacher you have a responsibility to know and follow these as well as at times review and develop them.

GROUP EXERCISE

In small groups of three to four choose one of the frameworks, guidance or legislation outlined in the list above and provide a clear overview of the key aspects of it in relation to teaching for everyone else. You will need to be able to:

- outline the key elements within the Act or guidance;
- show how this will impact on teaching in general;
- explain the implications it will have for you as teachers in your classroom;
- say how your placement schools have responded to the Act or guidance.

Summary

Teaching is a complex professional activity which we continually hone and develop over the years. We have a professional code of practice that we must be aware of as well as professional values. These are partly underpinned by legislation and guidance but also by our own professional nature. You will need to:

- understand what it means to be a professional as a teacher;
- be aware of and work within the frameworks and guidance that underpin our profession;
- consider new guidance which impacts on the profession.

Key reading

Berry, J. (2007) *Teachers' legal rights and responsibilities*. University of Hertfordshire Press

Hargreaves, D. (1994) 'The new professionalism: the synthesis of professional and institutional development'. *Teaching and Teacher Educator*, 10 (4), 423–438

Harrison, J. (2007) 'The assessment of ITT Standard One, Professional Values and Practice: measuring performance or what?'. *Journal of Education for Teaching*, 33 (3), 323–340

TDA (2007) *The Professional Standards for Teachers*. Available at: www.tda.gov.uk/teachers/professionalstandards.aspx.

References and bibliography

Caldwell, B. and Spinks, J. (1998) *Beyond the self-managing school*. London: Falmer Press

Carr, D. (2003) *Making sense of education*. London: Routledge

Cooper, H. and Hedges, L.V. (eds) (1994) *The handbook of research synthesis*. New York: Russell Sage Foundation

DfES (1999) *School Teachers' Pay and Conditions 1999*. Available at: www.dfes.gov.uk/publications/guidanceonthelaw/12_99/paycondoc99d9.doc

GTC (2004) *Code of Conduct and Practice for Registered Teachers*. Available at: www.gtce.org.uk

GTC (2006) *The Statement of Professional Values and Practice for Teachers*. Available at: www.gtce.org.uk

Hargreaves, D. (1994) 'The new professionalism: the synthesis of professional and institutional development'. *Teaching and Teacher Educator*, 10 (4), 423–438

Harrison, J. (2007) 'The assessment of ITT Standard One, Professional Values and Practice: measuring performance or what?'. *Journal of Education for Teaching*, 33 (3), 323–340

Hegarty, S. (2000) 'Teaching as a knowledge-based activity'. *Oxford Review of Education*, 26 (3 & 4), 451–465

Helsby, G. (1996) 'Defining and developing professionalism in English secondary schools'. *Journal of Education for Teaching*, 22 (2), 135–148

Hoyle, E. (2001) 'Teaching: prestige, status and esteem'. *Educational Management and Administration*, 29 (2), 139–152

Hoyle, E. & John, P. (1995) *Professional knowledge and professional practice*. London: Cassell

Humphreys, M. and Hyland, T. (2002) 'Theory, practice and performance in teaching: professionalism, intuition, and jazz'. *Educational Studies*. 28 (1), 5–15

Lonergan, B.J.F. (1957) *Insight: a study of human understanding*. London: Longman

Stenhouse, L. (1975) *An introduction to curriculum research and development*. London: Heinemann

TDA. (2003) *Raising Standards and tackling workload: a national agreement*. Available at http://www.tda. gov.uk/upload/resources/na_standards_workload.pdf

Winch, C. (2004) 'What do teachers need to know about teaching? A critical examination of the occupational knowledge of teachers'. *British Journal of Educational Studies*. Vol. 52 (2), 180–196

Yarker, P. (2005) 'On not being a teacher: the professional and personal costs of Workforce Remodelling'. *FORUM* 47 (2 & 3), 169–174

CHAPTER 4

COMMUNICATION AND COLLABORATION

Rod Robertson

Standards addressed

Q4 Communicate effectively with children, young people, colleagues, parents and carers.

Q6 Have a commitment to collaboration and cooperative working.

Q32 Work as a team member and identify opportunities for working with colleagues, sharing the development of effective practice with them.

Q33 Ensure that colleagues working with them are appropriately involved in supporting learning and understand the roles they are expected to fulfil.

Introduction

Schools are busy and complex places. When first encountering the school and the classroom you may be bewildered by the many interactions that you are expected to become involved in. It soon becomes apparent that classrooms and schools are populated not only by teachers and those that they teach. The school community includes learning support staff, pastoral officers, education welfare officers and a plethora of other professionals (not to mention the colleagues supporting in premises management, catering, administration support and so on) (see Chapter 6). If all of these adults are to bring about the most effective practice from which pupils are to benefit, then collaboration, cooperation and sharing of effective practice must take place before, during and after formal lesson times. As a teacher, you are also expected to communicate effectively with parents and carers. It is important that you see the need to be proactive in all of these opportunities for communication and collaboration.

This chapter will give some insight on how best to approach the challenging issues of communication, cooperation and collaboration.

Understanding expectations

It is succinctly stated in *Every Child Matters: change for children* (DfES 2004) that: 'The Children Act 2004 includes duties to co-operate to improve well-being and to safeguard and promote the welfare of children and young people' (p. 20). If you are to understand your role as a teacher within a particular setting then you need to ensure that what is expected of you in the context of Every Child Matters has been made clear. In many settings these procedures and protocols will be made explicit at the outset. However, if this hasn't happened during an initial induction period it is vital that clarification is sought. Understanding what is expected of you as a teacher is just as important as communicating, collaborating and cooperating effectively with children, young people, colleagues and parents/carers.

The following points highlight the issues that are addressed in this chapter:

- **Communicate** – establishing relationships (Q4).
- **Collaboration and cooperative working** – establishing effective practice (Q6).
- **Team working** – establishing a sense of team (Q32).
- **Being a team member** – establishing an understanding of your own role in the team (Q32).
- **Sharing effective practice** – establishing opportunities to share (Q32).
- **Encouraging involvement in supporting learning and understanding roles** – establishing clarity of roles (Q33).

Communicate

Communicating effectively with children and young people – building relationships

Most of your communication with young people and children will be in group contexts within the confines of the classroom – however, you will also constantly find yourself communicating with children and young people as you move to and from your classrooms and around the school. In this context you must see every situation where you encounter pupils, in your role as a teacher, as an opportunity. Seizing these opportunities to build relationships with children and young people will pay dividends for all. Communicating the notion that you are approachable is vital if you are to encourage children and young people to see you, and indeed all teachers like you, as people who are interested in their well-being.

A thought

Take the opportunity with a small group of children/young people to ask them what was the 'best' experience they have had at school – remind them this could be any activity, including after-school clubs and school trips. Listen carefully to what they say – they will very soon start describing events and the people involved, and what these people said and did. Reflect on what the pupils say about teacher involvement in these events – usually teacher participation/ supervision is intrinsically linked to the enjoyment of the activity. In some cases teacher participation is perceived as negative so be aware of this and how to deal with it.

You must never forget your role as responsible adult and teacher; however, this should not stop you being creative in your interactions with children and young people. Pupils will *perceive the boundaries* you set if you make them explicit. They will *continue to perceive* these boundaries if you consistently adhere to them in your interactions with them. Lack of clarity and inconsistency confuses young people and this confusion can lead to 'blurred boundaries'. Young people are capable of accepting that teachers (or any adults they encounter) have different personalities, interests, opinions and beliefs – but when teachers give out 'mixed messages' they are likely to become confused and unsure about what is appropriate.

A thought

Colleagues will often be willing to ask you to clarify something you have communicated to them if they are unsure what you mean. Children and young people are not always willing to do this. It is therefore important that you are sensitive to the non-verbal clues that children exhibit that may tell you they are unclear about what you have communicated, i.e. if you detect an individual or group looking doubtful about what you have said, get them to repeat back in their own words what has been said or asked of them.

Application to teaching

At the outset of a series of lessons remind pupils about the need for clear communication, i.e. use words like 'transmit' and 'receive'. Reiterate to the pupils your rules for the classroom, e.g. pupils listen when you talk, the pupils listen when another pupil is talking, no shouting out, etc.

Demonstrate clear communication by showing pupils semaphore (communicating using arm signals) – there is only need to do this for simple letters of the alphabet. Provide the class with a worksheet with various letters and their semaphore equivalent. Allow two small groups of pupils, located at opposite ends of the class, to send simple messages back and forward (obviously without talking). Allow other pupils to observe. At some point in the proceedings allow two pupils to unfurl a large piece of cloth or card that obscures the person sending the message from the person receiving – explain this is what happens when you get a breakdown in communication.

Pupils enjoy this activity and it often generates lots of discussion about the basics of effective communication. You can root the subject of the communication in your own subject or use it as a vehicle for setting classroom norms.

Communicating effectively with colleagues – building relationships

As teachers you should constantly be developing effective communication skills – you should be making sure that these skills are not just manifesting themselves in the classroom but in any forum where you are talking with, and sharing with, colleagues, parents and carers.

It is useful to acquire the organisation chart for your school to understand the roles and responsibilities of individuals. Reading the Staff Handbook will help you to understand any protocols and procedures that are in place. In addition, the school's calendar of meetings will allow you to prepare for any necessary input that you should make. For example, if there is an expectation that you should attend a regular meeting with teacher and learning support colleagues to discuss forthcoming projects and planned work then you should know this so that you can plan and prepare.

However, in a more pragmatic context, perhaps you may be expected to brief a learning support assistant (LSA) about a particular project that s/he will be working on with a pupil who will be in your class. It is absolutely vital that before the first lesson of this project you meet with the LSA to discuss with them the work to be covered. This may only take a few minutes but still has to be planned into the busy working day, i.e. it is not effective planning/teaching to 'grab' a minute at the start of the lesson to explain a complicated set of worksheets/resources. It is especially important that you are aware of, and follow, policy. For example, if there is a policy within the school that states all new resources that are to be used with classes/individuals should be forwarded to the special needs coordinator (SENCO) before the lesson you need to know about this and act accordingly!

Communicate effectively with parents and carers

It is vital that you know the formal ways (e.g. letter, detention slip, report card, Home/School Consultation Evening) by which the school communicates with parents and carers. It is also useful to know if other less formal ways are allowed. For example, it may be entirely appropriate (i.e. the school allows this) to telephone a parent. However, many schools will have a formal procedure for how to record the time, date and reason, and the outcome, of the telephone call and it is your responsibility to be aware of this (as well as the school's responsibility to make you aware). Some schools have a policy where the need to contact the parent is discussed with the relevant pastoral member of staff (e.g. form tutor) before the contact is made. Of course it is also possible that the school does not permit any telephone communication with a parent/carer unless it is instigated by a member of staff with a pastoral role – be aware of this.

When communicating with parents and carers it is important that at the outset of the communication they are made aware of the reason for the communication. Also, it should always be possible to give them an opportunity to ask any questions or seek further clarification (perhaps from someone else) at the conclusion of the meeting or telephone call.

Any face-to-face meeting must at all times be cordial but professional. The parent/carer must see you – the teacher – as approachable and concerned about the progress and well-being of the young person. In face-to-face meetings you can't underestimate the importance of communicating to the parent/carer that you know the pupil well and that you have an understanding of his or her abilities, achievements and areas to be developed.

Collaboration and cooperative working

Collaboration is when you work alongside others to achieve a common goal. Cooperation is where you plan together (and interlink with others) but don't then necessarily work alongside another professional to achieve that which is planned for.

Inherent in this is the acknowledgement that when meeting with colleagues, parents and carers, you are doing so in a spirit of both collaboration and cooperation. For example:

- An LSA that you are meeting with (and who you will be working with) may know of an effective strategy another class teacher uses with a particular behaviour or child. Remember, they may be supporting this child throughout the school day and are therefore able to observe how the child responds to different teaching styles. Obviously, it would be foolish of you not to listen to the suggestions that are made.
- A parent may suggest that their child really likes your lessons but does need to have longer to write the homework into the homework planner. You should be able to reassure the parent that you will make a little more time available to allow this to happen – and then make sure you do!
- You manage to cure Liam's pencil tapping habit (low-level disruption) by giving him some Blu-tack to play with. This occupies his hands but does not adversely affect his concentration (or the learning of others). Make sure that colleagues are aware of your strategy, maybe at staff briefing time.

A thought

Is there a difference between collaboration and cooperation? When do you work best with others – is it when *they* are working with *you* to achieve something you see (they see or you both see) as important? To demonstrate a commitment to collaborative and cooperative working you need to be involved in projects where colleagues work together to achieve a common (agreed) aim – not just your interests.

INDIVIDUAL REFLECTION

Select a period of 2/3 weeks in which there are a number of staff/department meetings where you will be in attendance. Reflect on the actual collaboration and cooperation that appears to take place – is it genuine or contrived? Is expediency the motivator for most discussions that take place? Then ask yourself how well planned the meetings were and how well prepared you were for them, i.e. was there a published agenda for the meeting (along with meeting papers) and did you (and others present) read the papers before the event?

Team working

To be an effective teacher you must accept that working independently in an educational setting is never an option. Teachers must constantly seek advice and information from a range of colleagues. You should also expect to be consulted (you are an expert, after all) and to be a willing source of information and advice for colleagues and others involved in the education or well-being of the young person.

Children and young people will be quick to discern whether or not the teachers they encounter are communicating effectively with one another. They will know because an effective dialogue will consistently communicate school expectations. This ongoing communication is also an important element of building and sustaining the team.

The reality of 'sharing effective practice' suggests that you should expect to make public, for others, strategies that you, as a teacher, find work well in your teaching situations. This provides your colleagues with the possibility of putting these strategies in place in their own teaching. However, if you are to be truly collaborative then you should be looking for this to be reciprocated. You should expect your colleagues to inform you of what works for them (being forthcoming yourself encourages this) and to reflect on these practices to determine how you might utilise them in your own context. We all need to be proactive if we are to identify opportunities to work together and maximise the benefits of these opportunities.

As a teacher, you should never lose sight of one of your primary roles and one of the primary outcomes you should desire – the support of learning. Remember that it is usually inefficient if more than one person is undertaking the same function. In this context you must be aware of how separate but complementary roles interlink. For example, as a teacher it would be ineffective for you to spend all of your time supporting a particular child to the exclusion of the other children in a class. It is your role instead to collaborate with the allocated LSA to allow her or him to support the child appropriately.

Theory

Communication

Barnard (1948) suggested the following:

- everyone should know the channels of communication;
- everyone should have access to a formal channel of communication;
- lines of communication should be as short and direct as possible.

Barnard, although writing some 60 years ago, saw the need for everyone to be clear about the channels of communication. (See Chapter 9 for Mehrabian's view.) He also implied that, while there should always be access to a formal channel of communication, there are often more expedient ways of arriving at a decision. For example, waiting for the next departmental meeting on the calendar may present problems if it is important to have a decision about a relatively minor matter before you meet with a class.

Thody *et al*. (2000) present a model to help understand communication – it places the individual at the centre of the model and has, radiating concentrically from this, 'values', 'attitudes', 'skills' and 'rationality'. Thody *et al*. suggest that as your 'values' are closer than your attitudes and skills then these 'values' will have more effect on your communication. Consequently, because your commitment to rationality (your desire to be objective, logical, etc.) is further removed from your values and attitudes this has less impact on your communication. This perhaps should make you aware of how your values and attitudes may have a disproportionate impact on how effectively (and objectively) you might communicate with colleagues, parents and carers. Effective practice comes about by a commitment to objectivity!

Collaboration

Brown *et al*. (1999), in the context of school effectiveness, highlight 'types' of schools. They identified the following.

- **Type A schools** – those schools which give opportunities for collaboration and where departmental priorities correlate with the school development plan. There are considered to be effective schools.
- **Type B schools** – those schools where there are fewer opportunities for collaboration. These are less effective schools.
- **Type C schools** – those schools where there is little collaboration – schools where effective practice is very much less evident.

Of course we would all like to be in effective schools and Brown *et al.* provide us with one test (are there opportunities for collaboration?) we can apply to determine if we are likely to be in an effective school! This test could quite appropriately be applied to a department or faculty context.

Leonard and Leonard (2003) tell us that from their research '... teachers themselves value attributes of collegial enterprise that are based upon strong customs of routine professional interaction ...'. Leonard and Leonard make explicit that teachers value regular interaction with colleagues in a climate of collegiality. In its truest sense collegiality is when colleagues are allowed to meet, discuss and arrive at a decision based on a consensus of those who have taken part in the discussion. This is very much focused on the setting where the discussion has taken place, i.e. teachers arriving at the best decisions for the children and young people in their school.

Teams

When first discussing the concepts of teams and 'team learning' it is instructive to look at the work of Tuckman (1965) and Belbin (1981). Tuckman was seeking to throw light on the 'stages' a team goes through when working together. Have you been aware of or experienced these team 'stages'?

* **Forming** – team members coming together, or a new member joining the team.
* **Storming** – team members experiencing initial tension between themselves.
* **Norming** – team members have a sense of the compromises that are necessary to act as a team.
* **Performing** – the team works collaboratively to achieve a goal or to work towards a target.

Tuckman suggested that a team must move through these stages in order to perform effectively. In this regard it is important to accept that while the 'storming' stage may be difficult it is necessary if you and the team are to ascertain your team 'norms' and thus perform better. There is a fifth stage that is often forgotten – adjournment – when the team breaks up or a number of members leave the team. Of course this necessitates the team reforming (even if some of the initial members are still present) and then moving through these stages again. You should not underestimate the number of times you will have to do this throughout your career.

Belbin was more interested in looking more carefully at the individuals that contribute to team effectiveness. He identified the following 'types' of team member through their positive and negative aspects:

- **Company worker** – is dutiful and hardworking *but* may lack flexibility.
- **Chairman** – appears self-confident, has a strong sense of objectives *but* is of ordinary 'intellect'.
- **Shaper** – is dynamic and will challenge complacency *but* can be impatient.
- **Plant** – displays individualistic tendencies *but* may disregard protocols.
- **Resource investigator** – constantly curious and will willingly contact people *but* may lose interest after period of time.
- **Monitor-evaluator** – sees being prudent and discreet as important *but* lacks inspiration.
- **Team worker** – sees being social as important and has the ability to respond well to changes *but* can be indecisive.
- **Completer-finisher** – is orderly and conscientious *but* will not readily 'let go' of task.

Belbin was suggesting that for the team to function most effectively each of these roles needs to be taken. In the context of schools this may be a little complicated because as a teacher you will be a member of more than one team. You are likely, for example, to be a member of a subject department and faculty while at the same time being a form tutor and consequently a member of a pastoral team. Further in your career you may lead one team (as a head of year), be a junior member of another (management) and a player in another (subject department). You will need to play a different role in each and to play each role effectively – this versatility is just one of the juggling acts that goes with being a good teacher!

Team learning

Hall (2001) highlighted the concept of 'team learning' and suggested that team learning (and personal effectiveness) is brought about by the following.

- **Appropriate team culture** – each individual recognises and identifies with the culture of the team.
- **'Team self-talk'** – open discussion within the team of concerns and ideas.
- **Group vision** – this has been arrived at and is shared by all team members.
- **Stimuli for group learning** – there are ongoing opportunities to develop team identity and learning is seen as important.

Hall went on to explain how these elements are interdependent. For the team to be effective the individual must therefore acknowledge s/he has an active part to play in bringing about and subsequently sustaining the team.

GROUP EXERCISE

In a small group (2–3) plan a lesson (that all involved will subsequently teach if possible) using a previously agreed lesson planning format.

- In the first instance agree the objectives for the lesson.
- After these have been agreed the group is to split up for about 30 minutes – each individual is to plan the lesson using the agreed lesson objectives.
- The group then reforms to agree the final lesson plan (bringing together the individual plans) with all to take responsibility for the outcome. If possible this small group should team teach this lesson.
- Together reflect on the lesson *outcomes* and the *process* of arriving at the lesson plan.

Summary

- It is important to communicate to children and young people that you are interested in their well-being.
- Know your school's policies and procedures for communicating with colleagues and parents/carers.
- Be proactive when meeting with colleagues and parents/carers – prevention is better than cure.
- Always prepare in advance for any meeting that you are to attend.
- At the outset of any interaction (meeting) you should agree the reason for the meeting.
- You should make explicit what you expect from the meeting or discussion.
- The meeting should be organised so that all planned activities can be addressed.
- At the conclusion of the meeting you should clarify what you understand to be the outcome and future implications.
- Team working is at the heart of any effective school.
- Effective and proactive team members are at heart of the effective team!

Key reading

Brown, M., Boyle, B. and Boyle, T. (1999) 'Commonalities between perception and practice in models of school decision-making in secondary schools'. *School Leadership and Management*, 19 (3), 319–330

Department for Education and Skills (2004) *Every Child Matters: change for children*. London: DfES. See Section 3: Integrated services and local change

Muijs, D. and Reynolds, D. (2005) *Effective teaching evidence and practice*, London: Paul Chapman. See Chapter 4: Collaborative small group work

References and bibliography

Barnard, C. (1948) *Organisation and management*. Cambridge, MA: Harvard University Press

Belbin, R.M. (1981) *Management teams: why they succeed or fail*. London: Heinemann

Brown, M., Boyle, B. and Boyle, T. (1999) 'Commonalities between perception and practice in models of school decision-making in secondary schools'. *School Leadership and Management*, 19 (3), 319–330

Department for Education and Skills (2004) *Every Child Matters: Change for Children*. London: DfES

Hall, V. (2001) 'Management Teams in Education: an unequal music', *School Leadership and Management*, 21 (3), 327–341

Leonard, L. and Leonard, P. (2003) 'The continuing trouble with collaboration: teachers talk'. *Current Issues in Education* [online], 6 (15). Available at: http://cie.ed.asu.edu/volume6/number15/

Thody, A., Gray, B. and Bowden, D. (2000) *The teacher's survival guide*. London: Continuum

Tuckman, B.W. (1965) 'Development sequence in small groups'. *Psychological Bulletin*, 63 (6), 384–399

CHAPTER 5

RESPONDING POSITIVELY TO COACHING AND MENTORING

Lesley-Anne Pearson

Standards addressed

Q8 Have a creative and constructively critical approach towards innovation, being prepared to adapt practice where benefits and improvements are identified.

Q9 Act upon advice and feedback and be open to coaching and mentoring.

Introduction

Teachers are not born, they are made. They improve their practice by learning. To learn, we need to be open to criticism. To be an effective teacher you need to be prepared to critically reflect on your practice and to adapt it in an innovative and creative manner. You must be observed teaching and be involved in discussions about your planning and preparation. You must work with experienced practitioners on monitoring, assessing and reporting on learners' progress. Ultimately you must be open to criticism from other teachers and be able to respond to this. This process is often referred to as coaching and mentoring. This chapter will establish what we mean by coaching and mentoring and analyse how the process of mentoring can encourage you to become reflective and innovative in your practice.

A thought

Throughout history the individuals who made the greatest impact, those producing the most outstanding achievements, have always been self-motivated. The most successful entrepreneurs and business leaders are always those who have acquired superior self-motivation skills. An important part of the coaching and mentoring process is to help performers find, harness and enhance their self-motivation. (MacLennan 1999: 19)

However, Blandford (2005) suggests that to become successful teachers, 'Trainee Teachers need support in school from mentors who are qualified to do the job and able to devote time to it' (in Child and Merrill, 2005).

What is coaching and mentoring?

Standard Q9 requires you to be open to coaching and mentoring but what is the difference? Downey (1999) suggests that:

> Coaching is an art in the sense that when practised with excellence, there is no attention on the techniques but instead the coach is fully engaged with the coachee and the process of coaching becomes a dance between two people moving in harmony and partnership. (In Parsloe and Wray 2000: 41)

In other words, coaching is a process in which the learner's performance develops and improves as a result of being supported by someone who has the subject knowledge, skills and techniques required in the area in which the coaching occurs (Parsloe and Wray 2000: 42). The DfES (2005) defines coaching as:

> ... a model of professional development designed to support and accelerate teachers' learning. It provides ongoing collaborative support for processes such as planning, trialling, reflecting on and evaluating lessons with the objective of enhancing teaching and pupils' learning. The focus is on deepening specific skills within a supportive and challenging relationship. (p. 4)

Mentoring has its roots in Greek mythology where Athena, the goddess of wisdom, crafts and the domestic arts, took on the form of Mentor, who was Odysseus' wise and trusted counsellor. The story goes that while Odysseus was away from home for ten years fighting in the Trojan Wars, Mentor was entrusted to become the guardian and teacher of his son, Telemachus. From this it became a Greek custom to pair young boys with older, wiser and trusted counsellors, usually a friend of the boy's father or an older relative. It was hoped that the boy would emulate these knowledgeable and experienced men. Such wise and trusted counsellors have since been known as mentors.

Murray (2001) defines mentoring as:

> a deliberate pairing of a more skilled or more experienced person with a less skilled or less experienced one, with a mutually agreed goal of having the less skilled person grow and develop specific competencies. (p. xiii)

According to MacLennan (1999) mentors will have the pedagogical acumen to provide you with the support you need to develop your new skills as a classroom practitioner. Parsloe (1999) suggests that a good mentor is someone who is a good motivator who can advise and instruct without interfering or imposing solutions. A good mentor allows the learner to make mistakes and encourages the self-management of the learning process. S/he should be adept at assisting in the evaluation process by being an effective questioner and listener without being judgemental. Therefore coaching is essentially an enabling process while mentoring is a supporting process (Parsloe 1999: 34). The key difference is that coaching helps performers to unlock their ability by learning *with* someone while mentoring is provided by someone *from* whom performers learn (MacLennan 1999: 4–5). You will experience both during your training.

A thought

Have you ever consciously acted as a coach or mentor yourself? For example, you may have coached youngsters in a sporting technique or an aspiring musician to tackle a difficult passage. Or have you ever done something which has made you think that you sounded like your parents, modelling their behaviour and mannerisms unconsciously? We are both consciously and unconsciously open to coaching and mentoring and our actions are influenced by those around us. However, our personalities also help us to define our behaviour and actions.

Consider ways in which you could coach or mentor in a lesson that you are teaching or supporting. Add these to lesson plans and check, once the lesson has been delivered, the effectiveness of your own mentoring.

The Centre for Understanding Research Evidence in Education (CUREE) suggests that coaching and mentoring make a significant contribution to a learner's professional development and are an effective form of continuing professional development (CPD) to 'embed change and sustain improvement' (DfES 2006). CUREE has produced a national framework for coaching and mentoring which shows that many features of coaching and mentoring naturally overlap. As a trainee teacher, you will be mentored by an experienced practitioner, normally the class teacher or specialist subject teacher in your placement school, who has taken on the role of supporting your development. It is also likely that you will be supported by other members of the school community acting as coaches.

The DfES (2006) outlines ten principles for effective coaching and mentoring. These describe coaching and mentoring as being 'a learning conversation' with an experienced practitioner who will help you to identify and clarify your learning needs and support you in your gradual development as a teacher. These practitioners should help you to reflect on, review and refine your practice and provide you with opportunities to develop and extend your repertoire through the sharing of planning and by observing them or other practitioners. They should encourage you to experiment and to 'take risks' while helping you to develop your teaching performance and professional skills over time in an atmosphere of mutual trust.

To summarise, you should not feel isolated in your training. You should have a mentor and access to coaches and mentors who are there to work with you. They will support and assist you through talking with you and by providing opportunities for you to observe excellent modelling. You should be encouraged to take risks and to try out new ideas or theories, all within an atmosphere of trust. Your learning environment must be low risk in which mistakes are seen as part of the process of learning and becoming an effective and even a good teacher. Mistakes and weaknesses must be recognised and reviewed and your targets agreed but, at the same time, your strengths and successes should be celebrated. However, this is a two-way process and you need to be highly proactive in the training process.

The world's most effective trainer

It is vital for you (and indeed your mentor) to understand that you are not expected to become a clone of your mentor. The role of your mentor is to be a facilitator to help you to develop as a teacher by encouraging you to make your own choices, decisions and mistakes (Kortman and Honaker 2002: 20). If you want to achieve your goals you need to be self-motivated; MacLennan (1999: 33) suggests that 'the world's most effective trainer is you!' and that self-motivational factors include:

- being focused on a purpose;
- having an intense sense of direction;
- having an opportunity and a requirement to learn new skills on an ongoing basis;
- being willing to experiment;
- having a feeling of total ownership;
- having a willingness to do whatever is required to achieve results;
- developing a willingness to persist in the face of adversity.

(MacLennan 1999: 10)

So, what is expected of you? Being open to coaching and mentoring is not enough; you cannot be complacent and need to be proactive in determining your own learning and development experiences in order to achieve them. You can adapt Shulman's (1987) cyclical principles for the knowledge required for teaching when you reflect on your own learning and on the feedback provided following coaching and mentoring activities that you have experienced. The cycle is comprehension, transformation, instruction, evaluation, reflection and new comprehensions (in Hoult 2005: 15). In the opinion of Argyris and Schön (1975) 'reflection is essential to educators' capacity to think not only about their practice but also about how they think, their implicit theories, and the sense they make of their experiences' (in Kortman and Honaker 2002: 25). Therefore, to be effective, reflection must be related to action, which can both precede or follow the reflection (Wragg 1994: 125).

Observations

It is part of your responsibility to make focused observations of others to identify ways of improving your practice. Wragg (1994: 78) suggests that 'looking at one's own or someone else's teaching can be an important part of initial teacher training'. The aims of classroom observation are to:

- analyse what is actually going on in the classroom, e.g. how space and time were used, what sort of questions were asked, what were the pupils actually doing;
- develop an understanding of what are acceptable standards for classroom teaching and what is not acceptable;
- broaden your knowledge of the variety of teaching and learning styles available;
- understand in what circumstances pupils will and/or will not achieve;
- discover the ways in which teachers perceive and think about classroom events.

INDIVIDUAL REFLECTION

1   Look at a recent evaluation. Did you set such specific SMART targets or are they vague? (SMART is the acronym for Specific, Measurable, Achievable, Realistic and Time-related goals.) Did you set yourself too many targets? Rewrite the evaluation being more specific about these targets, ensuring that they are SMART. Discuss this with your mentor and review a subsequent lesson plan taking account of the targets that you set yourself. Remember to increase the challenge and expectations that you set yourself over time.

2   Look at two or three of your most recent lesson evaluations and target-setting activities. Do you find that you keep setting the same targets for your development? If so, discuss this with your mentor and consider how you might address these targets successfully. For example, you might observe other teachers in the school who are successful with this issue and discuss with them how they deal with it. You could ask your mentor to teach a lesson that you planned together addressing your targets. Don't forget that there are lots of great books and useful articles out there designed to help you to address such issues!

Achieving focus

To improve teaching through observation you need to decide the focus of the observation with your school's coach or mentor. It is essential that you are clearly aware of what you are going to observe and how you are going to observe it before you go into the classroom. You must make written records of your observations and then, with reference to appropriate reading around your focus, evaluate and reflect on the observations that you have made. Finally, discuss these with your coach or mentor. You must be sensitive to the fact that such observations in school can lead very quickly into areas which are sensitive for the school, the teachers and its pupils. Thus observations should be conducted in a sensitive and unobtrusive way and with due regard to the confidential nature of the activity. Remember that both teachers and pupils have the moral right not to be observed or questioned by you and you should respect this at all times. If the observation produces results which are in any way contentious they should be discussed with the school staff before they are committed to paper.

The focus of observation activities should be related to the Standards and to areas identified by your coach or mentor. They include observations of both pupils and teachers. Observation of pupils is included as 'by studying what pupils do, observers can learn a great deal not only about the impact of teaching on the learner, but about the child's perspective and the influence that individual and groups of children have on the lesson' (Wragg 1994: 87). Observations of other teachers does not necessarily mean that you just observe them teaching; you could, for example, observe them supervising an activity outside the classroom, marking work or presenting at a parents' evening or school event. Alternatively you might observe them by focusing on a specific area such as inclusion, classroom management or their use of questioning. Some possibilities are outlined below.

Inclusion

- How curriculum support assistants are used to support teaching and learning.
- How pupils with special educational needs, children for whom English is an additional language, or gifted and talented children are supported in the mainstream curriculum.
- How teachers differentiate to encourage learning and to motivate pupils, for example by task, by outcome, by the use and deployment of resources and materials, by assessment or by organisation (seating).

Classroom or behaviour management

- How assertive discipline can be used to promote acceptable and good behaviour as a tool for classroom management.
- How behaviour modification encourages effective discipline and control in the classroom.
- How teachers use factors such as the amount of time allocated, room layout, whole-class and group work and different activities to ensure that pupils' interest and attention is maintained.
- How the teacher at different points manages transition effectively during the lesson, day or week.
- How the teaching and learning of pupils is affected by pace.
- How teachers either avoid or deal with confrontation.
- The effects of rewards and sanctions on control, motivation and discipline.

Other foci

- Verbal interaction (what teachers and pupils say to each other; who does the talking and about what; question and answer, choice of vocabulary and the pitch of the voice).
- Non-verbal interaction (movement, gesture, facial expression).
- Professional skills (questioning, explaining, arousing interest or curiosity).
- Teaching styles.
- Strategies relating to the assessment for and of learning.

To follow up these observation activities you could interview teachers. Of course, you also need to read the research around the issues addressed to enable you to reflect on these and put the theories into practice.

Planning and teaching collaboratively

Being able to plan is an essential aspect of learning how to teach. One of the best ways to learn this skill is by working collaboratively. Good coaches and mentors should encourage you to plan and teach collaboratively and should be prepared to model activities. However, as mentioned above, you are not expected to become their clone.

Time should be set aside regularly to enable you to check through your planning but also to observe the planning of your mentor. This will enable you both to review and reflect on the activities planned or proposed and for you to discuss or to anticipate possible problems with the planning. It is also a good idea to teach collaboratively and then review this teaching together following the lesson and to plan follow-up lessons. Another good activity is for you to teach using your mentor's plan with your mentor making a reflective observation of this or by your mentor teaching using your plan with you making an evaluative observation of this.

GROUP EXERCISE

Think about a lesson that you have recently evaluated and, using this evaluation and the lesson plan, discuss your reflection related to the targets set and consider different solutions to issues that arose in the lesson. Share different evaluations from other group members.

Self-reviewing techniques

Good teachers continually develop theories about what it is they are doing. By using self-reviewing techniques such as critical evaluation of your own teaching you can identify specific ways of improving your practice. Writing lesson evaluations helps you to record the journey through your development and allows you to review your thoughts and to refer back to earlier practice and experiences. It is useful to keep some form of log book on your development as a teacher so that you can easily refer back to it to trace key 'moments' in your development.

It is important for you to evaluate your teaching after the lesson as soon as you can do so in a calm and reflective manner. It is important to concentrate on whether learning has taken place within the lesson, and not to put too much emphasis on discipline or classroom management problems. Attempt to evaluate the lesson honestly by being reflective and analytical and by focusing on the targets that you set yourself. In order to make progress it is just as important to build on existing strengths as well as to overcome weaknesses and with this in mind, it is vital that you *identify good features of the lesson* along with *areas for improvement*. If the execution of the lesson differed in any way from the lesson plan, the reasons for this should be considered and discussed. You should evaluate your lesson by answering sets of reflective questions, which, according to Kortman and Honaker (2002: 25), 'creates opportunities for individuals to reflect aloud or be heard by one or more colleagues and to be prompted to expand and extend thinking through follow-up questions'.

The following set of questions could be used as a guide to encourage reflection. For your own development, you should aim to think of more or alternative questions:

- Were *all* the pupils actively engaged in their learning throughout and what evidence do you have for this?
- Were pupils motivated and enthused by the materials you chose to teach? Did you structure and present your material effectively?
- What did pupils learn and how do you know?
- Did you plan for the effective use of formative and summative assessment? How do you know?
- Were the materials and/or activities appropriate, stimulating and challenging? Why do you think this?
- Was the pace and timing right? How do you know this?
- Were your questions asked or phrased well, well-timed or at an appropriate level? How do you know?
- Was there too much or too little teacher input? What makes you say this?
- What were the learning problems and what was particularly successful? How do you know?
- What will you need to do differently next time and how do you know this?

Application to teaching

Observe your subject mentor teach a lesson and together evaluate this. Work together to plan the follow-up lesson which you should be prepared to teach.

Look at one of your lesson evaluations and the lesson plan for which it was written. Working with your subject mentor, reflect on this evaluation and plan a follow-up lesson. You will probably want to discuss how areas for development will be addressed and plan pupil tasks and activities to help address your targets. Your mentor will need to observe and evaluate you teaching this by discussing the strengths and weaknesses of the plan.

Setting goals and challenges

Whatever you do, do not focus on too much at once: pace yourself and increase the challenge within the targets that you set yourself. Then outline your new personal targets for the future and plan the follow-up lesson. Alternatively, you could look at your original lesson plan and annotate this by using questions such as those listed. (The problem with this method is that you tend to evaluate everything without focusing on your specific targets.)

Reflecting on your teaching and planning is integral to the learning process. To effectively evaluate your teaching you must set SMART targets for the achievement of these. Setting yourself such goals enables you both to evaluate your practice and to consider strategies for developing this practice. It is essential that SMART targets are set as a result of discussions with your mentor; however, you should be clear that they are your targets and not specified or imposed by your mentor. It is vital that you have ownership and that they are what you are comfortable with and clear about what you need to work on. For example, following discussions with her mentor and her self-evaluations of her own teaching, Jenny found that her questioning was disjointed and did not challenge the pupils. She produced a SMART target reflecting on this. She was specific about her problem – developing questioning and encouraging pupils to think more and thus be more challenged – and was encouraged by her mentor to write her questions down, thinking about possible answers and probing questions. Jenny also decided to observe other teachers, focusing her observation on the questioning of pupils. In addition, she read some materials and documents suggested by her mentor. To check she was achieving her goal, Jenny video recorded herself both at the start of the trial and after a week to see how she had developed. The results were positive, as she was able to use feedback from other mentors and the video recording to help her to develop her questioning skills.

Reading and researching into practice

Whatever you do, you cannot develop as a good teacher without understanding the theories related to the practice and then putting these theories to the test in your teaching.

> By thinking about the events, the observed person achieves a greater awareness of self and an increased understanding of how he or she enacts the role of school leader. This awareness and understanding encompasses areas such as personal and professional values and priorities, theoretical and applied knowledge, preferred modes of action, and strengths and limitations one brings to the leadership task. As participants carry out multiple cycles of observation and interviewing, they are able to examine how policies, practices, and resources are linked as a system in their school. (Barnett 1990, in Kortman and Honaker 2002: 25–6)

Reading around the areas that you are addressing through your goal setting helps you to move along the reflective cycle by encouraging you to review your beliefs and your practice in the context of other practitioners' experiences.

Summary

- Be proactive in your own learning and development by always being open to coaching and mentoring and by seeking help and advice.

- It's a good idea to evaluate by annotating your lesson plans and then using these to plan subsequent lessons but sticking to your foci.

- Be prepared to observe other practitioners with the focus on your own targets; evaluate how these practitioners were successful.

- Don't try to address everything at once – set yourself SMART targets.

- Review lesson plans and units of work regularly to make sure that different styles are catered for and that you are being creative and innovative.

- Ensure that you have regular meetings and feedback from your mentors.

- Be creative in how you evaluate yourself, for example using video to help you to reflect on your practice.

- Be prepared to do some reading round the issues being addressed.

Key reading

DfES (2005) *National Framework for Mentoring and Coaching*. Available online at: www. standards.dfes.gov.uk/local/ePDs/leading_on_intervention/site/u3/s3/ss3/sss4/index.htm

Lee, G.V. and Barnett, B.G. (2002) 'Using reflective questioning to promote collaborative dialogue'. In Kortman, S.A and Honaker, C.J. (eds), *The best mentoring experience*. Dubuque, I.A: Kendall Hunt, pp. 25–26

Parsloe, E. (1999) *The manager as coach and mentor*. London: Institute of Personnel & Development, pp. 8–34

Wragg, E. (1994) *An introduction to classroom observation*. London: Routledge, pp. 83–87 and 125

References and bibliography

Child, A. and Merrill, S. (2005) *Developing as a secondary school mentor: a case study approach for trainee mentors and their tutors*. Exeter: Learning Matters

DfES (2005) *National Framework for Mentoring and coaching*. Available online at: www. standards.dfes.gov.uk/local/ePDs/leading_on_intervention/site/u3/s3/ss3/sss4/index.htm

DfES (2006) 'Coaching in secondary schools' (DVD-ROM), *Secondary National Strategy for School Improvement*. Norwich: DfES

Hoult, S. (2005) *Secondary professional studies*. Exeter: Learning Matters

Kortman, S.A. and Honaker, C.J. (2002) *The best mentoring experience*. Dubuque, IA: Kendall Hunt

MacLennan, N. (1999) *Coaching and mentoring*. Aldershot: Gower

Murray, M. (2001) *Beyond the myths and magic of mentoring: how to facilitate an effective mentoring process*. San Francisco: Jossey-Bass

Parsloe, E. (1999) *The manager as coach and mentor*. London: Institute of Personnel & Development

Parsloe, E. and Wray, M. (2000) *Coaching and mentoring: practical methods to improve learning*. London: Kogan Page

Wragg, E. (1994) *An introduction to classroom observation*. London: Routledge

Website

www.tda.gov.uk/upload/resources/doc/q/qts_standards_guidance_2007.doc

CHAPTER 6

UNDERSTANDING THE ROLES OF SPECIALIST COLLEAGUES

Matthew Crowther

Standards addressed

Q5 Recognise and respect the contribution that colleagues, parents and carers can make to the development and well-being of children and young people and to raising their levels of attainment.

Q20 Know and understand the roles of colleagues with specific responsibilities, including those with responsibility for learners with special educational needs and disabilities and other individual learning needs.

Introduction

Schools are effectively large and complex communities where no two pupils are alike and all children have not just different educational needs, but different (and varied) personal, emotional and physical needs. Within schools every single person who comes into contact with a child has a responsibility for promoting the teaching, learning and welfare of that child. As someone embarking on a career in teaching you need to understand the roles and responsibilities of your fellow colleagues in meeting the needs of young people. By being aware of the wider roles of colleagues, parents and carers and how they all work together to raise achievement and promote learning you will be able to access a wealth of knowledge and expertise that will enhance your approach to teaching and help you with your own professional development.

A thought

The last time you spent a long period of time in a school may have been several years ago, or even when you were the pupil! Schools are constantly changing environments that need to be responsive to their pupils' needs. How aware are you of the school environment and how colleagues' roles and responsibilities have developed? Is it acceptable for a teacher to simply teach or are there other expected responsibilities? Within your first few weeks in school try to identify any major changes by finding out about key staff and arranging a time to meet with them to discuss any questions you may have.

Starting points

One of the key initiatives in schools over recent years has been the introduction of Every Child Matters (ECM). (This is covered in detail in Chapter 15 but cannot be divorced from content here and elsewhere.) This government initiative focuses on the well-being of children and young people. Within the framework there are five strands–the so-called 'outcomes' of ECM. Children should:

- Be healthy
- Stay safe
- Enjoy and achieve

- Make a positive contribution
- Achieve economic well-being.

(Children Act 2004)

As a teacher it is important that you have a clear understanding of the impact that this has on schools. The overriding aim of Every Child Matters is to protect children and young people and to help them accomplish what they want in life. This means all colleagues, parents and carers, external agencies and public services working together to help achieve each one of the five outcomes.

Within each school where you carry out your training there will be a large focus around Every Child Matters. Every colleague, whether teaching or not, has a responsibility to work within the framework. This places more emphasis on you to understand the roles and responsibilities of your various colleagues. It is important to understand, analyse and evaluate the impact that you, as a teacher, have on young people and through this evaluation to then communicate with relevant colleagues, parents and carers or appropriate external agencies. In this way you will become an integral part of the complex community that is the school.

Within schools

Some specialist colleagues are based in schools. A range of colleagues will have key responsibilities in assisting you in your role as a teacher. These colleagues cover a wide range of areas such as curriculum development, special educational needs, inclusion and pastoral duties. This builds on the roles and responsibilities within each teaching department that are based around the classroom and the curriculum.

The curriculum

School curricula have been developed to provide broad, personalised teaching that is accessible to all children and young people. According to the QCA, the curriculum should enable young people to become:

- **successful learners** who enjoy learning, make progress and achieve;
- **confident individuals** who are able to live safe, healthy and fulfilling lives;
- **responsible citizens** who make a positive contribution to society.

http://curriculum.qca.org.uk/aims/index.aspx

It is the role of senior management, usually a curriculum deputy, and the heads of teaching departments to ensure that the curriculum provided meets the above aims. Although in the majority of cases the curriculum is very much predefined, it must still cater for the range of abilities and needs of the pupils of your school. This includes those with special educational needs, the gifted and talented, and pupils from different social, moral, cultural and linguistic backgrounds. Catering for these groups must be evident in both planning and teaching the curriculum. Colleagues who can assist you with building on your delivery of the curriculum include fellow teachers, curriculum managers and departmental heads.

Fellow teaching colleagues will have a vast range of experience and will be happy to offer advice and help on planning teaching and learning strategies. Some schools will have advanced skills teachers (ASTs) who have constantly demonstrated a high level of expertise and effectiveness in their teaching. It is important as a teacher new to the profession that you draw on the experiences of other teachers and other curriculum specialists. Classroom observations are vital to this process.

Observation allows you to see a range of teaching and learning strategies, not just in your own subject area but across the curriculum. Cross-curricular observation is rewarding as other subject area colleagues may demonstrate particular strengths or techniques that can be incorporated into your own teaching. One aspect of teaching that needs particular focus is planning. By planning ahead and discussing your planning with your head of department or experienced colleagues you will have the opportunity to think about how you can maximise the welfare and achievement of all your pupils. Again, self-evaluation and reflection of your planning is critical.

Special educational needs and inclusion

SEN and inclusion dovetail into curriculum development. Schools work hard to ensure that the curriculum on offer provides effective learning opportunities for all pupils, whatever their needs. This is based around the following three key elements:

- Setting suitable learning challenges where all pupils can experience success in learning through teaching that is suitable to their individual abilities.
- Responding to pupils' diverse learning needs whether it be boys and girls, physical disabilities, pupils of different ethnic groups and social and cultural backgrounds or linguistic capabilities.
- Overcoming potential barriers to learning and assessment for individuals and groups of pupils by ensuring that teachers make provision for SEN pupils to be able to participate in assessment activities.

(www.nc.uk.net/nc_resources/html/inclusion.shtml)

Birkett (2003) states that teachers have a responsibility to support pupils with highly complex needs. Children and young people in mainstream school include disabled students and students with behaviour or learning difficulties.

Senior management and colleagues have a legal responsibility to make sure that both the curriculum and special educational needs policy within the school meet the needs of the pupils. The main aim of special needs is that every child reaches his or her full potential in school despite any disabilities or learning needs. As a teacher there are many ways in which this can be achieved. The appropriate specialists to advise on the school's policy towards SEN are lead colleagues such as the SEN coordinator (SENCO) or inclusion manager. SENCOs and their teams may create and distribute resources to help a teacher with special needs pupils; such resources may also be other colleagues. They can include a specialist higher-level teaching assistant (TA) or teaching support, technical support such as laptops or even simple classroom strategies to deal with the special needs within your classes. As a teacher you must plan on how best to utilise such colleagues and resources within your lessons. Lee (2002) identified several factors that influence working with TAs and included some of the following from a teacher's point of view:

- clarity of role for the TA;
- time for teachers and TAs to collaborate;
- guiding the TA on strategies to use with pupils;
- communicating effectively with the TA.

As part of the process, you should evaluate the effectiveness of the resources that have been used to help SEN pupils. From this, you can begin to develop strategies for individual pupils.

All teachers are essentially SEN teachers. They have a responsibility to their pupils as within any one class there can be a range of SEN needs. By speaking with and observing, not just members of your department, but colleagues across the school, and by using the expertise of the SEN co-ordinator you can effectively arm yourself with a range of strategies to help focus your teaching and understanding around inclusion and special educational needs.

A thought

Now that you are teaching have you considered the pupils seated in front of you in your classes? Do you feel that you have a good understanding of what teaching and learning, behavioural management, assessment and support is going to be most effective for them on a collective and individual basis? It may seem a difficult task to accommodate every single need but behind each pupil is a story. You are not teaching a class, but a set of individuals.

Pastoral system

All schools have a pastoral system which usually consists of a pastoral deputy head and learning managers (traditionally heads of year) along with form tutors in daily contact with the pupils. Each pupil is different and each has different learning, behaviour and emotional needs of which both you and the school must be aware. The role of the pastoral team is to promote an environment within school where positive teaching and learning can take place. They have a particular duty to monitor the mental and physical welfare of all students and to transmit concerns to other colleagues. This is achieved by supporting pupils' welfare, monitoring behaviour and achievement and ensuring that all pupils feel secure. Form tutors must learn to listen to pupils with as much respect or 'equality' as adults (Denby 2007).

As a teacher you have a responsibility to report any pupil concerns regarding behaviour, learning or other student welfare issues to the relevant pastoral colleague so that interventions and strategies can be used in order to support the pupil. The National Association for Pastoral Care in Education (www.napce.org.uk) has lots of useful information.

Application to teaching

In order to better understand your classes and build up a relationship with key colleagues start with one of your classes to compile information about your pupils. Make sure that you speak with all the colleagues who have some impact on that class. This may be the SEN coordinator who can give you background to SEN students or the curriculum deputy who can help compile attainment data about the students in the class. You may wish to speak with relevant pastoral staff to gain an insight into some of the family, behavioural, social and cultural issues to do with the pupils in the class.

Once you have compiled this information, consider how it can help you when planning your lessons. How can you incorporate the knowledge of individual needs into effective teaching and learning strategies through differentiation of work or addressing different learning styles?

Data managers (assessment)

Although covered in greater detail in Chapter 17 it is important in this context to recognise the increasing role of data within the management of a successful school. Teachers are expected to use a wide variety of data and there are specialist colleagues within school who have overall responsibility for the production and dissemination of data. Schools are data rich environments and, as a new teacher, it is important to familiarise yourself with the data and how it is used. Talk to colleagues responsible for data so that you can improve your teaching through a better understanding of your pupils. Data not only covers assessment but also behaviour. It facilitates the accurate use of interventions and teaching and learning strategies for pupils who are either underperforming or exceeding expectations.

Administration, technical support and caretaking colleagues

Schools have a whole range of support staff including administration and technical colleagues, buildings and caretaking staff. Often administration colleagues will come to your aid when you need to write letters to parents, to organise events or to deal with external agencies. Technical colleagues also help, in particular with new technology, and caretaking staff assist with the management of physical resources.

Your main focus will be teaching and learning; efficient administration and other support makes sure that it stays that way.

External colleagues

At one time, the word *colleagues* within education just meant fellow teachers, but not any more. Schools form a hub that is part of the wider community, they are not just dependent on teachers and support staff within them but on a whole range of outside agencies and individuals who can all be considered 'colleagues' in achieving the education and welfare of children (see Chapter 15). External colleagues include parents and carers and health, social and justice professionals.

INDIVIDUAL REFLECTION

Take three individuals as examples from one of the groups that you are teaching and, from your knowledge of their circumstances, list the external colleagues who have been involved in their education. Sort these into an order of priority and consider why particular colleagues are more important to particular young people. Repeat the exercise at your next placement. What does this tell you about the children in each school? What conclusions can you draw from this?

Parents and carers

The children in your care come from many differing backgrounds. The nuclear family, with both parents involved in the welfare of the child, may be the exception rather than the rule. Making assumptions about mothers and fathers is not wise, as many children will be cared for in different circumstances and by different people. Parents/carers[1] have a pivotal role in the development and well-being of children and young people. The communication channels between schools and carers should always be open. As a teacher, you will usually formally communicate through the school's reporting system and at consultation evenings. However, it is important to understand that the role carers have is much more and that, consequently, their involvement in school and education can be much larger.

The relationship between schools and carers needs to be positive. Communication between schools and families is becoming more frequent and thus more important, while possibly losing some of its 'formal' edge. To effectively deal with carers the following areas need to be considered:

- Staff must be approachable, communication is two-way and possible ethnic, social and cultural issues must be dealt with positively and sensitively.
- Carers and school staff can learn from one another and develop a relationship where both parties understand their role in promoting pupils' achievement.
- Carers of all social backgrounds should be involved in their child's progress and have an opportunity to express their views on the care and education being provided.
- Challenges and barriers such as busy or inactive carers must be overcome through creating flexibility within the communication process.

Source: www.teachernet.gov.uk/wholeschool/familyandcommunity/workingwithparents/ipratoolkit/ipra_taking_action/

The Children's Plan, launched in December 2007, contains a package of measures to improve teacher training, to enhance the role for school SEN coordinators and to supply better data to identify whether SEN pupils are progressing. Up to 20 per cent of families have one or more children identified as having a special educational need. The Plan also contains ideas to help parents and carers both to stay in contact with teachers and to learn alongside their children; it also proposes a greater role for the personal tutor.

At primary and early years stages, the idea of the 'red book'–a record of an individual's progress–will be developed so that parents can track development in key areas like mathematics and English.

GROUP EXERCISE

Review with your peers some of your experiences of dealing with colleagues. Some schools have different approaches to different issues and have a wider range of colleagues than others. Collect information on the colleagues and processes in your placement and, through discussion, compare them with those in other schools. Suggest an agreed list of priority colleagues and then make sure that you know exactly what each does in each of your placement schools.

---

1. To avoid repetition and as both are 'carers', this term is used to mean both groups.

Social services

As an external agency Children's Social Services (www.everychildmatters.gov.uk/social-care/socialservices/) may be called upon to intervene and support the school and specific pupils where there are children in need and looked-after children (children in care). Pastoral colleagues will involve Social Services if they believe a young person to be at high risk from harm, need looking after by the local authority or is a pupil seeking adoption.

As part of the children's trusts approach of ECM (www.everychildmatters.gov.uk/aims/childrenstrusts/) and multi-agency working you should understand that Children's Social Services form part of a wider menu of support that can be provided through school depending on the level of need of the pupil. You must recognise that pupils and their families may have contact with Social Services and a social worker due to being at risk or needing local authority intervention, so familiarising yourself with the needs of each pupil is paramount. The school will be central to all services as teachers spend significantly more time with children than do their families and can have considerable input into the welfare of the child.

Other key colleagues may include the school nurse, trained counsellors and mentors. These may provide confidential health advice, promote healthy living through the Healthy Schools Initiative or give additional support to pupils, carers and school in promoting student welfare.

Conclusion

Schools are not islands. They are part of a complex structure of experts, agencies and interested parties. All colleagues should be valued equally for their knowledge, experience and expertise.

Summary

- There is a vast range of colleagues with whom, as a teacher, you will have a professional relationship.
- These carry an enormous amount of knowledge and expertise and provide guidance and support so that you can promote teaching and learning and pupil welfare for the benefit of all
- By using these colleagues both your professional development and the pupils' learning experiences will be much improved.

Key reading

Information about roles and responsibilities in schools, including references to the SEN coordinator role and a link to the SEN Code of Practice, may be found at: www.teachernet.gov.uk

DfES (2005) *Every Child Matters: Common core of skills and knowledge for the children's workforce*. Available online at: www.everychildmatters.gov.uk/

GTC(E) *Statement of Professional Values and Practice for Teachers Practice*. Available online at: www.gtce.org.uk/publications/pub_reg

References and bibliography

Birkett, V. (2003) *How to support and teach children with special educational needs*. LDA McGraw-Hill Children's Publishing

Dendy, N. (2007) *Hawaii International Conference on Education*. Pepperdine University, CA

Lee, B. (2002) *Teaching assistants in schools: the current state of play*. Windsor: NFER

The National Curriculum Online website contains the National Curriculum inclusion statement, inclusion statements by subject and other inclusion materials published by the QCA. It is available at: www.nc.uk.net/nc_resources/html/inclusion.shtml

CHAPTER 7

LEARNING AT 'M' LEVEL AND CONTINUING PROFESSIONAL DEVELOPMENT

Helen Swift

Standards addressed

Q7

(a) Reflect on and improve their practice and take responsibility for identifying and meeting their developing professional needs.

(b) Identify priorities for early professional development in the context of induction.

Introduction

Many of you will be on a postgraduate course of teacher training. To be truly postgraduate, this means that you must show that you are capable of writing at Masters ('M') level. This chapter aims to develop your understanding of why M level modules have been included in PGCE courses and how you can succeed in producing them. It will examine some of the principles which differentiate postgraduate from undergraduate level assessment. The QTS Standards that you are reaching are just the first step in a career progression that then has an NQT (Newly Qualified Teacher) year and an expectation that you will continue to develop professionally. This chapter therefore also explores the nature and requirements of continuing professional development, particularly early professional development.

Table 7.1 A typical Masters course structure

Year/qualification	Credits	Assessed work
Year 1		
Postgraduate Certificate	60 credits	2 × 30 credit assignments
Year 2		
Postgraduate Diploma	120 credits	2 × 30 credit assignments
Year 3		
Masters	180 credits	1 × 60 credit dissertation

Masters level

Many of you may be wondering why Masters level credits are now part of a Postgraduate Certificate in Education (PGCE). This has stemmed from the fact that higher education (HE) has been reorganised within the newly created European Higher Education Area (Bologna Agreement 1999). This agreement established that no HE course should call itself postgraduate if it did not include 'M' level work. There has long been an anomaly in HE in that the first stage of a Masters course is called a Postgraduate Certificate (see Table 7.1).

This has often caused confusion among students who wondered if they had achieved 'M' level credit through undertaking a traditional – pre-Bologna – PGCE.

The Bologna Agreement led to PGCE educators having to make a decision from September 2007 as to whether to include 'M' level credit and retain the existing title, or for the course to change its name to Professional Certificate in Education – a qualification that did not incorporate 'M' level work. A survey conducted by the Universities Council for Education of Teachers (UCET) in December 2006 indicated that 39 per cent of HEIs were planning to offer PGCEs at just 'M' level and 48 per cent were planning to offer PGCEs at both 'H' (current) and 'M' level. This has created a two-tier system.

Structure of a traditional Masters

All Masters programmes in the UK are now a standard 180 Credit Accumulation Transfer (CATs) points. This is the system whereby credit can be transferred from one institution to another. Table 7.1 is a typical Masters course structure.

Different institutions may vary the size of their module credits, so, for example, the 2×30 credit assignments could be 3×20 credit assignments. Using the model in Table 7.1, as a trainee teacher on such a course, you will leave your PGCE with a third of a Masters, i.e. a Postgraduate Certificate at 'M' level. Due to the nature of the work undertaken on a PGCE course you will also have undertaken assessed work which does not contribute to the Masters element. Having achieved a third of a Masters it is obviously beneficial for trainee teachers to continue at some point in their career and acquire the remaining 120 credits to gain a full Masters qualification. This is discussed further below and now positively supported by government.

> ### 💭 A thought
>
> It is beneficial to have a clearly defined career path in teaching. Asking yourself where you want to be in five and ten years' time is a good way of assessing your early professional development needs

Types of postgraduate level study

There is a wide variety of ways of achieving postgraduate level outcomes through individual modules of assessment. HEIs are becoming ever more creative in their use of assessment which embodies the essence of postgraduate work. Three of the most common types of assignment offered are as follows:

- **Portfolio.** This asks you to build a portfolio which includes a range of evidence which demonstrates your professional achievement within aspects of the course. The evidence is not just a collection of documents; it is an active record which personifies the steps taken in pursuit of your goals. A portfolio is usually accompanied by a critical review which highlights the learning which has taken place through the development of the materials, along with a review of appropriate literature. An index, which clearly indicates the purpose of each piece of evidence, should accompany the portfolio. This must be clearly referenced within the critical review.

- **Presentation.** You may often be asked to give presentations during your postgraduate study. This method of assessment is a way of harnessing these presentations and formalising them through 'M' level credit. It also provides an opportunity for wider dissemination of assessment materials to other students on the course. Very strict criteria have to be applied to ensure that there is fairness in the judgement of what is a postgraduate level presentation, as opposed to what would be an undergraduate level presentation.

- **Essay.** This is a traditional piece of extended writing which can vary from 4–6,000 words and provides an opportunity for you to sharpen your writing skills. The quality of the reading to underpin the main arguments presented in the essay is very important, as is its structure and coherence and the synthesis of its main issues. This type of assessment is often tied in with a small practitioner action research study which could be designed to develop learning and teaching strategies, for example, to raise pupil achievement.

☁ A thought

As can be seen from the above range of assignments, postgraduate study is more varied and flexible than you may have imagined. It is generally related to meeting the needs of busy teachers and could focus on addressing performance management targets. It also offers the opportunity for accreditation of work you are already undertaking in your professional role, through mechanisms such as portfolio assessment.

Reflective practitioner

Many professionally focused Masters courses are designed with the underpinning philosophy of encouraging and stimulating the development of reflective practitioners (see Chapter 1). As a newly qualified practitioner you will be able to develop the tools to take responsibility for identifying and meeting your own early professional development needs. Reflective practice is set out in the theories of Schön (1983) and exemplified by such writers as Ghaye and Ghaye (1998), McEntee *et al.* (2003) and Farrell (2004). These theories emphasise the commonality of experience of professionals who are all called upon to exercise judgement and sensitivity in highly complex situations. You will join a group of professionals who need to develop 'situational understanding' by incorporating systematic reflection and self-evaluation into their practice. Schön (1983: 42) describes this as '… a reflective conversation with the situation'. Day (2002: 56) refers to three kinds of reflection:

- reflection about action (the goals and practices of one's profession);
- reflection on action (weighing competing viewpoints and then exploring alternative solutions); and
- reflection in action (drawing upon experience and knowledge).

He argues that reflection is a necessary process for learning, but that it is considerably promoted by interaction with others.

Application to teaching

Children and young people can also benefit from their own 'reflective' learning. Encourage them to think about their own development needs at an early stage. They too need to develop responsibility for enhancing their own profile. An exercise with children of any age can be to imagine where they would like to be in five or ten years' time. They can have great fun imagining themselves as astronauts, pop singers or Formula 1 drivers. The exercise is then to track backwards over the five- or ten-year period to see what skills, knowledge and experiences they will need to develop if they are going to reach their ambition. This can be used as a planning project in almost any subject and with almost any age group.

Aims of postgraduate level study

The overall aim of 'M' level postgraduate courses which are professionally focused, as opposed to undergraduate courses, is to assimilate material at a deeper level. You will need to demonstrate greater intellectual activity, enhanced professional competence and critical reflective awareness. The learning outcomes of 'M' level modules can be divided into two distinct areas: knowledge and understanding, and ability. Knowledge and understanding relate to the content of your course. Ability relates to the skills you can demonstrate after completion of the course. Typical examples of these are:

- *Knowledge and understanding*

  - identifies and understands strategies for improving own practice within the institution;
  - analyses and evaluates strategies for supporting different learners.

- *Ability*
  - critically evaluates established and emergent theories of teaching and learning;
  - produces a well planned and innovative set of materials which enhances teaching and learning within an identified curriculum area.

Meeting the knowledge and understanding and ability outcomes is related to the concept of the reflective practitioner and requires demonstration of professional knowledge and ability exemplified in:

- engaging in analysis and critical reflection;
- employing independent learning strategies;
- integrating practical and theoretical understanding;
- applying learning to evaluate and inform practice.

Below, these four overall aims are examined further and related to the requirements of Masters level study on a PGCE course.

Engaging in analysis and critical reflection

Postgraduate level work requires critical engagement with the ideas of those in 'authority'. These are people with a wide range of experience and expertise in the field. They have often undertaken practical research studies and the published findings are regarded as a useful starting point in building up a body of understanding.

There are several kinds of literature, e.g. theoretical, research, practice and policy. Different types of literature will tend to emphasise claims to different kinds of knowledge and have different sets of strengths and limitations.

- **Theoretical knowledge** – deals with systems of interrelated concepts. It may well draw from other writers' work.
- **Research-based knowledge** – is based on focused and systematic enquiry using various methods of data collection and analysis resulting in a set of research findings. It is important to consider the nature of the research and whether it has been commissioned by a particular body, such as the DCSF. This can influence the findings of the research.
- **Practice-based knowledge** – concerns knowledge of everyday activity, such as professional practice. This may be implicit know-how, i.e. used without awareness. Reflection is the means whereby this knowledge is brought into full consciousness in order to inform and challenge practice.
- **Policy literature** – policy-makers tend to emphasise practice knowledge. A policy is based on a set of values and assumptions in keeping with a particular political ideology. It is important to critically review this literature in relation to theory and not assume it is ideal.

Therefore, learning to engage in critical analysis and reflection within academic enquiry necessitates a questioning approach to your studies. It requires an interrogative tactic to be used to examine the literature and not believe it as authoritative and indisputable. This is particularly relevant in terms of government policy documents.

Central points include using a range of literature from different sources, not relying on individual authors' beliefs and recognising that a wider viewpoint gives a more balanced perspective. Key texts are usually recommended as part of the assessment and these are a guide to the level of reading required.

Employing independent learning strategies

A key aspect of engaging in analysis and critical reflection is demonstrating, through your assignments, your competence in employing independent learning strategies, i.e. the extent to which you have used your capability to interrogate and critically examine the literature and research to form your own well-informed judgement.

The choice, range and depth of literature used are key elements in employing independent learning strategies. The degree to which this is achieved is, in part, judged by the extent to which your work draws together the views of a range of theorists and highlights the strengths and weaknesses inherent within them. The articulation and support of a case or argument with a breakdown and analysis of issues and inherent relationships between them is critical in demonstrating how you have engaged in 'critical activity'. The conclusions you have developed highlight how you have employed judgement in the appropriate treatment, interpretation and reporting of evidence and research findings.

INDIVIDUAL REFLECTION

Think about the following key points in relation to the production of M level material and decide how you can:

- adopt an attitude of scepticism not cynicism;
- use a questioning approach to claims being made;
- scrutinise – checking the coherence of a theory, sufficiency of evidence and underpinning values and assumptions.

How useful do you think these are as guides to producing good M level work? What would you add to them?

Integrating practical and theoretical understanding

The demonstration of critical evaluation of theory/research in relation to professional practice is an important tool on a PGCE 'M' level course. This is demonstrated in assignments by underpinning comments about your own practice with references to appropriate theory.

As mentioned above there is a wide range of educational literature available and a great deal of this is related to theoretical knowledge of learning and teaching. Much of what is written is very accessible and easy to relate to the reality of the classroom because it has been written by practitioners. For example, the late Professor Ted Wragg was a very interesting, amusing and, above all, readable writer.

Therefore the theory that you cover as part of your 'M' level PGCE is not turgid, nor is it unrelated to your everyday experiences in school. Critical incidents that you have to deal with in practice are often less problematical when reading demonstrates that there are good examples and practical solutions to be found in literature. Classroom management, for example, is often of great concern to the trainee teacher but authors such as those referred to in Chapter 8 on behaviour management are able to use a wealth of experience and expertise to relate the theory to the practice. Thus the reading will enable you to feel more confident that your own practice relates to what others have experienced and written about.

In essence, read widely and gain knowledge about your professional role, try to be receptive to new ideas obtained from theory and remember most incidents from practice can be related to theory.

Applying learning to evaluate and inform practice

At Masters level you will be expected to demonstrate a critical understanding of appropriate knowledge gained from a theoretical perspective and to be able to apply this theory to evaluate and inform professional practice. This includes the application of conceptual ideas and research findings.

Becoming a reflective practitioner requires taking responsibility for your own academic learning and having the motivation to inform your own and others' practice. The key to this element of a Masters programme is using the ideas and theories you have established from your reading and any course lectures to engage in critical dialogue with colleagues, both fellow learners and within your school placement. This allows you to broaden the scope of your thinking and evaluate and inform practice using a more knowledgeable approach. The underlying principle is to provide you with skills of critical analysis and deepening understanding of professional practice to give you the confidence to develop strategies for the improvement of your own professional practice.

It is important that you *engage* in critical dialogue with professional colleagues, discuss ideas for the development of professional practice with colleagues and develop a well-grounded standpoint to inform your own and others' practice.

Continuing professional development

The TDA (2007) website (www.tda.gov.uk) determines that continuing professional development (CPD)

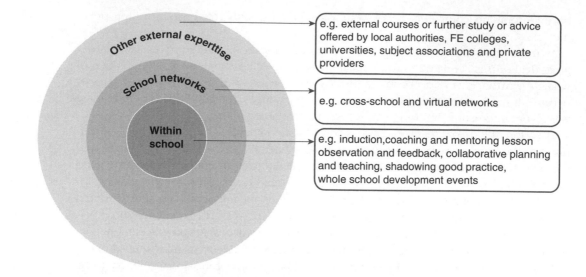

e.g. external courses or further study or advice offered by local authorities, FE colleges, universities, subject associations and private providers

e.g. cross-school and virtual networks

e.g. induction,coaching and mentoring lesson observation and feedback, collaborative planning and teaching, shadowing good practice, whole school development events

Figure 7.1   CPD links within school, school networks and external expertise
Source: tda.gov.uk (accessed 2 November 2007)

consists of reflective activity designed to improve an individual's attributes, knowledge, understanding and skills. It supports individual needs and improves professional practice.

Figure 7.1 shows how CPD is interlinked between elements from the school, school networks and other external expertise.

Blandford (2001) outlines the key issues which schools need to work towards when deciding professional development requirements for their staff. These include: reflecting on experiences, individual and collaborative research and practice, keeping up to date with educational thinking and giving critical deliberation to education policy, with the emphasis being on raising pupil achievement.

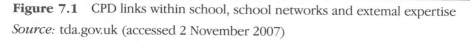

A thought

As a teacher you're used to thinking about the needs of your pupils. It's also important that you're able to further your own development.

Early professional development (induction)

Early professional development (EPD) is described by Turner (2006: 00) as:

the development of knowledge, understanding, skills and attitudes of teachers that might occur in the induction plus the two immediate years after induction.

Blandford (2000: 06) contends that:

> teachers and support staff will normally associate professional development with In-Service Education for Teachers (INSET).

She describes this as planned training activities to develop knowledge and skills which can take place both within the school or at another venue. INSET was the original term used to refer to professional development and still is to some extent. However, the term 'continuing professional development' is becoming more widely used within the teaching profession. To broadly differentiate between the two: INSET could be described as a short training course with no assessment requirements. It could, for example, be the requirements of non-contact days (NCD) where staff development is organised for the whole school. CPD, as outlined above, could be described as more sustained professional development with learning outcomes and often includes assessed work.

Newly qualified teachers who engage in 'early professional development' will have the opportunity to engage in both kinds of development. The development of a profile in teaching which demonstrates that professional development has been undertaken is a useful tool in terms of performance management, threshold assessment and promotional prospects. Some examples of what could be classed as INSET and CPD are:

- **INSET:**
  - training from examination boards (GCSE, A Level, etc.);
  - local authority short courses;
  - classroom observation to improve practice;
  - conference attendance;
  - shadowing a pupil.
- **CPD:**
  - accredited Masters modules;
  - NQT Standards portfolio;
  - mentoring/coaching;
  - writing curriculum materials.

Both types of professional development should be related to the 'school improvement plan' (SIP) and individual 'performance management targets' (PMTs). Performance management is the appraisal system operating in schools whereby senior managers embark on an appraisal interview with all their teachers. This is to assess how well the teacher has performed during the year against predetermined targets and to set new targets for the forthcoming cycle. These should be set within the context of the SIP to ensure that all teachers are working towards the same goals. When developing skills and attributes for performance management and reflecting on early professional development you will have to be proactive in considering in which direction you would like your career to develop. Clarity of what is expected at each career stage can be accessed by reference to the Professional Standards for Teachers in England which are 'statements of a teacher's professional attributes, professional knowledge and understanding, and professional skills'.

Early professional development of the CPD kind would seem to offer some opportunity to step outside the working environment and examine, review and reflect on teaching and learning, as outlined in the section above on the reflective practitioner. Whether this opportunity is offered or encouraged is often dependent on your own initiative and school finances. This may be easier in future. The Children's Plan, an ambitious 'blueprint' for the future published by the DCSF in December 2007, includes plans to encourage *all* practitioners to reach Masters level. It says:

> We already have many teachers and headteachers who are among the best in the world. However, to deliver a teaching workforce and a new generation of headteachers which is consistently world class we will allocate £44m over the next three years to make teaching a Masters-level profession, with all new teachers able to study for a Masters-level qualification through a focus on continued professional development.

The variety of assignments now on offer on Masters courses enables you as an NQT/new teacher to select modules which best suit your needs and are easier to fit into your busy professional lives. Many higher education institutions are now offering an NQT module during the induction year which is linked to the work that you will have to undertake anyway to meet the NQT standards.

GROUP EXERCISE

- Working in pairs, list as many examples you can of what could be classed as either CPD or INSET activities. Categorise them by CPD or INSET and be prepared to defend why you think an activity is one or the other.
- Working in a small group identify any CPD/INSET activities you have been involved in on your course and discuss what impact they could have had on trainee teachers, schools and pupils.

Share your findings with the whole group.

Postgraduate professional development

The Training and Development Agency (TDA) allows HE institutions and other relevant bodies to bid for funding to contribute towards postgraduate professional development (PPD) which is professional development at Masters level. A number of providers are using this funding to reduce the cost of Masters provision. The funding criteria for PPD require the institution to demonstrate that it has impacted on teachers, schools and pupils. With these criteria in place it means that PPD can really add value to the new teacher's profile. The TDA (2007) website gives examples of what these benefits could be:

School:

> PPD programmes give teachers the time and opportunities to develop as reflective practitioners and have a positive impact on classroom performance.

Teacher:

> There have been a substantial number of promoted posts gained by participants in the programme . . . in one school alone with 20 participants, over 50% have gained promotions internally and externally.

Pupils:

> With PPD in place the school has achieved its best results ever.

Evidence shows that professional development enhances a teacher's well-being and provides an opportunity to step outside the classroom and reflect on practice. This is what you should be aiming for as a new practitioner. Developing reflective practitioners is an important aspect of encouraging you – and indeed all teachers – to identify and fulfil learning needs. A wealth of professional development opportunities are available for you as a newly qualified teacher to cultivate a high-quality profile which enhances 'learning and teaching' and addresses your individual needs. Due to the nature of schools the teacher has to be proactive in seeking out and taking responsibility for identifying and meeting professional development needs – this means *you*: to continue with your professional development you will need to be keen and proactive, to seek out appropriate opportunities and ensure that you are aware of the funding arrangements that go with them. In this way you will enhance and accelerate your progress through your career.

Summary

- 'M' level assessment is now part of PGCE courses.
- Postgraduate assessment is now more flexible to meet changing professional needs.
- The aims of postgraduate study include both knowledge and ability.
- Postgraduate students should engage in analysis and critical reflection, employ independent learning strategies, integrate practical and theoretical understanding and apply learning to evaluate and inform practice.
- Development of the reflective practitioner is encouraged at 'M' level and gives teachers the tools to identify their continuing professional development needs.
- Early professional development in the context of continuing professional development and postgraduate professional development is encouraged.
- Government is planning to make teaching a Masters level profession.

Key reading

Burton, D. and Bartless, S. (2005) *Practitioner research for teachers.* London: Paul Chapman

Pickering, J., Daly, C. and Pachier, N. (2007) *New designs for teachers' professional learning.* London: Bedford Way Papers

Wallace, M. and Poulson, L. (2003) (eds) *Learning to read critically in teaching and learning.* London: Sage

Training and Development Agency (2007) – www.tda.gov.uk/teachers/continuing professional development/ppd (accessed 2 November 2007)

Turner, C. (2006) 'Informal learning and its relevance to the early professional development of teachers in secondary schools in England and Wales'. *Journal of In-service Education,* 32 (3), 301–319

References and bibliography

Blandford, S. (2000) *Managing professional development in schools.* London: Routledge

Blandford, S. (2001) 'Professional development in schools'. In Banks, A. and Mayers, A.S. (eds), *Early professional development for teachers.* London: David Fulton

Day, C. (2002) Revisiting the Purposes of Continuing Professional Development. In Trorey, G. and Cullingford, C. (eds) *Professional Development and Institutional Needs.* Aldershot: Ashgate Publishing Ltd.

Farell, T.S.C. (2004) *Reflective practice in action: 80 reflection breaks for busy teachers.* Thousand Oaks, CA and London: Corwin.

Ghaye, T. and Ghaye, K. (1998) *Teaching and learning through critical reflective practice.* London: David Fulton Publishers.

McEntee, G.H. (2003) *At the heart of teaching: a guide to reflective practice.* New York and London: Teachers College Press.

Schön, D.A. (1983) *The reflective practitioner.* London: Temple Smith

Training and Development Agency (2007) www.tda.gov.uk/teachers/continuing professionaldevelopment/cpd. accessed 2 November 2007

Part 2

STRATEGIES FOR TEACHING, FOR LEARNING AND FOR DEVELOPING PUPILS

CHAPTER 8

CLASSROOM MANAGEMENT AND BEHAVIOUR STRATEGIES

Jayne Price

Standards addressed

Q30 Establish a purposeful and safe learning environment conducive to learning and identify opportunities for learners to learn in and out of school contexts.

Q31 Establish a clear framework for classroom discipline to manage learners' behaviour constructively and promote their self-control and independence.

Introduction

As a teacher the creation of a positive classroom environment in which pupils are safe, secure and able to learn underpins everything that you do. Making relationships with pupils is fundamental to teaching and learning. You need to develop methods by which you plan lessons that engage and motivate pupils, use assessment for learning strategies (see Chapter 13) and organise your classroom for lesson activities. The ways in which you interact with pupils as a class and individually, how you deal with low-level disruption and how you cope with more challenging aspects of behaviour all define your classroom environment and create and cement your relationships with pupils.

Behaviour and learning

Managing behaviour and promoting learning are not separate issues, they are interdependent. This is one of the most essential constructs with which you need to come to terms. Powell and Tod (2004) suggest that we use the term 'learning behaviour' in order to emphasise this link and define behaviours that are exhibited in the classroom. Powell and Tod argue that learning behaviour arises from the learner's relationships and offer the model in Figure 8.1 as a conceptual framework by which we can come to understand the determinates of learning behaviour.

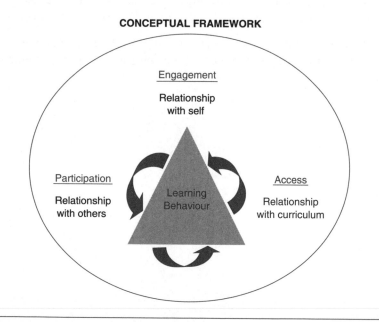

Figure 8.1   Model of learning behaviour

Relationship with the curriculum – promoting access and engagement

There is a direct link between the way that you plan a lesson and behaviour. To succeed, pupils must understand the purpose and relevance of their work. They need to perceive how the new work builds on existing knowledge and previous learning activities, and how what they are doing fits into the big picture of how they are progressing as musicians, scientists, historians, etc. Smith *et al.* (2003) talk about building motivation by 'selling the benefits' of what the pupils are going to learn.

Active learning

Pupils are more likely to display positive learning behaviours when they experience variety in the way in which the lesson is presented, in the activities and materials with which they will engage and in how they demonstrate their learning to you. Expositions and explanations supported with a variety of stimuli – props, photographs, video, ICT, music, discussion, etc. – will help pupils to stay focused on you and the point you are teaching. Pupils stay on task and incidences of low-level disruption are reduced when they are involved in activities to develop and consolidate their learning that generate curiosity and encourage them to construct their own solutions to given problems. Asking pupils to demonstrate their learning in a variety of different ways acknowledges that not all pupils process and remember information in the same way. Examples could include drawing a mind map, making a board game, writing a report, making a presentation, teaching someone else the concept, role playing a process, developing a storyboard or cartoon. Many possible behaviour problems will be prevented or minimised by having a clearly structured lesson which is well paced with a variety of tasks which truly engage pupils. In particular, avoid 'occupying' tasks; instead concentrate on developing activities that will really push the pupils forward in their learning.

A thought

How often when we are working do we take comfort breaks without realising we're doing it? We just go and get a coffee, or we'll just put the washing on or we'll just ring someone to see if they're OK before we get on with our work. Think about how you process information and the length of your own concentration span – when sitting in a long lecture for example. Do you stay fully focused for the whole time? Crowley (2006) reminds us that when planning a lesson, we have to be reasonable; it's perfectly acceptable to expect the pupils to be silent during your explanation as long as you don't proceed to talk without any other stimulus for 20 minutes. Similarly, it's possible to have pupils working on their own in silence as long as it's not for the whole lesson. How much variety do you have in your lessons?

Expectations

Pupils must understand your expectations; this is a vital concept in helping them to engage fully in their learning. Pupils need to know what they are aiming for when they set off on a task and how to improve their work in order to get there. Using assessment for learning strategies not only motivates pupils but also improves their work and therefore increases self-esteem and a feeling of satisfaction from their work. Research has shown that if we have high expectations of our pupils, they will often surprise us. Be wary of always giving lower-ability pupils low-level knowledge and comprehension-type tasks to do. Involve them in group tasks that really require them to think and to engage with their own learning.

Access

Perhaps the most important factor in pupils' relationship to the curriculum is the question of access. Is the lesson manageable, understandable or challenging enough for all the

Application to teaching

Low-level disruption may still happen, however well you have structured the lesson. It is less likely, and less likely to be a problem, if you ensure that each lesson has a range of learning activities. This is the first principle you should apply to lesson planning. Should low-level disruption occur the following strategies are useful:

» **Use non-verbal communication** – develop the 'look' that means I'm not pleased, use hand gestures to indicate turn round or put your pen down. The benefit of using this strategy is that the lesson can continue without interruption.
» **Allow take-up time** – ask a pupil to get on with their work and tell them that you will come and see how they are doing in two minutes. The benefit of this strategy is that you have given them an assertive instruction but in a positive way.
» **Refocus the pupils on their work** – 'Lisa, what should you be doing now?' This reinforces the positive learning behaviour you expect. Another way of doing this is to ask the pupil 'what's our rule about ....?'
» **Create a diversion** – when you see a misdemeanour occurring ask the pupil 'Alright, Emma?' this positive question makes it difficult for the pupil to be confrontational with you.
» **Proximity praise** – rather than confront the inappropriate behaviour, praise another pupil nearby who is doing what you want. This strategy works well with behaviour that is basically attention-seeking.

learners in the group? Many behaviour issues in the classroom arise from not getting this right, when pupils demonstrate behaviours that are related to task avoidance, frustration or boredom. Teachers need to develop differentiation strategies that enable all pupils to make progress. These could include targeting support from other adults, actively engaging pupils in group tasks that encourage all to contribute at their own level, pitched questions, guided learning and so on.

These are fundamental principles of planning effective lessons which are developed further in Chapters 9, 10, 11, 12 and 13.

Relationship with others – developing a positive climate for learning

Your own relationship with the pupils is the most important factor in determining learning behaviour in your classroom. Relationships are built over time and are defined by the way in which you interact with the pupils in groups and on an individual basis and also in the wider classroom climate you create. Pupils appreciate most a teacher who they know is committed to teaching them and who shows interest in and engagement with them and their progress.

Effective routines

One way to build a positive climate is to establish a routine for the start of lessons. Your relationship with pupils will develop and grow if you are ready for the arrival of the pupils and greet them at the door, say something positive to them, perhaps have an informal quick word with individual pupils as they come in. An interactive starter activity at the beginning of the lesson will help to get the pupils immediately involved in the lesson and set an atmosphere of real purpose. If registers have to be taken at the very start of the lesson it's useful to have something on the board or on their desks for them to do while this is completed.

Hard though it is, you must not bear grudges from one lesson to the next with particular groups or individual pupils that have been challenging. In these circumstances it is even more important to plan lessons carefully for active engagement. In such situations it is important to build bridges rather than set up further resentment by being negative and officious. Establish the routine – and stick to it regardless of what might have gone before. ('We are copying from the board at the start of this lesson due to your behaviour last lesson' fails on any number of counts – copying is not learning, writing should not be a punishment, the negative atmosphere created will pervade the whole lesson and the pupils may have either forgotten the behaviour or be looking for the chance to show they regretted it.)

Plenary activities allow you to help pupils to reflect on what they have learned during the lesson and to set the lesson objectives in context by showing how this will lead to further learning in the next lesson. It's an opportunity to praise pupils and celebrate their achievements in the lesson, and even perhaps just to thank them for their hard work and participation. Praise is free and effective – this cannot be overemphasised! Leaving the classroom in an organised way helps to improve corridor behaviour and again sets the tone of your relationship with them.

Developing other effective routines will further develop a positive classroom climate. Managing transitions between activities is important particularly if pupils will move and/or will be collecting equipment and resources. When planning the lesson, you will need to think through the sequence of activities to ensure that it is logical to avoid unnecessary movement during the lesson. Is it possible to set up equipment before the lesson begins? A useful tip is to organise the equipment needed for a group activity into boxes so that one pupil from each group can collect a box. Can pupil monitors help you to give out resources? The collection of resources and equipment at the end of the task needs just as much careful planning as distributing them at the start of the task. When observing other teachers these transition points and organisational factors seem to happen automatically, but these routines will have been planned and reinforced over time with the pupils. As a new teacher it is useful to continue the routines that have already been established with the pupils.

It is also appropriate to develop routines for dealing with certain types of interactions with pupils, such as when pupils arrive late to your lesson. This helps to develop consistency, saves time and avoids confrontations. These routines need to support any whole-school policies for dealing with such issues.

INDIVIDUAL REFLECTION

Make classroom management routines a focus of your observations. Talk to teachers about how they have reinforced these routines over time with the pupils. Develop some routines that you will use in your own teaching to suit particular aspects of your subject specialism or age range, or for particular types of activities or interventions. For example, you could develop a routine for pupils working in groups with a range of equipment or resources, for pupils arriving late or for involving pupils in discussion activities. Use these in a lesson and reflect on whether the routines you developed were successful.

The physical environment

When planning effective lessons you will need to consider the layout of tables and chairs in the teaching space. In some classrooms the furniture is fixed and there is little opportunity for different arrangements, but in these circumstances it may be possible to provide opportunities to move chairs appropriately for different types of activities. For example:

- Tables and chairs arranged in a double horseshoe allow for all pupils to focus on the front of the classroom during teacher expositions, but are flexible in allowing pupils at the front to turn round and work on discussion activities in groups of four or to work with the person seated next to them in pairs, but is an arrangement less conducive to individual work.
- Seats arranged in circles are good for discussion activities and ensuring that pupils respect the rights of others to speak.
- Desks and chairs arranged in rows are good for individual or paired work.
- Desks and chairs arranged so that four pupils can sit facing each other but angled so that all children can see the front, are most useful for concentrated group work. Placing resources centrally allows pupils to collect them as needed throughout the task.

Whatever is decided it's important that as a teacher you can move around the room freely to talk to individual pupils, pairs and small groups. Even when addressing the whole class you must be able to move, to make sure that you ask questions of and involve all pupils, to spot and deal with any misdemeanours that are going on secretly and just to keep the pupils on their toes. Careful consideration needs to be placed on how to group pupils for different activities. Many schools now have a policy of boy/girl pairing in all lessons, but when placing them in groups, you may wish to consider whether these will be friendship, mixed ability or ability groups. This will vary depending on the activity but the choices you make can have a direct bearing on both the effectiveness of learning and behaviour.

Use displays to make the classroom an interesting place to be. This also reflects your enthusiasm for the subject and reinforces your commitment to the pupils' learning. Good displays can inspire and celebrate pupils' work. They can provide further information for the topic through the display of key words, concepts or key facts, can stimulate curiosity by offering a challenge and can introduce new information about a topic. They can reinforce good subject-specific and/or learning habits through the use of key questions (DfES 2004).

Pupil–teacher interactions

A prerequisite for positive learning behaviour is to develop relationships where pupils feel physically and emotionally secure. When giving instructions you must ensure that all pupils understand them and that they feel secure enough to ask questions. It is possible to encourage this by acknowledging that you may not have explained it clearly enough for them. The relationship between you and the pupils can also be defined by how you deal with a wrong answer. Encouraging pupils to explain why they think that or how they have reached their conclusion can make it more comfortable for them to be confident and to take risks when answering. Another strategy to encourage pupils to answer questions is to let them prepare answers individually, in pairs or in small groups.

> ### 💭 A thought
>
> Another way of building security is to devise strategies that the pupils can try when they are stuck, before they ask you for help. Making these processes visible through display and the provision of the resources needed for them while they are working builds self-confidence and also has the advantage of making your time go further. Consider sharing with pupils the strategies that you use when you are in the same situation. This lets them see that being challenged and developing strategies for dealing with challenge is part of becoming a successful and independent learner.

Relationship with self – building self-esteem and confidence

Praise is a powerful tool in building pupils' self-esteem and developing their confidence as successful learners. It is recognised as one of the most successful strategies for encouraging positive learning behaviour in the classroom. Focus on the pupils' positive behaviour and reward it with praise that is personal, genuine, specific and age-appropriate. Examples might be 'Well done, Thomas, for being the first to be ready to listen to me'. Or to the whole class: 'Well done for working so quietly' or 'Thank you for coming in and getting your things out without any fuss'. The important point is that the praise is genuine but happens frequently, and that you find language with which you feel comfortable. Sometimes it is not appropriate to publicly praise as some pupils find this embarrassing. In these cases it may be more appropriate to leave a comment in a book or have a quiet word when the pupils are working on their own or on the way in or out of the classroom.

GROUP EXERCISE

As a teacher you have tremendous power and influence over pupils. You can escalate a confrontation or diffuse it, can build self-esteem or dash it. Think back to your own time at school and think of a teacher that you would describe as having a negative impact on you as a pupil. Contrast this with a teacher who had a positive impact on you. Share these experiences in your group and discuss what defined the teachers' different teaching styles, behaviour management strategies and interactions with you. Make a list of teacher behaviours that harm self-esteem and behaviours that support it.

Using positive correction as a strategy for encouraging positive behaviour is a development of this positive approach to discipline. Rather then telling pupils not to do something, such as 'Stop talking, Daniel', state the positive behaviour that you want the pupil to demonstrate: 'Daniel, I need you to listen please, thank you'. Using a pre-emptive close in this way also assumes that the pupil is going to do what you want.

Another way to deal positively with low-level disruption in the classroom is to offer pupils choices. 'Sarah, if you continue to talk while I am then you will have to be moved. Stop and there's no problem. You decide.' The strength of this strategy is that the pupils take responsibility for their own actions. It is also effective in allowing you to then focus on the behaviour, not on the student, by asking questions such as 'How can we avoid this happening again?' (Dix 2007).

Consistency

Being consistent is a key skill when teaching as pupils regard consistency and fairness as important qualities of a 'good' teacher. Being consistent allows you to be more assertive in the classroom. The pupils know what to expect and the consequences of their actions, and therefore confrontational situations become less frequent.

Respect

At all times you must avoid using inappropriate language or body language with pupils as this is likely to encourage and escalate confrontational interactions and harm pupils' self-esteem. Inappropriate teacher behaviour includes invading personal body space, intimidating pupils by being aggressive, throwing personal insults and using rude non-verbal communication such as pointing, rolling eyes, etc. Although it is sometimes difficult to manage your temper when in a confrontational situation, you must remain professional at all times. Dix (2007) argues that managing a confrontation should always be about an adult behaving appropriately and teaching a child about expectations of behaviour. And anyway, it's less stressful and more fun to be pleasant all the time!

Summary

- The prerequisite of positive learning behaviour is effective teaching that actively engages pupils in their learning.
- Negative behaviour is minimised if you develop a positive classroom climate, with effective classroom routines, where the pupils feel safe and secure.
- Praise is the most powerful tool for building pupils' self-esteem in the classroom.
- One of your priorities, as a teacher new to the profession, is to develop a range of strategies for dealing with low-level disruption and for maintaining a professional approach to more challenging behaviour.

Key reading

Crowley, S. (2006) *Getting the buggers to behave*. 3rd edition. London: Continuum, chapter 1

DfES (2004) *Pedagogy and Practice: Teaching and learning in secondary schools*. London: HMSO, Unit 18: Improving the climate for learning, and Unit 20: Classroom management

Dix, P. (2007) *Taking care of behaviour: practical skills for teachers*. Harlow: Pearson Education, Part 1

Lee, C. (2007) *Resolving behaviour problems in your school: a practical guide for teachers and support staff.* London: Paul Chapman, Chapter 5

References and bibliography

Crowley, S. (2006) *Getting the buggers to behave,* 3rd edition. London: Continuum

DfES (2004) *Pedagogy and Practice: Teaching and learning in secondary schools.* London: HMSO

Dix, P. (2007) *Taking care of behaviour: practical skills for teachers.* Harlow: Pearson Education

Powell, S. and Tod, J. (2004) 'A systematic review of how theories explain learning behaviour in school contexts'. In *Research Evidence in Education Library*. London: EPPI-Centre, Social Science Research Unit, Institute of Education

Smith, A., Lovett, M. and Wise, D. (2003) *Accelerated learning: a user's guide.* Stafford: Network Educational Press

CHAPTER 9

BEGINNING TO UNDERSTAND HOW YOUNG PEOPLE LEARN

Neil Denby

Standards addressed

Q14 Have a secure knowledge and understanding of their subjects/curriculum areas and related pedagogy to enable them to teach effectively across the age and ability range for which they are trained.

Q18 Understand how children and young people develop and that the progress and well-being of learners are affected by a range of developmental, social, religious, ethnic, cultural and linguistic influences.

Q7 (a) Reflect on and improve their practice, and take responsibility for identifying and meeting their developing professional needs.

   (b) Identify priorities for their early professional development in the context of induction.

Introduction

As one new to the profession, it is easy to think that teaching is pretty much one-way traffic. The teacher teaches, the children learn. But if you remember your own time at school, or as a parent, you will remember that the process of teaching and learning is very much a two-way one. Teaching and learning have to take place together – even though they are often separated as subject matter, they are intertwined and mutually dependent. Learning is just part of the process of communication and communication itself is only effective if it is two-way.

Communication

The traditional model of communication is shown in Figure 9.1. In this model there is any amount of coding and decoding taking place and therefore there are vast possibilities for misunderstanding. In the learning situation, the teacher has to first code the message – this means putting it into a form that can be understood such as writing, pictures or images. Even at this stage, some codes may be better understood than others. The teacher then decides how the message will be transmitted, in what format and through what medium. The child receives the message and, first, has to separate it from what communication theory refers to as 'noise'. This is all the other messages and distractions that are being dealt with. In the classroom these include cultural influences, peer pressure, the outside world, interruptions from peers and physical messages such as 'I'm too hot' or 'I'm hungry'. Only when the noise is dealt with can the receiver then concentrate on the message. They can only understand it if they understand the coding and have access to the medium; they can only demonstrate that they understand it by supplying the appropriate feedback – another transmission, in another medium and also coded.

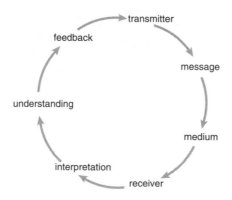

Figure 9.1 Traditional model of communication

> ### A thought
>
> Think about it. To ask the simple question 'what is 2 + 2?' and receive the answer '4' is a complex process. The questioner has coded the question in language and symbols. The '+' or the word 'plus' may not be within the child's understanding (which is probably why we always used to do 'guzinters' instead of 'divisions'). There is an implied notion that this is a sum, but no concrete instruction. The respondent has to deal with abstracts and respond with the appropriate symbol. Now think about some of the questions you have asked in class and you may realise why you did not get an instant response!

If we accept Mehrabian's (1971, 1981) model of communication then things become even more difficult. Mehrabian claims that communication has three clear facets, and that only one of these (and a minor one) is the actual words spoken. Just 7 per cent of meaning is in the words that are spoken, whereas 38 per cent of meaning is in the way that the words are said (called paralinguistic) and 55 per cent of meaning is in facial expression and body language. For the words of the teacher to carry meaning, the message must be conveyed in a way that clarifies meaning, rather than obscures it. So, for example, the child who cannot properly see the teacher is at an immediate disadvantage. Vygotsky (1978) claimed that if we are to define a species by the tools that it uses, then communication is the main tool that defines homo sapiens.

> ### A thought
>
> The message can often be misunderstood because of cultural differences. For example, in certain African cultures, to look straight at a superior (such as a teacher) is seen as an act of bravado or defiance. In a Western culture that insists that 'you look at me when I'm telling you off' this creates a problem. The child shows a culturally correct attitude by keeping his eyes downcast; the teacher expects acknowledgement of the reprimand through eye contact ...

Children learn and respond in many different ways, so it is necessary to develop teaching strategies that feed into as many of those ways as possible. This is why we have the term 'pedagogy' and link it to pedagogical strategies – really just a way of saying that we need a set of plans and methods of operation for any class, because there is a set of different learners in front of us. You may think that you are teaching a 'class'. In fact, you are teaching a set of individual young people. It is an area that you can take a great deal further in assignments and in your CPD as you will find, inevitably, that you develop a theory or set of theories of your own. No single theory from the many theorists will suffice. You will take parts of many theories to develop your own unique and effective style of teaching.

Why do children learn?

> One of the most deeply held beliefs about learning is that learning is undertaken 'for its own sake' ... But the idea of learning as a marketable commodity and the idea of learning for its own sake both leave out the use that learning can be to the individual and to the quality of thought. Learning is never for its own sake in the sense of some higher reach of abstraction that enables each person to escape the realities of life. Learning continues to have a distinct purpose for the individual and for the individual's relationship to others. (Cullingford 1990: 206–7)

Children and young people (and everyone else) learn because they want to. This may be triggered by a need that may be utilitarian – survival, a better job, an enjoyable skill – or by a desire to learn for more esoteric reasons (although Cullingford would see a more selfish purpose to such learning). If young people don't want to learn a specific concept, method or process, it will be because they don't see the need for it or its application to their lives. If we can introduce a need, the learning becomes imperative. When people need to learn, they are much more efficient learners. Should you ever find yourself in a foreign country and not proficient in the language of that country, you will understand what is meant by the need to learn. Often the need is strongly linked to a survival instinct and may involve the learning of a skill. The first major steps in learning that a child takes are walking and talking – both extremely complex operations which carry some risk. Parents know instinctively what sort of progress their child should be making and may reintroduce a need if progress appears to be halted. For example, the child who can crawl effectively and efficiently may be slow to learn to walk. Parents therefore move the furniture to reinforce the need. As Moylett (2006: 111) says:

> We are all competent learners from birth and it is usually our parents who give us the confidence to keep learning and stretch the boundaries of our understanding.

Speech is learnt through copying, repetition and reward. The child needs to learn language if s/he is to be efficient at expressing needs – 'I am hungry, I want that, let me go …' – in ways other than gesture and crying. The child is even proficient enough to learn much of the code that messages are couched in both verbally and non-verbally. The child needs to learn, so learns efficiently and effectively. According to Tony Buzan (1995: 28):

The young child's ability to learn language involves him in processes which include a subtle control of, and an inherent understanding of, rhythm, mathematics, music, physics, linguistics, spatial relations, memory, integration, creativity, logical reasoning and thinking …

Teachers may try to introduce a 'need' at various stages ('you need this examination result in order to …' is typical) but the focus should really be on the 'want'. What is it that can make a child or young person want to learn?

Wanting to learn

The word that we use for 'wanting' to do something is motivation. What motivates a person to work harder or do better? There are many external influences on the child (and much research into their effects) that are, in the main, beyond the control of the teacher. The influence of culture or society, for example, may be extremely powerful. There may be cultural events or obligations taking place that serve as 'noise' as far as learning is concerned. There may be mixed messages – with the home teaching one outlook or set of values and the school another.

The influence of parents and the home is also paramount. How well educated are the parents? Are there books in the home? Is access to knowledge easy? Is there a quiet space to work? Is there access to technology? All of these will have an effect on the child's ability to study and learn (see Chapters 6 and 15). Social factors have a significant effect on learning. According to the Rowntree Foundation (Hirsch 2007):

> Children growing up in poverty and disadvantage are less likely to do well at school. This feeds into disadvantage in later life and in turn affects their children.

Peer group pressure is also influential. Is the child part of a social group where learning is applauded – or where it is seen as 'soft' or conformist and therefore to be avoided? This is the home territory for much bullying behaviour.

A thought

Praise is free and extremely powerful. Use praise as a tool in the classroom. Smile and give positive feedback. Even if the child has it wrong, you should find some area to praise before putting them on the right lines. This builds self-esteem and creates feelings of security and social acceptance – the first steps before Maslow's higher order needs can be tackled and the basis for Herzberg's ideas (see below).

Motivation theory in business and industry provides a useful guide for the classroom. There are several theories as to what it is that makes people work harder or better which can be applied to motivating children to learn. Below are some of the major ones.

- **Frederick W. Taylor (1856–1917)** was an American who sought greater efficiency in engineering plants. He pioneered a 'carrot and stick' approach through Scientific Management Theory. This meant rewards for those who worked hard enough, penalties for those who didn't. Although now pretty much defunct in industry, this model does still find its way into the classroom.

- **Elton Mayo (1880–1949)** carried out the Hawthorne Experiments at a plant in Chicago to try to find out how different conditions affected work rate. His conclusion was that the subjects of his study increased their work rate less because of changes in conditions and more because they were being studied, responding because they were being shown extra attention. His Relay Assembly Test identified that other motivators included being able to direct their own work, teamwork and good communications between management and team. This has obvious classroom implications, so much so that the new diplomas include skills like teamwork, effective participation and creative thinking as central cross-curricular planks (see Chapter 12).

- **A.H. Maslow (1908–1970)** is perhaps the best known motivational theorist. He said that people worked in order to climb a 'hierarchy of needs'. Starting with survival, people then sought safety and security, then social and family fulfilment, then status and finally what Maslow called self-actualisation needs. We might think of it better as ambition or fulfilment. This implies that children must feel safe, secure and socially accepted before there is any real motivation to learn 'outside' of this structure.

- **Frederick Herzberg (1923–2000)** came to similar conclusions to Maslow. He asked workers what motivated them and found out that the main things were a 'job well done', a feeling of being appreciated, trust, responsibility and promotion. One of the major factors which demotivated people was if a job was boring. Some conditions, which Herzberg called 'hygiene' factors, were discovered to make people unhappy, to demotivate them, if they were missing or poor. In work terms, these were good pay and working conditions. In learning terms, they are the creation of an atmosphere for learning – a clean, bright, safe and attractive classroom space, for example, where the children feel that they have some ownership.

- **Victor Vroom (b.1932)** introduced expectancy theory or the path-goal concept. His contention was that motivation is linked to goals. If these goals are seen to be attainable, workers will work towards them. If they are seen to be out of reach, workers are demotivated. This is important when you are thinking of setting targets – there must be intermediate targets, small incremental steps that can be attained by each individual on his or her way to the main goal.

Ability to learn

You may think that one of the main factors that influences learning is the innate ability to learn carried by each child. But here the science becomes, at best, fuzzy. There is no accepted measure of intelligence. It has long been accepted that IQ tests are more to do with technique and repetition than any objective measurement. Neuro-scientists (and their imitators) have discovered much more about the brain than was ever known before. It can grow; it can become more efficient; it can recover from serious trauma in unexpected ways; it responds to certain stimuli. Everything from hydration to cross-word and number puzzles is claimed to increase brain power, along with vitamin supplements, exercise and fish-oil.[1]

Learning theories

This is a necessarily brief round-up of some key learning theories. Never forget that there are many others, including that one of your own that you are just developing to cope with that particularly intransigent class or individual. Those below are recognised as key theories and ideas on which many more variations have been built. Some are directly related to education, others to areas of science, psychology or even business; all can be adapted and adopted to improve learning in your classroom.

Piaget

Jean Piaget (1896–1980) is responsible for cognitive development theory. This is based on the notion that the child constructs 'cognitive structures' in order to understand and respond to its environment. The structure is the child's reality and it is within this structure that learning takes place. As the child gets older s/he moves to more complex structures. The school age stages are 'concrete operations' (approximating to ages 7–11) and 'formal operations (approximating to ages 11–16). In the first of these, the child can create structures to explain experiences. S/he gains the ability to see from other perspectives and can tackle a problem using several aspects of it. In the second of these, the child can 'conceptualise'. S/he can think in abstract terms and does not need the experience in order to learn. This has implications for the stages in which we introduce learning (and therefore for curricular content) and for knowing how far the teacher can step outside the construct. If the learning is sufficiently different, then the child reforms the construct to take account of it. If it is too different, it lies outside the realm of possible learning (see Vygotsky).

---

1. Commercial concerns are not averse to skewing 'research' to try to make it look as if their product is effective. Read about the Durham fish-oil 'trials' at: www.badscience.net/2007/09/the-fishy-reckoning/.

Vygotsky

Lev Vygotsky (1896–1934) moved away from the notion of 'stages of development'. It is his contention that development is too complex to be divided into stages, but presents a continuum. His social constructivist theory examines the idea of a 'zone of proximal development' (ZPD). This requires an analysis of where the child is now and where the teacher wants them to be. The teacher then provides the 'scaffolding' to get them there. Vygotsky describes it as follows:

> the distance between the actual development level as determined by independent problem solving and the level of potential development as determined through problem solving under adult guidance or in collaboration with more capable peers. (Vygotsky 1978: 86)

Learning outside the ZPD is not assimilated by the child (see Piaget) so learning must be incremental, based on current knowledge and understanding. The notion of collaboration is also an important one. The implications for the classroom are that learning should take place in a spirit of teamwork and cooperation; desks should be grouped; teachers should be supportive facilitators rather than instructors.

Skinner

B.F. Skinner (1904–1990) first aired his ideas of operant conditioning in the 1930s. His work is built on the classical conditioning work of Pavlov. Operant conditioning means that learning has taken place when there is an observable change in the behaviour of the learner as a result of teaching. Learning in operant conditioning occurs when 'a proper response is demonstrated following the presentation of a stimulus' (Ertmer and Newby 1993: 55). There are three stages to the learning which may be looked at as a question and answer technique:

- a stimulus (the question);
- a response (the answer); and
- reinforcement (praise for the right answer or correction).

The major criticism of behaviourism is that it gives the learner only a passive role. There is no journey of discovery, just a response to what is being taught. Skinner refutes this and sees the learner as active. He sees three necessary parts for learning: doing, experiencing and practising, which together form a change in behaviour which is measurable. The implications for modern teaching lie in taking small steps, building learning and reinforcement.

INDIVIDUAL REFLECTION

Look at two or three of your lesson plans that form a sequence. State how each addressed different learning styles. Consider if you could have introduced other styles. Look at the progression of the lessons. Consider whether or not you are building in incremental steps, or making leaps from one level to another. What exercises or activities could you build in to ensure that learning is taking place and understanding is growing?

Bruner

Jerome Bruner (b. 1915) is another constructivist.[2] He maintains that learning is an active process. Learners build further knowledge on that which they already possess. There are appropriate classroom conditions to make this happen. The learning space and atmosphere must be conducive to learning, making the learner ready to learn (readiness). Spiral organisation of knowledge should make it more accessible to the learner; learning should be sequential, and a process of building. Learners should be encouraged to extrapolate or extend from knowledge to fill in the gaps for themselves in what has been termed a 'learning journey'. The implications of this for teaching are that the teacher should act as a facilitator to enable learners to discover for themselves. A question and answer technique creates a dialogue where discovery can take place. The curriculum should be designed as a spiral, so that the learner is continually building on knowledge already gained. Bruner's final proposition is often overlooked – that there should be appropriate rewards and punishments (see motivation, above).

Kolb

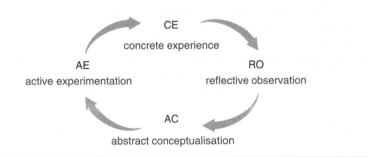

Figure 9.2   Kolb's experiential learning circle

Kolb, David A., *Experiential Learning: Experience as a Source of Learning and Development* © 1984. Reprinted with permission of Pearson Education Inc., Upper Saddle River, NJ

---

2. You can listen to Bruner being interviewed by visiting http://luria.ucsd.edu/Luria.mov.

Kolb's (b. 1941) experiential learning cycle draws on the work of Piaget and others. He sees a cycle of learning, which he represents diagrammatically as a circle (see Figure 9.2), emphasising that learning is a continual process rather than having a single measurable outcome. Its four stages are concrete experience, reflective observation, abstract conceptualisation and active experimentation. It can be summarised as 'do, review, learn, apply'. The teacher provides pupils with a concrete experience. This should be active rather than passive, so verbal 'I talk, you listen' instruction is weak. Role play, trying out, a demonstration or other stimulus close to 'doing' is needed. Students then review the experience and discuss what happened and why. Phase three sees learners asking why this happened, would it happen again and using 'what if' questions to build general principles. Finally, they test or apply these principles, which feeds into another round of 'doing'. As a teacher, you would be encouraging pupils to learn from experience and then apply that learning in new situations.

Gardner

Howard Gardner's (b. 1943)[3] concept of multiple intelligences was published in the book *Frames of Mind* in 1983 and, although not specific to education, was immediately seized on by the educational community. He posited seven 'intelligences'. While these were not directly related to learning styles, nevertheless they suggest that each intelligence is closely linked to a particular way of learning. In more recent work Gardner has added three more (naturalist, linked to the natural environment; spiritual/existential, linked to religion; and moral or ethical).

The seven original intelligences (*very* briefly outlined) are:

- **Linguistic** – learning through words and language. Would typically be comfortable learning from or doing writing, reading, speaking out loud.
- **Logical-mathematical** – learning through logical thinking. Typically learns best when involved in analysis, measurement, logic, problem-solving, incremental learning.
- **Musical** – learning through music. Happiest when performing, writing about music, detecting rhythm.
- **Bodily-kinaesthetic** – learning through bodily movement. Would typically be comfortable learning through role play, drama, construction activities.
- **Spatio-visual** – learning through pictures and images. Typically learns best when creating a picture or design or working with shapes.
- **Interpersonal** – learning through the ability to relate to others. Happiest when involved in human contact, empathising, working in teams or groups, relying on others.
- **Intrapersonal** – learning through understanding self, being adaptable, negotiating positive outcomes. Works best when working for self-improvement, or when personal gain or reward can be seen from a learning activity.

---

3. Gardner can be heard via podcast and seen via video on his own website at www.howard gardner.com/.

Gardner's criticism was that schools and teaching focused too closely on linguistic and logical-mathematical intelligences, and insufficiently on the others, denying some children the opportunity to succeed. The theory of multiple intelligences gained the attention of the educational world and has led to some significant rethinking of styles of teaching.

GROUP EXERCISE

Discuss with other members of your cohort how each of you feels that s/he learns best. Write three lesson plans in your subject area. Each should be attempting to teach the same content, but approaching it in a different style. Exchange lesson plans so that each is reviewed by a person who stated a preference for that style. How would they improve it? Now exchange plans so that each is reviewed by someone who preferred a different style. Discuss how the plan could be changed to incorporate both styles.

Buzan

Tony Buzan (b. 1942) has pioneered the 'two brain' theory of cognition and learning and is the inventor of mind-mapping. (You should note that this is a trade protected name, whose creation is according to strict rules, and not the same as a bubble or spider diagram.) The left side of the brain (numbers, lists, words, logic, analysis, sequence, linearity) must be paired with the right side (rhythm, spatial, Gestalt, imagination, colour, creativity) to bring about true learning and begin to open up the potential of the brain. Learning activities which engage both sides of the brain result in 'synergy' – meaning a greater gain than the addition alone would achieve. Mind-mapping helps learning through assisting study, recall and understanding.

VAK

The Visual-Auditory-Kinaesthetic or VAK model is probably most closely associated with the Montessori schools in the Victorian era. Maria Montessori was the first woman to receive a medical degree from the University of Rome. Her research and innovations concentrated on early years education and the key developmental periods of the child. She, and colleagues, used the scientific method to study ways to educate those with physical or mental problems that prevented them from learning. VAK was promoted as a way of reaching this group for whom conventional teaching could be a problem. It recognises that people have broadly different preferred learning styles. Learning may be preferred through pictures and images, sound and speech or movement and touch. It is a feature of much good teaching that it builds in opportunities for each style into a lesson. VARK adds a fourth 'Read/Write' area originally subsumed into Visual-Auditory.

There are numerous free tests available on the Internet for checking which is your (or a pupil's) preferred learning style. However, beware of nailing your colours to any one mast – learning styles will change with subject, situation, mood, context – even the weather! The key to good teaching (and therefore good learning) is variation and variety in approach. VAK is not a cure-all, and the inclusion of it in lesson plans does not mean that you are necessarily reaching everyone in a class. It should therefore be treated with some caution, as many see it as some kind of panacea. What VAK does do is to ensure that you have a variety of approaches in a lesson, and this is something that is good practice anyway. Different approaches, changes in activities, transition activities – all contribute towards better learning by providing variety and maintaining interest.

Application to teaching

One way to build in a variety of learning approaches, adaptable to any subject, is to introduce a topic in such a way that learners feel they have ownership. Separate the class into groups of (if possible) four. Each group is given a particular set of arguments or a point of view. For example, in Business Education or Economics (or PSHE) the groups could be looking at a proposed project from the viewpoints of different stakeholder groups. A new supermarket development, for example, may be welcomed by one part of the community for cheapness and ease of access, unwelcome to local businesses, supported by a local authority that will gain revenue, opposed by conservationists, and supported by shareholders for increased profit. Each group is presented with just one point of view and has to develop an argument to support this viewpoint. This encourages collaboration and expression. Ownership usually becomes so embedded that finding a solution is difficult, and participants can empathise with similar real-world situations. This allows for group and team work, for participants to build on their own experiences, for different learning styles to be adopted by group members in a natural style and for ownership of the learning. All of these are powerful influences on good learning.

Conclusion

As teachers, we have to recognise that every child is good at something, every child has an area where s/he can shine. All children have immense potential which is often, sadly, not realised. At least part of our job is to remove any extraneous factors that may be preventing that potential being reached and add any factors that we think might smooth the path. So there is no harm in making sure that the learner is comfortable, feels safe and is not put under undue pressure or tension. We can use music and movement, pictures and stories, role play and drama, to reach as many learners and learning styles as possible. We can look at Maslow again really – if the learner is hungry or thirsty, tired or threatened, uncomfortable or bullied, then learning will suffer. Theorists use such methodology in accelerated learning techniques and in developing memory and thinking techniques such as mind-mapping (Buzan 1974).

Summary

■ You should develop your own theory of learning, cherry picking from those outlined here the ones which work for you, in your classroom, at this time.

■ Don't forget the common-sense notions about comfort, safety and security – creating an atmosphere where learning will take place.

■ Use a variety of approaches and you will reach a variety of learners.

■ Review lesson plans and units and schemes of work regularly to make sure that different styles are catered for.

■ Individuals learn better than groups. Giving individual attention, or facilitating discussion, is still teaching – you don't have to stand at the front and expound!

Key reading

Buzan, T. (1995) *Use your head.* London: BBC Books
Ertmer, P.A. and Newby, T.J. (1993) 'Behaviorism, cognitivism, constructivism: comparing critical features from an instructional design perspective'. *Performance Improvement Quarterly*, 6 (4), 50–72
Moylett, H. (2006) 'Supporting children's development and learning'. In Bruce, T. (ed.), *Early childhood*. London: Sage, pp. 106–126

References and Bibliography

Bruner, J. (1960) *The process of education.* Cambridge, MA: Harvard University Press
Bruner, J. (1996) *The culture of education.* Cambridge, MA: Harvard University Press
Buzan, T. (1995) *Use your head.* London: BBC Books
Cullingford, C. (1990) *The nature of learning.* London: Cassell
Ertmer, P.A., and Newby, T.J. (1993) 'Behaviorism, cognitivism, constructivism: Comparing critical features from an instructional design perspective'. *Performance Improvement Quarterly*, 6 (4), 50–72

Gardner, H. (1993) *Frames of mind: the theory of multiple intelligences.* New York: Basic Books

Hirsch, D. (2007) *Experiences of poverty and educational disadvantage*, 'Round-up'. Joseph Rowntree Foundation. Available at: www.jrf.org.uk/knowledge/findings/socialpolicy/2123.asp

Kolb, D.A. (1984) *Experiential learning: experience as the source of learning and development.* Englewood Cliffs, NJ: Prentice-Hall

Mehrabian, A. (1971) *Silent messages.* Belmont, CA: Wadsworth

Mehrabian, A. (1981) *Silent messages: implicit communication of emotions and attitudes*, 2nd edition. Belmont, CA: Wadsworth

Moylett, H. (2006) *'Supporting children's development and learning'*. In Bruce, T. (ed.), *Early childhood*. London: Sage, pp. 106–126

Vygotsky, L.S. (1978) *Mind and society: the development of higher mental processes*, eds M. Cole, V. John-Steiner, S. Scribner, and E. Souberman. Cambridge, MA: Harvard University Press.

CHAPTER 10

APPROACHES TO TEACHING AND LEARNING 1: DEVELOPING A RANGE

Joanne Pearson

Standards addressed

Q10 Have a knowledge and understanding of a range of teaching, learning and behaviour management strategies and know how to use and adapt them, including how to personalise learning and provide opportunities for all learners to achieve their potential.

Q24 Plan homework or other out-of-class work to sustain learners' progress and to extend and consolidate their learning.

Introduction

You do not need to be very long in the teaching profession before you realise that it is impossible to separate teaching, learning and behaviour. They cannot be viewed in isolation – to do so is to reduce teaching to telling, learning to listening and behaviour to sitting still and being quiet. It is perfectly possible to imagine a lesson in which the teacher talked, the pupils copied from a book and were quiet and stayed in their seats (you may even recall such lessons from your own schooldays), but was anything learned? This example is an exercise in the occupation of children rather than in their learning. The aim of teaching is to add to the pupils' learning; therefore, as a teacher, you need to be able to plan for lessons in which the children learn rather than just behave.

Establishing effective relationships

The relationship between teaching and learning takes place within a personal relationship, that of the teacher and the pupil. Every pupil, and teacher, arrives at each lesson with a different set of needs and expectations. Managing these differing needs, adapting to the demands of 30 different people within one room, is one of the most challenging aspects of teaching. Some aspects of this are beyond the control of one teacher. For example, the previous experiences of pupils will affect their attitude to school, to the teacher and to the subject being taught. Within the classroom you need to establish ways of creating positive relationships with pupils that aid their learning, rather than just their behaviour. This can be termed 'affective learning' – the learning of emotions or attitudes. This affective learning supports the cognitive learning of knowledge and skills; indeed it is difficult to imagine how pupils can achieve their cognitive potential in a subject towards which they have very negative feelings. How then can you create positive and effective learning relationships with your pupils?

The art (and heart) of teaching

At the centre of the effective teacher/learner relationship is caring. Do you effectively communicate that you care about, and indeed are passionate about, what you teach? Do you communicate the importance, relevance and purpose of the subject you are teaching? Do the pupils have a sense of the potential, of the infinite possibilities of learning? As a teacher you should always remember the privilege and power the job holds; if you do not seem to believe in what you are teaching, if you cannot be enthusiastic, excited and engaged in the learning, then how can you expect the pupils to feel any different?

Caring also applies to the pupils. Are you interested in them? Do you believe that they can achieve? A passion for a subject will not be enough to establish a positive learning relationship if it is not matched with a passion and belief that all children can achieve and make progress. One of the common fears of beginning teachers is that they will fail, will not be able to 'control' a class or answer a child's question. Children have exactly the same fears in the classroom – they too are afraid of failing, of being labelled as unsuccessful (Cullingford 2006). Just as trainee teachers need a mentor who believes in them, even when things sometimes go wrong, so pupils need teachers who believe in them, who support them and acknowledge that they have the potential to get better. This can be as simple as learning every child's name, but also encompasses a recognition of the differing needs and achievements of children. Every human enjoys being praised and having their achievements acknowledged; children are no different. As a teacher, it is your job to know and recognise individual pupil achievement. This requires:

- an understanding of the levels of attainment the pupil has already demonstrated;
- a clear and realistic target for each pupil's further progression;
- an understanding of the specific and particular learning needs that some pupils may have.

Creating a positive learning relationship is the responsibility of the teacher. It can be characterised as the communication that the teacher enjoys their job, the subject they are teaching and the pupils themselves.

> Teaching is more than just a job, more than an intellectual challenge, more than a management task, for whom vocation and commitment are essential features of professionalism. It is for teachers who are concerned through their work, with education in its broader sense, who acknowledge that emotional engagement and care are essential to good teaching, who are committed to service, and who are, have been or wish to be again, passionate. (Day 2004: 10).

A thought

There will be some days when you do not want to be in the classroom, some aspects of a subject that you hate to teach and some pupils that you groan at the thought of teaching. These are the days/lessons/pupils with which you will need to work the hardest. Sometimes this is as simple as being honest with children; 'I know that iron and steel production is not as exciting as children working in coal mines, but if we do not understand this it means we will not be able to explain why so many children ended up working in coal mines.' On other occasions it is a determination to catch that difficult pupil doing something right and praise them for it. It is the building over time of small bridges like this that can change a pupil's attitude to learning or school.

Range

There are many different approaches that can be taken to the teaching of a subject. Consider the Five Pillars of Islam as a topic. Pupils could be asked to:

- write a description of each of the Pillars;
- draw an illustration to symbolise each of the Pillars;
- interview a practising Muslim about the role of the Five Pillars in their life;
- make a mobile with the Pillars as branches and examples of the role of each Pillar in practice hanging from underneath;
- a word search;
- a role play exploring the practice of each of the Pillars.

The list could go on for much longer. There are three questions to be considered here. Which of these teaching and learning strategies:

- is most appropriate for the pupils?
- will motivate and enthuse them?
- will enable pupils to make progress in their understanding of the concepts and processes of RE?

Teaching strategies need to meet all these needs. The above activities vary in their level of challenge and engagement; it is for the teacher to consider the appropriateness of an activity for the class and the individual pupils within the class. In Chapter 11 we examine how to put together sequences of lessons and plan for progression.

A priority for any good teacher is to have a range of types of activity/teaching strategy to draw upon when planning for pupil learning. These could encompass:

- group work
- paired work
- discussion work
- active learning
- listening
- reading
- observing
- teacher-centred activities
- pupil-centred activities
- question and answer session
- hot seating
- role play
- playing games.

Again the list could be extended much further; for example, none of the above need necessitate any writing from the pupils. The list forms a part of your repertoire as a teacher. Careful management of the list, and making appropriate choices from it for different situations, can mean children experiencing a wider variety of learning experiences and a positive learning environment in the classroom, resulting in more motivated pupils who achieve better.

A thought

In any one teaching day you may adopt a variety of strategies as part of your planning. In the bigger picture, however, you may be relying on a small number of those strategies with each class. You are experiencing your range, but your individual classes are not. How can you monitor the range of teaching and learning strategies that your pupils are experiencing?

Personalised learning

Learning to teach can be divided into three phases (Leask 2002):

- the first in which you evaluate the experience you as a teacher have gone through;
- the second in which you start to focus on the experience of the class as a whole;
- the third in which you focus on the individual learning of pupils. This can be termed personalised learning.

Personalised learning – the need to cater for all children in schools – may be a relatively recent term, but it has been part of the job of a teacher for much longer. It is important enough that we have devoted a whole chapter to it (see Chapter 12) but it is still worth exploring here. All children have different needs, not just those who may be identified in a formal way as having additional needs. A single lesson plan will illuminate the strategies you will adopt on a holistic level (and indeed may highlight specific strategies for some individuals within the class), but it is in the lesson itself that the interaction and support for the individuals within that class will be evidenced. What then might this look like?

One of the key indicators is the amount of time you as a teacher spend at the front of the class talking. There are some times within a planning cycle, for example at the start of a new topic or when explaining a new concept or skill, when you may need to have some didactic teacher talk. However, over a number of lessons your time with a class will need to be more equitably distributed. One of the ways a teacher can personalise a lesson is by talking, supporting, questioning and challenging individual pupils. This cannot always be done from the front of the room. It is also useful to ask the following questions as part of your reflection both during and after the lesson:

- How many of the pupils grasped the main points I was trying to get across?
- To which aspects might I need to return?
- How can I revisit areas of learning in a new way to support those who have struggled in this lesson?
- How can I, later on, reinforce and consolidate what they have learned successfully?

INDIVIDUAL REFLECTION

Observe two or three lessons and note down the movement of the teacher and his/her contact with individual pupils. How much of the lesson was spent talking to the whole class? How much time was spent working with individual pupils? What was the nature of the whole-class talk? Was it instructions, explanations, classroom management, praise? What was the nature of the individual teacher/pupil talk? Was it clarification of content or instruction, questioning, praise or chastisement? Who talked most in these exchanges – the teacher or the pupils? What evidence could you observe about the effect of the teacher/pupil talk?

Whole-class questioning and discussion can inform you about much of the understanding and learning in the room, but it frequently does not allow you as a teacher to monitor the individual understanding and learning of pupils.

Equally, productive interaction between teacher and pupil is not just conversations in which the teacher repeats instructions or clarifies concepts; it is also conversation that asks the pupils to talk, to clarify or explain their thinking, to reconsider their thoughts and answers in new ways with prompting and support from the teacher.

A thought

In some lessons pupils are engaged and enjoy themselves but believe they have not 'worked' and therefore not 'learned'. They think they have 'learned' where a lot of 'work' has taken place. By this, they often mean a lot of listening or writing. Which type of lesson do you think is the most effective?

Behaviour management strategies

Developing a variety of effective teaching and learning strategies is an essential prerequisite to the promotion of good behaviour. If children are interested, engaged and motivated, behaviour is unlikely to be an issue. But what if they aren't? What if a single child (or group of children) decides that this learning activity, this lesson, this teacher or even this subject is not for them? Maybe it is due to 'baggage' that they are carrying with them – a dispute spilled over from another lesson, a row at home or a problem in the community? Maybe it's a child who craves attention or needs to be noticed? Maybe the child is distracted or tired – just arrived from getting a bad decision in PE perhaps, or a particularly strenuous maths lesson. Sometimes it's just the weather, a high wind or a wasp at the window. Chapter 8 covers the ground of establishing the framework and environment for good behaviour, but what individual strategies might you develop? First you need to be very familiar with your school's policies for dealing with individual behaviour issues. For example, do they have an exit policy? Is there an on-call system? Then consider the following:

- **Distraction techniques**. If a child is being very unwilling and difficult, are you able to divert them from the unwanted behaviour with a new stimulus? This might be doing a job for you in the classroom or a new task to complete.
- **Anticipating good behaviour**. Sometimes thanking children in anticipation that they will cooperate can be a useful management tool. 'Thank you for sitting down' instead of 'sit down now' can help to diffuse an escalating or potential problem.
- **Make time for calm talk**. Rather than let a situation with an individual pupil escalate, create time after a difficulty for you to be able to talk calmly with the pupil about the behaviour and to explore any underlying issues behind that behaviour.

Application to teaching

Teachers need to plan for productive interventions with individual pupils that allow them to explore their understanding and support their further development. This means letting the pupils do much of the talking, listening to their answers and prompting/questioning them to allow them to make progress. Plan a lesson in which you will spend most of your time working with the pupils in the class and consider how you might talk to pupils about their work in a way that demonstrated their understanding. Holt (1982) gave seven ways in which pupils might demonstrate their understanding. They were when:

(Continued)

(Continued)

» **They can state something in their own words.** *This can be a discussion between the teacher and the pupil about the things they need to consider when producing a presentation or a pupil retelling a story in their own words.*

» **They can give examples.** *This might be when pupils are able to describe or perform various poses in order to demonstrate balance. It could also be a conversation or activity in which the pupils identify examples of franchised businesses.*

» **They can state or identify the opposite.** *This could be an exploration of a child's understanding of the mechanics of subtraction discussing what its opposite (i.e. addition) might look like. The same could apply to abstract concepts such as capitalism or democracy.*

» **They can recognise it in other situations.** *This may be recognising monotheism in religions other than Islam. In geography it may be asking a pupil to give you examples of a natural disaster other than an earthquake.*

» **They can make connections between it and other facts or concepts.** *This could be asking pupils to make connections between the weapons the Romans used and those used in the Crimean War. It can also be asking them to explain the relationship between the music of Negro spirituals and rap music.*

» **They can make use of it in other ways.** *This could be asking them how addition can help them to tell the time. It can also be asking them to tell you how else they can use rhyme in a poem to change meaning/tone etc.*

» **They can foresee some of its consequences.** *These are conversations along the lines of what would happen if ... you used a different material to make your hat ... you lowered the temperature of the water instead of raising it?*

Strategies such as these enable the teacher not only to monitor the understanding of the pupil and support their individual progress, but can also act as useful language modelling for students who do not have English as their first language.

The place and purpose of homework

Teaching timetables are often pressured. It is important that as a teacher you recognise that learning does not always have to happen in a formal classroom situation with a teacher directing it. It is, however, also important to see homework, and learning outside the classroom, as a meaningful activity that is more than just filling up time for children. Does it move their learning forward from the lesson, or is it more of the same but to be done at home? If it is the latter consider why you have set it. If they have already understood and demonstrated their understanding in the lesson is this the right time to consolidate? If they have not understood in the lesson are they going to be able to do the work at home?

As a group consider the last three homework tasks you have each set to a class. Think about why you set them. Were they consolidating the learning? Moving it forward? Why was this the right time for that work to be set? Now consider ways in which the homework activities may be improved.

There are some questions to consider when planning homework:

- Have you left enough time in your lesson plan to be able to explain the demands of the homework adequately?
- Have you considered some of the barriers to the pupils completing the homework successfully? Not all children have access to paints/fabric/art materials in their home; not all have Internet access. Some children do not have a room of their own or quiet space in which to work. How can you manage this kind of task in these circumstances?
- Have you thought about how long the homework task will take to complete? Is it reasonable?
- Have you given the pupils the tools to be able to complete the homework? A typical example of this is a task that asks pupils to 'research' Peru or Florence Nightingale. Do pupils know what you mean by 'research'? If they do not they will copy and paste a page from a website or a book and may not even read it! Is this what you meant by research? If not then you will need to support their understanding of the true nature of research.
- What is the potential impact of the homework on their attitude and achievement in your subject? If they regularly get mechanistic tasks, or complete work at home that you then never look at or mark, how will this impact upon their motivation and engagement when they are back in the classroom?
- Are there support mechanisms in your school for pupil homework, e.g. homework clubs, and how can you help pupils to use them effectively? Are there resources in the community that you could make use of in out-of-school learning?

Out-of-school learning

Out-of-school learning can be seen as an opportunity to develop pupils' enthusiasms and interests and an opportunity to involve parents and carers more closely in the school life of their children. For example, if the children have made a board game to explain the dangers to public health of living in a city in the nineteenth century, the homework could be to play the game with a parent or carer and ask them what they learned from playing it. Perhaps a child's engagement with reading might be more effectively developed if parents/carers are given the resources and support to read a book with their child rather than asking the pupils to undertake a comprehension exercise. This might involve communicating with parents and carers about the purpose of out-of-school learning and helping them to develop their own confidence that they can help their children not only to learn but also to enjoy learning.

Summary

- Effective learning environments are created when behaviour is connected to learning.

- Teachers must see their pupils as individuals who have different and changing needs.

- No one lesson strategy or teaching activity will work with pupils all the time. Pupils and teachers need variety.

- Learning can often be most effectively personalised when teachers plan for time to be spent talking to pupils as individuals.

- Homework should have a clear learning purpose and rationale. It should be realistic and achievable for pupils in differing circumstances.

Key reading

Cullingford, C. (2006) 'Children's own vision of schooling'. *Education 3–13*, 34 (3), 211–221
Leask, M. (2002) 'The student teacher's role and responsibilities'. In Capel, S., Leask, M. and Turner, T. (eds), *Learning to teach in the secondary school*. London: RoutledgeFalmer, pp.18–28
Information on how to help parents and carers support learners in their homework and other out-of-class learning may be found at: www.parentscentre.gov.uk

References and bibliography

Cullingford, C. (2006) 'Children's own vision of schooling'. *Education 3–13*, 34 (3), 211–221
Day, C. (2004) *A passion for teaching*. London: RoutledgeFalmer
DfES (2005) *Learning Behaviour: The Report of the Practitioners' Group on School Behaviour and Discipline*. London: HMSO
Holt, J. (1982) *How children fail*. New York: Delacorte/Seymour Lawrence
The 2020 Group (2006) *A vision for teaching and Learning in 2020*. London: HMSO
Leask, M. (2002) 'The student teacher's role and responsibilities'. In Capel, S., Leask, M. and Turner, T. (eds), *Learning to teach in the secondary school*. London: Routledge Falmer

Information on how to help parents and carers support learners in their homework and other out-of-class learning may be found at: www.parentscentre.gov.uk

CHAPTER 11

APPROACHES TO TEACHING AND LEARNING 2: PLANNING, PROGRESSION AND SEQUENCE

Joanne Pearson

Standards addressed

Q22 Plan for progression across the age and ability range for which they are trained, designing effective learning sequences within lessons and across series of lessons and demonstrating secure subject/curriculum knowledge.

Q25 Teach lessons and sequences of lessons across the age and ability range for which they are trained in which they:

(a) use a range of teaching strategies and resources, including e-learning, taking practical account of diversity and promoting equality and inclusion;

(b) build on prior knowledge, develop concepts and processes, enable learners to apply new knowledge, understanding and skills and meet learning objectives;

(c) adapt their language to suit the learners they teach, introducing new ideas and concepts clearly, and using explanations, questions, discussions and plenaries effectively;

(d) manage the learning of individuals, groups and whole classes, modifying their teaching to suit the stage of the lesson.

Introduction

As teachers, we have a passion for our subject; we know intimately the content, the particular distinctive features, the methods and theories that underlie and support it. As teachers. we are already successful learners. This can make us forget key aspects of teaching and learning; we are not just teaching children more about biology, the Second World War or quadratic equations, we are teaching them to become better biologists, historians and mathematicians. This means not just teaching more content, but planning for progression. The problem is how to plan lessons that build together to allow children to become better at subjects rather than just knowing more. How can we use what children are already able to do and what they already know to make them better at individual subjects? And what does 'being better' at a subject really mean?

A thought

What does it mean to get better at a subject? What does getting better at geography or music look like? Is it the acquisition of more facts – knowing the names of 12 rivers rather than five, or the compositions of three composers rather than two? This is a complicated area that provokes much discussion. Think about the nature of a particular subject, its features, unique and otherwise. Can you describe what it means to get better at these features? What progressive journey did you undertake to get better at the subject?

Starting points

There are several questions that must be answered when planning for progression:

- What does it mean to get better in a subject/area?
- What can the pupil already do (skills)?
- What does the pupil already know (knowledge)?
- What concepts and skills can the pupil apply (understanding)?
- What is the next step to progress them in their knowledge and understanding?
- How can we plan teaching and learning experiences that will allow the journey to take place?

Defining and describing progression

There are national models for progression in a number of subjects in English schools. These are the National Curriculum documents for subjects such as English, mathematics and science. Within these documents are the 'key concepts' and 'key processes' that define particular subjects. There are also the 'level descriptors' that describe progression in a particular subject. For subjects that are not part of the National Curriculum such as business studies, sociology and psychology there are the national 14–19 subject criteria that describe the aims, assessment objectives and grade descriptions for each subject. Such documents may be described as a model for progression that helps to inform the planning of teaching and learning (see Chapter 14).

GROUP EXERCISE

In small groups of two or three download a copy of the National Curriculum programme of study for a subject or the QCA grading criteria for a subject. Discuss the aims, concepts, processes and assessment objectives contained in these documents. To what extent do they match with your own definition of the subject? Examine the level/grade descriptions – how useful do they seem as a description of progress within the subject?

Although these national models do provide a framework they do not provide a definitive model of progression. They are designed to describe progress over a long period of time whereas teachers need to plan for progression over a much shorter time period, over a matter of weeks rather than years. An additional consideration is that children do not make progress evenly; individuals make progress in one concept or skill at different rates to one another, meaning that pupils can reflect several levels in the same subject. The levels are therefore 'best fit' rather than accurate reflections of a pupil's abilities. Finally the steps between the levels may not be uniform. For example, in one subject, progression from level 3 to 4 may be easier than from level 5 to 6. National Curriculum levels and exam grade descriptions are useful tools for longer-term planning and assessment of children, but they are not in themselves models of progression that allow teachers to plan for children to improve in the shorter term.

The task for the teacher is therefore to explore progression within and between the levels described in national criteria. This means thinking about how children learn (see Chapter 9), and exploring the levels of difficulty in the tasks that pupils are being asked to perform in lessons. One model for this is Bloom's taxonomy (Bloom 1984). Bloom looked at the demands of different activities and categorised these into levels of challenge, creating a hierarchy of 'skills' ranging from 'knowledge' (lower level) to 'evaluation' (higher level). These are described as:

1 **Knowledge**. This can be the recall of information, for example dates or facts.
2 **Comprehension**. This is the understanding of facts, the interpretation of recalled data, for example comparing one fact with another.
3 **Application**. This is the ability to apply the information in other settings or solve problems using the knowledge and skills they have acquired.
4 **Analysis**. This is when pupils might begin to see patterns, to make connections and classifications.
5 **Synthesis**. Here pupils use old knowledge to create new knowledge. They pull together knowledge from several areas, they predict.
6 **Evaluation**. Here pupils make judgements about competing theories and beliefs. They formulate arguments and are able to support them.

This model has been further revised by Anderson and Krathwohl (2001), who came up with the following model:

1 Remembering
2 Understanding
3 Applying
4 Analysing
5 Evaluating
6 Creating.

Both these models are based upon the cognitive model of learning (see Chapter 9) and have had their critics. For example, 'understanding' is a slippery word – what does it mean and what would it look like in the classroom? There is also no suggestion that these levels are chronologically based. For example, younger pupils cannot just remember, they can (and do) create or evaluate. Rather, the levels are a general model of how new knowledge may be processed and used at any age. These models, even with their flaws, are another tool by which teachers can explore progression and plan for pupils to improve within a particular subject.

INDIVIDUAL REFLECTION

Look at two or three of your lesson plans that form a sequence. Use either Bloom's taxonomy or Anderson and Krathwohl's model and analyse the level of demand and difficulty in the tasks the pupils undertook. To what extent was there any progression across the lessons? Go back to the National Curriculum document/subject specification and explore the skills, concepts and assessment objectives developed in these lessons (do not focus on content). To what extent is progression evident in these areas? Finally, look at a piece of work produced by the pupils in one or more of the lessons. Have they made any progress as a result of the lesson (use both the taxonomy and the national guidance)?

Prior knowledge and understanding

Allowing pupils to get better at a subject means that we as teachers need to know what they *already* know and can do when they arrive at a particular lesson. There are several sources of information available to teachers to help them do this. They include the following:

- The National Curriculum document for the key stage preceding the stage being taught. For example, what content, skills and processes should children at Key Stage 2 have undertaken in Geography? What are the expected numeracy levels of a pupil ending Key Stage 1?
- The departmental scheme of work for the key stage being currently taught. What content, skills and processes have the children already been taught during this key stage?
- The individual assessment records for each pupil. This may be in the form of Standard Attainment Test (SAT) results, National Curriculum levels or departmental subject achievement descriptors (see Chapter 17).

While all of these sources are available and can be useful, in themselves they may be something of a blunt tool. As discussed above National Curriculum levels are broad brush strokes rather than accurate snapshots and primary schools may have devoted very different amounts of time to subjects, especially those in the foundation rather than the core. You may be teaching a subject at GCSE or A Level that the pupils have never tackled before, such as business studies. How then can teachers plan for the progression of individual pupils?

A thought

Teaching a subject does not automatically mean that children have learned anything. The coverage of any content, skills or processes by the teacher does not always result in pupil learning. In fact it can result in the opposite. In 1993 Lightman and Sadler found that pupil understanding of a topic, in this case physics, could actually decrease as a result of being taught it in a lesson.

The most obvious starting point for this is the pupils themselves. As teachers, you should think about beginning new topics with an exploration of what they already know and can do rather than assuming no knowledge or assuming too much. The former results in no progress because if the pupils already know and can do before coming to the lesson, then the lesson has added nothing. The latter results in no progress because if the teacher assumes pupils know and can do things they cannot, then the lesson will be beyond the pupils.

Application to teaching

When planning a new unit of work consider the opening lesson as a means to assess pupil knowledge and understanding. This can be done in several ways.

» Produce an overview map of the content, skills and processes that will be covered in the unit. The pupils can add to the headings, or colour the map in using a traffic light system – green for the areas they feel confident in already, orange for those they feel they are familiar with but lack full confidence, red for the unfamiliar.

» Put the title of the unit on the board and ask the pupils to generate questions they would like to be able to answer about this topic by the end of the unit. Having done this explore as a class any questions they have asked that they may already be able to answer in part or in total. For example, if the topic is the First World War, pupils may ask: why did it start? why did it end? how was it fought? who fought? who won? who were the soldiers? Some of these questions, e.g. who fought, they may already as a class be able to answer (at least in part); others, such as why the war began, they may have no understanding of.

» Allow the pupils to generate their own mind maps. Put the title of the unit on the board and ask them to put down words, questions and/or images they think may be involved in this topic.

» Try a 3-2-1 approach. Given a topic heading, ask the pupils to write down three things they already know/can do that will help them in this topic, two questions they would like to be able to answer at the end of the unit and one target for their own progression during the unit.

Next steps

Once teachers feel confident about what their pupils do know and/or can do, the next challenge is to plan lessons that allow all the pupils to move forward. This means thinking again about progression models and about how children learn. Take, for example, extended writing: the level of challenge involved here can depend on several variables:

• some questions may be harder than others – describing events is less challenging than explaining events;
• the level of support provided – pupils may be given a rigid writing frame or may be given no supporting framework;

- content may be more or less challenging – concrete concepts such as a person or event may be easier to understand than abstract concepts such as capitalism or romanticism;
- the teaching strategies adopted can affect the challenge – are pupils working together to discuss and draft ideas or are they working alone?

These examples are all factors which teachers take into account when planning lessons to accommodate progression. Pupils may begin in Year 7 with extended writing about concrete concepts, in groups with writing frames, and by Year 9 may be writing individual pieces, unsupported, about abstract ideas, but it is unlikely to be a journey taken in one leap.

Implicit in all planning therefore is teacher knowledge and an understanding of what will be asked of the pupils at the end of the journey, i.e. what destination are we preparing them for? What are the final demands required of A Level RE, Key Stage 1 SATs, GCSE mathematics …?

Teaching and learning

Knowledge of your pupils, of your subject and of different and varied pedagogical approaches all precede the planning of sequences of lessons. The reality of this in the classroom means that you will never teach any lesson in exactly the same way twice. The content may be the same, but the pupils are not. They will have learned at different rates, made different mistakes, started with different prior knowledge. Planning needs to start with the pupils in front of you. Some factors that you may need to consider are as follows:

- **What learning experiences you have already given them**.   Even if a class seem to respond very well to one particular teaching strategy, using it too often, while ignoring others, may result in boredom, disengagement and a lack of progress. It is useful to audit the teaching strategies you have used with each of your classes regularly to ensure variety. It is also useful to audit the knowledge and resources you use in lessons; how inclusive is your subject content? For example, many primary school children will experience no Black History in their experiences at Key Stages 1 and 2 – how can you develop content that reflects a diverse society?
- **Being adversely affected by demands other than learning**.   Do not avoid certain teaching strategies because of the age of the pupils or the demands of external assessment. If group work and discussion produce learning in Key Stage 2 English, then why should they not do the same in Post-16 English? If role play aids the learning of a five-year-old do not assume that it no longer aids learning at age 15.

- **Explicitly thinking about the teaching 'style' you might adopt as part of the planning**. There are times, for example when introducing a new concept, skill or area of content, that an 'expert' style may be most appropriate. This will involve the teacher taking the role of the experienced learner and explaining to the pupils. When revisiting a concept, skill or content, it may be more appropriate for a 'facilitator' style of teaching. This involves very little teacher explanation and much more teacher support as the pupils work. Your style of teaching may also need to change as each lesson progresses and as you respond to the pupils' needs and changing situations. If pupils are clearly demonstrating misconceptions at any point during a lesson think about pulling the class together and addressing these misconceptions; if individual pupils or groups need support, then facilitation at the appropriate level will be more effective than a whole-class approach. (There are several models of teaching styles – see for example Grasha's (1996) five styles.)

- **The role of language in teaching**. Your use of language in a lesson needs to be carefully considered. For example, when explaining a new concept how much subject-specific language are you going to use? Are there terms and phrases that pupils may misconceive? 'The Church' has a particular meaning in an RE or history lesson; it may have a different association for a pupil. Similarly in mathematics, 'product' has a particular meaning that differs from other uses of the word (for example, in business education). Questions need to be clearly planned. Will they be closed or open? Who will you ask? How will you ensure most children participate? How will you monitor/manage the participation of children in the lesson? How demanding are your questions – are pupils being challenged? Consider Bloom's taxonomy to support your planning of questions. For example, 'who wrote Romeo and Juliet?' is 'recall of knowledge' and is at the bottom of the taxonomy; 'how good do you think it is?' is evaluative and of a much higher-order skill. It is often at the end of a lesson when teacher talk becomes less focused and planned. Think about the purpose of the plenary – are you reviewing learning that has taken place or looking ahead to the next lesson's learning? Are you calming and settling or enthusing and exciting? Do you intend to review the lesson objectives or link the lesson to the bigger teaching objective? Are you dealing with misconceptions now or covering them next lesson? These are all decisions to be made both prior to a lesson and during a lesson as the pupils' learning becomes apparent.

- **The link between the activity you have chosen in a lesson and the learning**. Make sure this link is clear. How is note-taking going to develop learning and help achieve the lesson objective? If it is not then consider alternative activities. Be careful of finding a 'good' activity for a class and using it in a lesson without considering how it aids the pupils' progress. The same applies to e-learning. This offers enormous opportunities for teaching and learning. It can give access to resources and images, create opportunities for independent learning and give pupils the tools to revise and redraft work. E-learning is not just 'word processing'; it encompasses podcasts, interactive learning, use of e-mail and the Internet. However, it is not a panacea; like any other activity it needs to meet the learning objective. It is a tool that should be used when appropriate – if listening to Martin Luther King's 'I have a dream' speech, or seeing film of Gandhi's march to make salt aids learning and understanding, then the presence of these clips on the Internet is priceless. Adding clipart to a document may not be quite so useful! The purpose of e-learning is to extend the subject learning – for example, to improve English, geography, design & technology; it is not an end in itself (see Chapter 18).

- **The role of language in learning**.   This is twofold. It is the role that pupils' talk can play in their own learning and the role of talk between the teacher and an individual pupil in learning. Pupils talking to the whole class and one another about their learning is invaluable to teachers. Like any other part of a lesson it needs to be planned with care. If an open-ended, challenging question has been planned as part of the lesson, give pupils the opportunity to consider their thoughts, to discuss and revise their opinions with a partner, before expecting an answer. The skills of discussion work such as listening to others, articulating opinion along with supporting evidence and avoiding shouting out do not happen naturally. They need to be explained and articulated. The potential of teacher/pupil talk is enormous. It is often when the most effective differentiation can occur. You decide to whom you will talk, how you will use this talk to support and challenge individual pupils and how you will help to develop their ability to talk about their own learning.

- **Linking teaching and learning objectives**.   Keep making links between the learning objectives in individual lessons and your overall teaching objectives. Teaching objectives are longer term – they are linked to progress. For example, as a PE or dance teacher, your teaching objective may be to develop the pupils' control of *whole-body skills*; this will be achieved over a longer period of time than one lesson and you will need to link your learning objectives for the children in each individual lesson to this overall teaching objective. This might be a lesson objective that states the children will be able to perform a balance. The lesson objective alone cannot achieve the overall teaching objective, but instead is one step towards it. Other lessons will need to be planned to support the medium-term teaching objective.

Planning a lesson can therefore never be carried out in isolation. Pupils have had learning experiences before they arrive in our classrooms. We are not just giving them a single lesson. For teaching *and* learning to be meaningful we need to have a bigger plan in mind. Where have they come from and how did they get here? Where are you taking them and how will you get them there?

Summary

- Teachers need to have an understanding of what it means to improve at a subject.

- Progression is supported by planning that considers the learning journey of pupils.

- Lessons need to be linked together to support the learning over the longer term.

- Each class and pupil will be at a different stage in their learning and planning needs to consider who we are planning for.

Key reading

DfES (2004a) *Pedagogy and Practice: teaching and learning in secondary schools.* London: HMSO

DfES (2004b) *Excellence and Enjoyment: learning and teaching in the primary years.* London: HMSO

References and bibliography

Anderson, L. and Krathwohl, D. (eds) (2001) *A taxonomy for learning, teaching, and assessing: a revision of Bloom's taxonomy of educational objectives.* New York: Longman

Bloom, B. (1984) *Taxonomy of educational objectives.* Boston: Pearson

DfES (2004a) *Pedagogy and Practice: teaching and learning in secondary schools.* London: HMSO

DfES (2004b) *Excellence and Enjoyment: learning and teaching in the primary years.* London: HMSO

Grasha, A. (1996) *Teaching with style.* Pittsburgh: Alliance

Lightman, A. and Sadler, P. (1993) 'Teacher predictions versus actual student gains'. *The Physics Teacher*, 31, 162–167.

CHAPTER 12

APPROACHES TO TEACHING AND LEARNING 3: DIFFERENTIATION AND PERSONALISATION

Neil Denby

Standard addressed

Q19 Know how to make effective personalised provision for those they teach, including those for whom English is an additional language or who have special educational needs or disabilities, and how to take practical account of diversity and promote equality and inclusion in their teaching.

Introduction

All pupils are different. They have different backgrounds, different needs and different ways of learning. Some of these differences may be physical, some more learning orientated, some more culturally or socially embedded. If the needs are seen as a particular cause for concern, or specialist intervention, then they will gain a category description of their own. Not having English as a first language can obviously be a barrier to learning in an English classroom, so there are special provisions for English as an additional language (EAL) learners. Similarly, special arrangements may be made for those with physical difficulties such as speech, sight, hearing and mobility. Special educational needs of all types are generally put under the heading of Special Educational Needs (SEN) or Learning Difficulties and Disorders (LDD). The first encompasses both ends of the spectrum, from those who have difficulty learning to those considered to be 'gifted and talented'; the second covers a whole range of physical and mental problems.

A thought

Who are the 'gifted and talented'? The DfES Standards Unit defines 'talented' students in just three subjects: art, music and PE. Talented students are the top 5–10 per cent of pupils per school as measured by actual or potential achievement in these areas. Gifted pupils are measured as the top 5–10 per cent of pupils by actual or potential achievement in the other curriculum subjects. Welding (1998) suggests the generic characteristics of gifted students: in general they have a *'thirst for knowledge'*, high powers of reasoning and the ability to understand abstract and/or difficult concepts quickly. They can also express themselves lucidly and show analytical and independent thinking.

In your local authority there will be special schools for those for whom mainstream education is not possible. Many parents, however, would like their children to be educated with their peers, so opt for normal school with special arrangements. Certain schools in the authority will therefore be designated as having special arrangements for certain groups and will receive appropriate funding for this.

As well as these specific groups and individuals, you will be faced with a range of diverse needs. Every class that you teach will, to a greater or lesser extent, be of mixed ability. You must therefore develop an 'inclusive' approach to ensure that all are reaching their potential. The school will have collected a wide range of statistics and information regarding pupils and you should use this information to help plan lessons. Expert colleagues will help you to identify the needs of specific groups for which they have responsibility. Accessing and understanding data, and how to make best use of support colleagues, is detailed in Chapters 6 and 17 while the focus on diversity occasioned by the Ajegbo Report is discussed in Chapter 16.

Having a range of activities or routes through a lesson is called differentiation. Taking differentiation to its logical conclusion would mean creating a different learning plan or route for each pupil, called personalisation. Each is a step on the road to providing excellent education by meeting children's individual needs.

> To ensure children are confident, happy and engaged in learning, their individual needs must be met. This may sound simple, but it is a highly complex task, requiring practitioners to be constantly alert and responsive. (Hutchin 2006: 30)

Differentiation

Differentiation means creating a variety of learning experiences for pupils and can be linked to various 'learning styles' theories. Materials and methods in the classroom should be adapted to each different level of learning and each different learning style. At its most extreme, it becomes a personal curriculum for each child – hence its inevitable link with the concept of personalisation. Joyce *et al*. (1997: 15) conclude that different experiences help pupils to develop:

> Increasing the range of learning experiences provided in our schools increases the likelihood of more students becoming more adept learners.

Differentiation may be achieved through any number of routes – it does not just mean preparing work at different levels for different individuals, or having easier materials for part of your class. Differentiation by outcome – i.e. in a set situation like a test or class exercise each pupil will perform differently – is not really differentiation at all, but can be useful as a way of ranking young people by ability. You should aim to assess learning regularly, both in formal ways and through formative assessment for learning (see Chapter 13). Assessing learners' progress allows you to provide timely interventions, to issue tasks of greater or less complexity and/or to arrange appropriate support. Self-assessment – encouraging pupils to think about their own learning – is also appropriate.

For any learner you should have a five-phase 'map' so that you can set appropriate, personalised, targets. These phases are:

- Where are they now?
- How do you know this?
- Where do you want them to be?
- How will they get there?
- How will you know that they have arrived?

INDIVIDUAL REFLECTION

The curriculum in Scotland is different, and has already gone some way to meeting some of the targets sought by the QCA. Its 'Curriculum for Excellence' is a programme that runs through the entire age range from 3 to18 and is based around young people needing to become successful learners, confident individuals, responsible citizens and effective contributors. All of these, you will notice, are personal skills rather than wedded to the subject matter of the curriculum.

Consider, in percentage terms, how much of your teaching is based on developing personal skills. Plan to increase this and monitor the effects on learning.

Planning for differentiation

In what might be termed the 'traditional' teacher-centred lesson, the lesson is designed for the whole class with class learning outcomes and pupils are set the same tasks to complete. Differentiation is by 'outcome', i.e. how well each pupil performs. In the differentiated lesson, targets and outcomes are set for individuals, pupils are set different tasks and there is less teacher-talk and more facilitation. The first has the advantage of being easier to prepare and manage, but for many of the pupils, the level will not be right (whether too high or too low is equally problematic). The second makes whole-class interaction a lot harder and takes more preparation but, as a pupil-centred approach, is better for the learners. Your differentiated learning objectives become key signposts of learning within the lesson and within sequences of lessons. From a practical point of view, you may be able to aim for a lesson that falls part way between these two: one, for example, where different groups have different learning objectives with separate targets set for a few individuals. In this way you may only be monitoring and facilitating four or five pathways rather than 20 plus. For each lesson or series of lessons you will need to decide what the underlying essential learning is going to be for each group or individual, and how they can best achieve this. In addition, you will need further targets for the more able and possibly more complex tasks, and to plan appropriate support and interventions for weaker pupils. A good general rule is to work to objectives that state by the end of the lesson:

- All pupils will …
- Most pupils will …
- Some pupils will …

It is then easier, within these broad groupings, to set individual targets. In practice, some whole-class teaching will take place and you will need to find a balance that allows all pupils to progress at a satisfactory rate. Differentiated approaches to learning include people, methods and materials.

People

The people involved should not just be designated support teachers such as TLAs, but also technicians, librarians, parents and other pupils. Mentoring – from a parent, a member of a community or even an older student – can be an effective way of personalising a curriculum. It is a particularly useful way of ensuring that EAL pupils or those from diverse backgrounds understand concepts and ideas. Collaborative work within a group can also help learning. A more able pupil may learn a concept better by explaining it to a less able one (the motto of a good teacher should be *docendo discimus* – we learn by teaching), creating better and more individualised learning for both. Similarly, group work can allow pupils to follow different paths and use different skills within the group.

Methods

Many of the methods of differentiation involve encouraging children and young people to think more deeply. Challenging pupils' assumptions and values, for example, will provoke a response coloured by diverse backgrounds and cultures and promote thinking. Questions should be cognitively demanding and in question sessions you must leave time for thought processes to take place. Open questions of course encourage more differentiated responses than closed questions. You should also make room for young people to respond in different ways – there is no reason for a response to always be written down. Encourage pupils to pace themselves, manage their own time and work at a rate which they find comfortable but within parameters within which you know they can achieve. Tasks should be set that require solutions to be thought out and measured. This can be encouraged by setting tasks or problems with no single solution and, crucially, requiring pupils to justify choices and decisions. These skills of analysis and evaluation are often thought to be difficult, but are actually inherent in the human psyche. (Think about the thought processes involved in crossing a busy road, or ask any 14-year-old why such-and-such a team lost a match or so-and-so didn't win the *X Factor*, and you will see how good people are at analysis and evaluation.) These skills can be further honed by using homework to extend the range or depth of a project.

Application to teaching

Set a homework for a whole class on the same topic but promote different ways to respond. You could ask for responses of, for example, a piece of writing, a picture, a cartoon, a poem, a rap, a piece of music, a text message, a speech, a diagram, a spider diagram, a webpage, song lyrics, a mnemonic … You will be pleasantly surprised by the number of different responses that you receive and by how much more the pupils will enjoy the homework.

Materials

Materials can be prepared with different levels of support within them. A crossword, for example, could have cryptic clues, easy clues, first letters given or partial answers given. Tasks or activities can be graded by difficulty, with pupils moving on to more demanding work as they succeed. Be careful that, once a concept is understood and practised, it is not unnecessarily repeated. It is easy to think that you are providing harder work when actually it is more of the same. You can also differentiate by making more information available at different levels and in different formats. Pupils can then access the information they need in a form with which they are comfortable and at a level they understand.

Finding a balance

Some or all of these strategies can be used to differentiate both within lessons and across series of lessons. Using a single approach has problems so you will need to combine several techniques to ensure inclusive teaching. For example, differentiating by providing increasingly difficult tasks within a lesson is likely to bore higher ability pupils at the start of the lesson and leave weaker ones frustrated at the end. To reach all pupils and thus qualify as inclusive, the approach would need the addition of, for example, extra support, group collaboration and targeted intervention. The combination of people, tasks and materials will lead to pupils being able to take different routes through lessons, heading for individualised or personalised learning targets.

GROUP EXERCISE

How do you test what children have learned as individuals and is transferable rather than that which can only be recalled as a 'class' effort or in a specific context? 'Deep' learning involves a set of skills or knowledge that is transferable. Perkins (1993) suggests that, to succeed in transferring problem-solving skills, learners need to be:

- able to spot the problem;
- motivated to solve it;
- able to select and use appropriate tools.

For example, a learner taught Pythagoras' theorem in mathematics could be set the problem of deciding which trees should be felled in which direction to clear a space and miss buildings. Can they adapt the learning to work out the height of trees and thus where they will fall in order to give appropriate directions to the tree fellers? Discuss how different subjects within your learning group could devise ways to test that learning is transferable.

Personalisation

The idea of personalised learning in an educational context is not a new one as Ken Boston, Chief Executive of the Qualifications and Curriculum Authority (QCA), explains:

> The learning theory on which personalized learning is based goes back 30 years: that for each individual in each domain of learning there is a zone of proximal development – or achievable challenge – in which learning can occur. Teaching is effective only when it is sufficiently precise and focused to build directly on what the individual pupil knows, and takes him or her to the next level of attainment. If the learning task is beyond the zone of achievable challenge, no learning will occur and the child will be frustrated and disaffected. If the learning task is too easy and does not extend the child, again no learning will occur, and the child will be bored. (Boston 2006)

It is, however, a concept that has been readily adopted by politicians in recent years. David Miliband, the Minister for School Standards in 2004, said the government's aim was to make personalised learning a key feature of the education system. He claimed that:

> ... decisive progress in educational standards occurs where every child matters; careful attention is paid to their individual learning styles, motivations, and needs; there is rigorous use of pupil target setting linked to high-quality assessment; lessons are well placed and enjoyable; and pupils are supported by partnership with others well beyond the classroom. (Miliband 2004)

The concept has also been promoted by the then Schools Minister Jacqui Smith and Prime Minister Tony Blair and has found its way into several government proposals such as the White Papers *Higher standards, better schools for all* (DfES 2005) and *Further Education: raising skills, improving life chances* (DfES 2006). In 2006, on the launch of the Education and Inspections Bill, Education Minister Ruth Kelly said:

> Our best schools have been personalizing learning with great success for many years. It is the key to raising standards and the Education and Inspections Bill has at its core a commitment to ensure every school is delivering for every child.

Christine Gilbert, Her Majesty's Chief Inspector (HMCI), has produced a report (Gilbert 2006) that outlines the skills required for and benefits to be gained from personalised learning. The skills are:

- analysing and using data, with a specific focus on assessment for learning;
- understanding how children learn and develop;
- working with other adults (including parents and other children's service professionals);
- engaging pupils as active participants in learning.

She adds that personalised learning is learner centred, knowledge centred and assessment centred and:

> Put simply, personalizing learning and teaching means taking a highly structured and responsive approach to each child's and young person's learning, in order that all are able to progress, achieve and participate. (Gilbert 2006: 6)

It is an idea that has resonance in all public services where the 'person' is at the centre of service provision, particularly with multi-agency services. The philosophy of Every Child Matters (see Chapter 15) is a natural manifestation of the idea with the child set at the centre of service provision. The concept of personalisation recognises that each learner is different, and that the 'hydra curriculum' (Lewis 2007), where as each subject is cut another one or more takes its place, is no longer sustainable. The 2007 QCA curriculum review has thus put less emphasis on subject and the new National Curriculum places more responsibility on the learner. Learners are more central and are expected to develop their own skill sets within descriptors that include teamwork, creativity and reflection on their own learning. According to the Director of Curriculum at QCA, Mick Waters, this means that:

> Curriculum subjects need to emphasise the possible routes through schooling and the application of specific learning in the world … [This means] … rejuvenating content within the curriculum to use subject disciplines to develop skills and personal qualities in context, and demonstrate links between the traditional and emerging subjects. (Waters 2007)

A thought

How possible is choice within an already overcrowded curriculum?

Charlie Brown: I learned something in school today. I signed up for folk guitar, computer programming, stained glass art, shoemaking and natural foods workshop. I got spelling, history, arithmetic and two study periods.

Lucy: What did you learn?

Charlie Brown: I learned that what you sign up for and what you get are two different things.

(Charles Schultz, quoted in Reimer 1971)

To truly deliver personalised learning, you need both a flexible curriculum and the ability to access a wide range of teaching and learning strategies, including groupwork, mentoring, involving parents and community and, indeed, involving children and young people directly in their own learning. Five key strands are:

- the use of assessment for learning (Black and Wiliam 1998, 2001) to establish where pupils are and how to move them on;
- teaching for learning – planning teaching to be motivating and transferable;
- creating choice within the curriculum;
- engaging parents and communities so that learners perceive themselves as members of a wider social body;
- listening to the student voice.

The importance of listening to the pupils' voice is vital. MacGilchrist *et al.* (2005: 65) believe that pupils have much to teach us:

> Particularly, we learn how articulate and in touch even the youngest pupils can be when they are given time to talk about their learning and their experience of it at school.

Gray *et al.* (1999) agree that schools which combine paying heed to pupils' views with any of the suggested approaches to school improvement will achieve a more speedy improvement while Hannam (1998: 3) is of the opinion that:

> The views of pupils/students represent the single most neglected source of potential data for school improvement.

The future

The Children's Plan, an ambitious 'blueprint' for the future published by the DCSF in December 2007, suggests more moves away from the structures and systems that stand in the way of individualised learning. It suggests that children should be taught according to their 'stage not age' and, on the whole, should be 'tested when ready' rather than at pre-set times. By 2009, key stage tests could be abandoned in favour of individual tests when individuals are ready for them, but only after pilots have been evaluated and proved to be effective.

Of course, there is an obvious and dangerous conflict between the target-driven statistics, testing and ordering of Chapter 17, the subject-based curriculum described in Chapter 14 and the idea of a curriculum geared to individual learning needs. Governments, parents and statisticians need the measurements to be able to chart progress and make comparisons. Individuals need to be able to chart and reflect on their own progress. This is a tension that you, in the classroom, will need to manage. You must take cognisance of figures and forecasts but also plan and deliver a curriculum aimed at the individual learner.

Summary

- All pupils are different and every class is to some extent mixed ability.
- Differences include learning, language and social and cultural backgrounds.
- You need to take account of these differences in planning and teaching.
- Differentiation can be achieved using a combination of people, methods and materials.
- Personalisation is the concept that, where services are involved, the 'person' should be at the centre.
- Its application to education puts the learner at the centre and involves them directly in their own learning.

Key reading

Black, P. and Wiliam, D. (2001) 'BERA Final Draft'. In *Inside the black box. Raising standards through classroom assessment.* Available online at: http://ditc.missouri.edu/docs/blackBox.pdf

Gilbert, C. (2006) *Report of the Teaching and Learning in 2020 Review Group.* DfES. Available to download from: http://publications.teachernet.gov.uk

Hannam, A. (1998), cited in Ruddock, J. and Flutter, J. (2000) 'Pupil participation and pupil perspective: "Carving a new order of experience"'. *Cambridge Journal of Education*, 30 (1), 75–89

Hutchin, V. (2006) 'Meeting individual needs'. In Bruce, T. (ed.), *Early childhood: a guide for students.* London: Sage, Chapter 4.

References and bibliography

Black, P. and Wiliam, D. (2001) 'BERA Final Draft'. In *Inside the black box. Raising standards through classroom assessment.* Available online at: http:// ditc.missouri.edu/docs/blackBox.pdf

Boston, K. (2006) *Tipping points in education and skills*, speech to QCA Annual Review 2006. Available online at: www.qca.org.uk/qca_11280.aspx

Gilbert, C. (2006) *Report of the Teaching and Learning in 2020 Review Group*. DfES. Available to download from: http://publications.teachernet.gov.uk

Gray, J., Hopkins, D., Reynolds, D., Wilcox, B., Farrell, S. and Jesson, D. (1999) *Improving schools: performance and potential*. Buckingham: Open University Press

Hannam, A. (1998), cited in Ruddock, J. and Flutter, J. (2000) 'Pupil participation and pupil perspective: "carving a new order of experience"'. *Cambridge Journal of Education*, 30 (1), 75–89

Hutchin, V. (2006) 'Meeting individual needs'. In Bruce, T. (ed.), *Early childhood: a guide for students*. London: Sage, Chapter 4

Joyce, B., Calhoun, E. and Hopkins, D. (1997) *Models of learning – tools for teaching.* Buckingham: Open University Press

Lewis, P. (2007) *How we think but not in school.* Rotterdam: Sense Publishers

MacGilchrist, B., Myers, K. and Reed, J. (2005) *The intelligent school,* 2nd edition. London: Sage

Miliband, D. (2004) *Personalised learning: building a new relationship with schools.* Speech delivered at the North of England Education Conference, 8 January

Perkins, D. (1993) 'Teaching for understanding'. *Journal of the American Federation of Teachers,* 17 (3), 28–35

Reimer, E. (1971) 'Peanuts', quoted in 'School is dead, an essay on alternatives to education'. *Interchange,* 2 (1)

Waters, M. (2007) 'New curriculum, exciting learning'. Comment, *Guardian,* 5 February

Welding, J. (1998) 'The identification of able children in a secondary school: a study of the issues involved and their practical implications'. *Educating Able Children,* 2

CHAPTER 13

UNDERSTANDING AND USING ASSESSMENT AND DELIVERING FEEDBACK

Roger Crawford

Standards addressed

Q11 Know the assessment requirements and arrangements for the subjects/ curriculum areas they are trained to teach, including those relating to public examinations and qualifications.

Q12 Know a range of approaches to assessment, including the importance of formative assessment.

Q26 (a) Make effective use of a range of assessment, monitoring and recording strategies.
(b) Assess the learning needs of those they teach in order to set challenging learning objectives.

Q27 Provide timely, accurate and constructive feedback on learners' attainment, progress and areas for development.

Q28 Support and guide learners to reflect on their learning, identify the progress they have made and identify their emerging learning needs.

Introduction

As a teacher, you will be expected to assess pupils' work and feed back the results of this assessment to help them to develop. You will also need to use assessment to feed forward into your planning. This is a skill that has to be learned. Teachers tend to be rated highly on general professional knowledge and planning but they do not always make effective use of assessment (Ofsted Annual Reports, cited in Stanley 2007). For teacher trainees, it is perhaps understandable that specific provision for assessment may be left out initially as concerns about presentation of subject content and classroom management can be more pressing. But to become a good teacher you will need to be aware of the importance of assessment for public accountability and will need to understand how assessment can significantly improve teaching and learning. You will assess pupils both during and after learning. These assessments are usually called assessment for learning (AfL) or formative assessment, and assessment of learning (AoL) or summative assessment. However:

> Assessments in themselves are not inherently formative or summative – it is the process and how the information is used that is important. (DfES 2004: 17)

Assessment for learning

> Assessment for Learning is the process of seeking and interpreting evidence for use by learners and their teachers to decide where the learners are in their learning, where they need to go and how to get there. (Assessment Reform Group 2002: 2)

Assessment for learning (AfL) or formative assessment is one of the most powerful ways of promoting improved learning. It is central to more effective classroom practice as it can improve the focus and pace of teaching and enhance pupils' learning significantly (Black and Wiliam 1998; Assessment Reform Group 1999).

Every interaction with a pupil is an opportunity for AfL, and it is embedded in the ongoing dialogue between teacher and pupil that informs and develops teaching and learning. At its most informal this could be a conversation between a teacher and a pupil that leads to the teacher identifying what the pupil does or does not understand. As a teacher, you will give feedback to the pupil that acknowledges and praises what is understood and use the conversation to help them to overcome misconceptions so that more effective learning takes place. You now have information about the success (or otherwise) of your teaching plans and strategies in relation to the specific pupil, and can investigate whether the misconceptions identified are more widespread. You can use this to reshape and refocus your teaching so that other pupils are helped to overcome the misconceptions.

From the pupil's perspective, the quality of the teacher's feedback is most important as knowing what is fully understood and what is less secure helps learners concentrate their efforts. From the teacher's perspective, it is the reshaping and refocusing of their teaching that is important as this can increase the pace of learning for more pupils.

GROUP EXERCISE

Whatever style of assessment is being used, in practice there are some common issues that should be considered and some questions that you will need to ask when planning assessment.

- **What? Is it clear what is being assessed?** Both pupils and teachers should know before and during the assessment exactly what will be assessed. Look at your lesson plan and decide whether the assessment is relevant and valid. Assessment should focus on the intended topics. For example, the AfL planned within a lesson should focus on the learning objectives that you have written for the lesson.
- **How? Is the assessment feasible?** The precise details of how the assessment will be carried out and marked should be decided in advance. This will help ensure that all the tasks can be done, that they can be done in the time available and that marking is fair and consistent.
- **When? When will assessment take place?** It should be clear in your planning at what points pupils will be assessed. For example, lesson plans need to include explicit planning for AfL, and pupils should be given ample warning of important AoL events, such as end-of-unit tests.

Look at a series of four lesson plans of people in your group and see where they have included assessment opportunities. Suggest other places where you would have included assessment. Make sure that you are not only providing opportunities for assessment, but also opportunities for feeding back the results and for feeding the information forward into future lesson plans.

AfL strategies

There is a wide variety of AfL strategies that you can use (DfES 2004). These will vary considerably from subject to subject and in their formality and the general applicability of the information they yield. Informal dialogue with individual pupils and the class, and formal end-of-unit written tests, are the extremes in the continuum of assessment strategies. Some of the strategies you might employ to find out whether each pupil in a class understands are as follows:

- Have a one-to-one conversation with each child. This provides very specific opportunities to redirect an individual pupil's learning but is less efficient than talking to the whole class.
- Ask the whole class a question and judge their response, for example by requiring pupils to raise their hands if they know the answer. The proportion of the class responding gives a broad indication of the extent of understanding. Teaching can be modified immediately building on pupils' answers.
- Ask the whole class a question and choose a particular pupil of known ability to answer it. If the pupil is generally slow to understand, an accurate response gives a broad indication that the class understands; if the pupil is generally quick to understand, an inaccurate response gives a broad indication that the class does not understand.
- Quickly circulate and note whether each pupil has done a specific task correctly. This provides information about the progress of the class and may lead to an immediate review with the whole class, a group of pupils or individuals. Acknowledging each pupil's efforts as you circulate and checking their work can help build confidence and engagement and refocus learning.
- Devise a short oral quiz that covers the learning objectives of the lesson and ask pupils to write down their answers. Mark this quickly in class (probably self- or peer-assessment – see below). Ask pupils to raise their hands if they, for example, gave the correct answer for four out of five questions. If all the class raise their hands, this can be taken as a broad indication that the lesson has been successful and vice versa.
- Set homework so that pupils can independently and individually demonstrate that they have understood the lesson. When you mark the homework, diagnostic comments and grades or marks will help pupils understand the progress they have made and the standard achieved. However, it is important to take into account that pupils may have had help doing homework, pupils may copy others' work and homework may not be well supported by parents or not done. These factors affect the reliability of homework as a tool for assessing the progress of individual pupils and the class.
- Ask pupils to produce a piece of work at the end of a task to demonstrate what they have done, or set a short test or a formal end-of-topic assessment. Mark this yourself and make sure that the feedback pupils receive includes a grade or mark and a written commentary on the strengths and weaknesses of their work and how they can improve it. The grade is important to pupils who want to do well; they will compete with one another to achieve the highest grade. Some pupils may apparently ignore the written feedback which has taken you considerable time and effort to produce and this can be frustrating. However, this written feedback is central to the learning process and should not be omitted. It will be helpful to all pupils but can be particularly helpful to those of lower ability.

> ### 💭 A thought
>
> When teachers return marked work, pupils often appear to be very interested in the grade or mark awarded but may show little interest in the teacher's diagnostic comments that are essential to help them improve their work.
>
> Why are some pupils more interested in the grade or mark they receive than in the diagnostic comments that will help them improve?
>
> How can teachers encourage pupils to carefully consider the diagnostic comments?

Self- and peer-assessment

You should build into your planning opportunities for self- and peer-assessment and explain to pupils why they need to do this. As with other aspects of assessment, pupils are likely to perform better at self- and peer-assessment if they know why they are doing it and recognise its advantages and disadvantages.

Self-assessment helps pupils develop their ability to learn and it is 'necessary for effective learning' (Boud 1995: 14). 'Pupils are more likely to make rapid progress in their learning if they understand what they are aiming for' (DfES 2004: 10), and learning can be more effective when learners are able to identify for themselves what they understand and what they do not, as this enables them to learn independently without feedback from the teacher. If pupils are not engaged in self-assessment, the effect 'is to remove them from participation in the core processes of learning' (Boud 1995: 12). 'This can lead to disengagement with the learning process and sometimes to poor behaviour' (DfES 2004: 1).

Pupils develop confidence in what they know through self-assessment and can focus their learning more accurately. This form of assessment also enables pupils to learn more quickly and efficiently. Prompt feedback on success helps shape learning more quickly so that understanding of concepts can be adjusted while the pupil is engaged with tasks. Delays mean that the tasks and the assessment may not be well remembered. Immediate feedback is intrinsic in self-assessment.

Peer assessment helps pupils increase their understanding of the assessment process and improve their self-assessment. It is difficult to assess one's own work accurately; however, in order to make progress with learning, it is important to learn to do this (Boud 1995). Robust discussion with other pupils about the quality of their work can help them to discover the strengths and weaknesses of their own work. Assessing others' work helps pupils view their own work more objectively and assess its worth more accurately.

Even so, teachers need to be aware of the disadvantages of self- and peer-assessment. Self-assessment may be inaccurate (Rees and Shepherd 2005), and learners may overestimate their own abilities or be unrealistic about their potential achievements. They may also underestimate what they can do and become downhearted and discouraged. Peer assessment should lead to robust discussion between pupils but can lead to inaccurate assessments (Platt 2002) and mutual hostility if pupils resent criticism. A more dominant pupil may persuade other pupils that their good work is of a lower quality. You will need to manage carefully self- and peer-assessment to minimise any downside.

A thought

AfL is a powerful technique for improving the focus and pace of teaching and learning. AoL is a snapshot of a pupil's achievement.

Is assessment either formative or summative or can it be both?

INDIVIDUAL REFLECTION

Think about a lesson you planned and taught recently and how you planned for and used AfL within the lesson.

- Did the AfL cover the learning objectives and the topics you had taught?
- Did the lesson plan indicate specific opportunities for AfL?
- Did you incorporate self- and peer-assessment and explain why?
- Was assessment fair and reasonable? Did you encourage pupils to judge this for themselves?
- Did you modify your teaching and future lesson plans as a result of the assessment?

Key areas

All assessment must be fair and reasonable. You should encourage pupils to check and challenge your assessments so that they become more engaged with and have a greater understanding of the assessment process. For example, when returning marked work, you could give pupils a copy of the mark scheme you used. If assessment is open and well understood, pupils will know that they have been assessed fairly and that there is no favouritism on the part of the teacher. You will soon discover that young people have a very well developed sense of justice and respond positively to fair treatment. In addition, this approach can help pupils develop a greater understanding of the topic.

Assessment results need to be recorded so that you can monitor participation and actual performance relative to expectations. At a minimum, you should note whether pupils have completed homework and other set work and to what standard. After each formal assessment, you should record a grade or mark for each pupil. It is also useful to record a comment that characterises each pupil's progress, in preparation for parent–teacher consultation and written reporting to parents. There is government and commercial software to support the recording of assessment results, for example the DfES pupil achievement tracker (2007) and the Primary Progress Toolkit (Watson 2007).

Any assessment impacts on pupils' willingness to learn, so you need to look at how you can use assessment as a vehicle for motivation. Pupils who are more enthusiastic and engaged achieve better than those who are not. You will need to differentiate between pupils but this should be done in ways that encourage pupils to persist with their studies. An assessment designed so that all pupils achieve between 50 and 90 per cent success will have a more positive effect on motivation than a test where all pupils achieve between 10 and 50 per cent, even though the range of marks is the same.

Application to teaching

The purpose of the exercise is to emphasise that pupils' achievements in assessed work can be improved by ensuring they understand what they are required to do and know the criteria that will be used to assess their work. The clapping exercise is subject neutral so can be used to reinforce assessment in any subject.

The exercise works best with a group of around 15 to 30 pupils in an informal session.

» Ask for three volunteers. Don't explain what they are volunteering for. Foster a sense of relaxed excitement, anticipation and good humour throughout.

» Ask the volunteers to stand at the front facing the class.

» Explain that the teacher is going to set a task for the volunteers and that the rest of the group will be asked to assess them and write down their assessment without conferring with other pupils.

» Describe the task briefly: each volunteer will clap their hands for one minute.

» The volunteers do this in turn. The teacher should time each volunteer and allow a short period of time for the class to write down their assessment.

» When all the volunteers have completed the task, they remain at the front of the class, and the teacher asks the pupils to consider which volunteer is best at performing the task.

» Ask the class to vote for each volunteer in turn with a show of hands.

» Ask pupils for explanations of their judgements. For each volunteer, choose at least one pupil who believed the volunteer was the best.

» Discuss the exercise with the class. Note that when the assessment took place, the volunteers had no prior knowledge of the task and did not know the criteria that would be used to assess them. During the discussion, derive criteria for assessing the task, for example variation in rhythm, variation in volume, movement and dance, and audience participation and engagement.

» Ask each volunteer to repeat the task but for 30 seconds only.

» The volunteers' performances are usually much improved.

Summarise: improvement can only be due to prior knowledge of the task and how it will be assessed.

Assessment of learning

Assessment of learning (AoL) or summative assessment is a snapshot of achievement and 'tends to be carried out periodically, e.g. at the end of a unit or term, year or key stage' (DfES 2004: 17). As teachers we are familiar with this type of assessment as it is how we have ourselves been assessed. Public examinations such as GCSE, A Level and degree examinations are all summative. The outcome of AoL is usually reported as a grade or level which is intended to summarise a level of achievement. A detailed description of what a pupil is expected to have done to achieve a particular grade or level is often available; for example, GCSE specifications include grade descriptions and there are level descriptions for National Curriculum subjects.

External assessment

AoL at the end of a module or course is often external assessment, that is the tasks are set and marked by an organisation external to the educational institution attended by the pupil. Well-known examples are the end of key stage tests in English, Mathematics and Science, and GCSE, AS and A Levels which are set by the three major English awarding bodies, AQA, Edexcel and OCR. For more information on awarding bodies, browse their websites (see the Key Reading section). Although these awarding bodies are large, they do not have a monopoly. There are hundreds of awarding bodies in the UK, ranging from the specialist (banking, accounting, sports coaching) to the more general.

External AoL helps further or higher education institutions and employers summarise the individual achievement of prospective students and employees, and enables them to choose the best students and employees.

> ## 💭 A thought
>
> Grade and level descriptions attempt to characterise the achievements of pupils who are awarded a particular grade or level. However, they do not describe the achievement of a particular pupil.
>
> Grades and levels tend to be very broad. For example, a very good grade D in GCSE Mathematics may differ only very slightly from a very weak grade C.
>
> How useful are grade and level descriptions in helping pupils and teachers plan future learning and employers in deciding who to employ?

League tables

Statistics summarising the achievements of pupils attending a particular school are publicly available and these are used in compiling school league tables. As a result, parents have information about schools that could help them choose a school for their children, and schools are publicly accountable for the progress of their pupils. This is designed to stimulate competition between schools and drive up the quality of education.

Resources

The government does not directly fund awarding bodies. When schools and colleges enter pupils and students for an external assessment, for example GCSE, a fee is paid to the awarding body. As a result, awarding bodies compete for pupils and strive to offer the best service to schools and colleges and their websites have a wide range of useful resources for teachers and pupils. For example, for GCSE there could be:

- a specification that clarifies exactly what should be studied and how it will be assessed;
- specimen or previous examination papers;
- marked examples of coursework;

- advice on how to prepare for the examination;
- reports that identify the areas where pupils have been successful or less successful in the assessments;
- statistics showing how many pupils achieved a particular grade and the standard required to achieve it.

The resources available from the awarding bodies can be very useful when planning teaching. They describe the knowledge, skills and understanding that will be assessed, and can help teachers identify topics that pupils in general find difficult, so that teaching can be planned to include these. Specimen or previous examination papers with answers and marked examples of coursework can be helpful when teachers prepare summative assessment for use in schools and colleges. (If using past papers for your own tests, remember that pupils and parents also have access to the awarding body websites!)

Similarly, there are useful resources on the National Curriculum in Action website (see Key Reading). There is helpful advice to support teachers assessing the level of their pupils' work, and a particularly useful feature is the embedded hyperlinks in the level descriptions that link to examples of pupils' work at that level.

Awarding bodies are using ICT to improve efficiency and lower costs. For example, they are developing online, on-demand tests with immediate feedback on performance, and e-portfolios so that pupils' coursework can be submitted for assessment in electronic form. They have changed the way paper-based examination scripts are marked: these may be scanned, distributed to examiners over the Internet and marked online, as this is more accurate and efficient. The detailed results of computer-based assessment are more easily recorded using ICT, and more information about the performance of each individual pupil is becoming available. Currently, the feedback each pupil receives can be only a grade or level but it is likely that in the very near future each pupil will receive personalised and detailed feedback on success in every aspect of an assessment.

School tests and examinations

AoL also takes place in schools when teachers assess their pupils' work. Many schools assess their pupils every year, often using assessment methods similar to those that will be used when pupils are externally assessed. This gives pupils practice with these methods of assessment and often leads to a summative grade or level so that schools can report pupils' attainment to parents. However, because teachers set and mark these assessments, they have access to detailed information about their pupils' learning and can use this to improve teaching and learning. In this case, summative assessment can also be used for formative assessment. In addition, when personalised and detailed feedback is available from the awarding bodies, it is likely that this will also be used for formative assessment.

Summary

- Assessment for learning (AfL) or formative assessment helps teachers judge pupils' progress and improve the focus and pace of teaching and learning.

- Every interaction with a pupil is an opportunity for AfL.

- Feedback to pupils should let them know what is understood and what is not so that they gain confidence and can concentrate their efforts to improve.

- Self-assessment helps pupils develop the ability to learn independently, and learn more quickly and efficiently.

- Peer-assessment helps pupils increase their understanding of the assessment process and improve their self-assessment.

- Teachers need to be aware of the negative consequences of self- and peer-assessment and carefully manage these.

- Assessment of learning (AoL) or summative assessment is a snapshot of what pupils have achieved. It is often external assessment, for example GCSE, and is important for public accountability.

Key reading

A concise summary of the principles of assessment for learning:

Assessment Reform Group (2002) *Assessment for learning: 10 principles to guide classroom practice*. Assessment Reform Group. Available online at: www.assessment-reform-group.org.uk (accessed 10 July 2007)

An extensive review of the practice of assessment for learning:

DfES (2004) *Pedagogy and Practice: Unit 12: Assessment for learning*. London: DfES

The content and assessment of the National Curriculum in most subjects, with examples of pupils' work at each level of the relevant Attainment Target:

National Curriculum in Action website. www.ncaction.org.uk/ (accessed 10 July 2007)

Awarding body websites where you can download external assessment specifications and supporting resources:

AQA – www.aqa.org.uk (accessed 10 July 2007)
Edexcel – www.edexcel.org.uk (accessed 10 July 2007)
OCR – www.ocr.org.uk (accessed 10 July 2007)

References and bibliography

Assessment Reform Group (1999) *Assessment for learning: beyond the black box.* University of Cambridge, Faculty of Education

Black, P. and Wiliam, D. (1998) *Inside the black box: raising standards through classroom assessment.* London: King's College

Boud, D. (1995) *Enhancing learning through self-assessment.* London: RoutledgeFalmer

DfES (2004) *Pedagogy and Practice. Unit 12: Assessment for learning.* London: DfES

DfES (2007) *Pupil achievement tracker.* Available online at: www.standards.dfes.gov.uk/performance/pat/ (accessed 2007)

Platt, J.A. (2002) *Peer and self-assessment: some issues and problems.* School of Social Sciences, Sussex University. Available online at: www.c-sap.bham.ac.uk/resources/project_reports/findings/ShowFinding.htm?id=Platt/1 (accessed 9 November 2007)

Rees, C. and Shepherd, M. (2005) 'Students' and assessors' attitudes towards students' self-assessment of their personal and professional behaviours' in *Medical Education.* 39 (1), 30–39.

Stanley, N. (2007) *Assessment.* Available online at: www.ict-tutors.co.uk/ (accessed 2007)

Watson, R. (2007) *Primary progress toolkit.* Available online at: www.primaryprogresstoolkit.co.uk/(accessed 2007)

Part 3

THE KNOWLEDGE BASE

CHAPTER 14

QUALIFICATIONS AND EXAMINATIONS IN ENGLAND AND WALES

John Trafford

Standard addressed

 Know the assessment requirements and arrangements for the subjects/ curriculum areas in the age ranges they are trained to teach, including those related to public examinations and qualifications.

Introduction

Much of the discussion and publicity surrounding education over the past 20 years has centred on the effectiveness of schools and colleges as measured by statistics. Most prominent among these are the results of public examinations, often measured through local and national comparisons, commonly referred to as 'league tables'. One rationale for the introduction of a national curriculum in 1988 was that it would provide for a commonality of experience for pupils on which schools would build. The curriculum, and the examination systems which accompanied it or predated it, have nevertheless proved highly complex, and you will need to ensure that you are familiar with those components of the national system which apply to your pupils and your situation. At the same time, you have the opportunity (and, it can be argued, responsibility) to know about the phases of education before and after that in which you teach – where your pupils came from and where they might be heading.

The National Curriculum

The existence of a national curriculum has become such an unquestioned feature of our education system that it is worth reminding ourselves that it was as recently as 1988 that the Education Reform Act was passed which introduced it. This was no less than a revolution in children's schooling. Prior to this, apart from a legal requirement to provide religious education, which schools interpreted very liberally, there was no specification for the curriculum to contain any particular subjects, strands or themes. What existed, therefore, was a curriculum by consensus – there was generally similarity between the curricula offered by schools, but there could also be significant differences from school to school.

The 1988 Act made schools aware of an important concept, little considered before – the fact that a 'statutory requirement' places a legal obligation on schools and teachers to offer a certain subject or incorporate a certain theme into their curriculum. The word 'statutory' is very important for you to consider when reading the multiplicity of documents that relate to the National Curriculum. If something is statutory, it is a legal requirement. Much of the content of the curriculum, being statutory, is still not negotiable, even though the manner in which it is taught, and accessed by pupils, often allows for considerable flexibility. Indeed, the spirit of the latest revisions of the curriculum is to allow schools considerably more room for manoeuvre than earlier versions.

INDIVIDUAL REFLECTION

If you are working in primary schools, or when you visit them as a secondary trainee, what is the status of the subjects that are not in the core curriculum?

Find out about the time allocation that subjects have. Do teachers' perceptions of their own areas of expertise determine the weight they give to certain subjects?

Familiarising yourself with the curriculum

It will be very important for you, and for your professional progress as a teacher, to keep pace with developments in the curriculum, whatever phase of education you are working in. Since the introduction of a statutory curriculum, it has been adapted, rewritten, added to and modified on many occasions and in many ways. One example is the more structured approach to Early Years education introduced over recent years with the establishment of the Foundation Stage and the Early Learning Goals, which extended formal learning and formal requirements for learning to younger children. More experienced teachers will remember early versions of the National Curriculum, characterised by ring binders of information, published subject by subject, with the links between them not always clear. Electronic communication has, not surprisingly, made your task as a new teacher much easier in reading and assimilating documents about the curriculum and its assessment, now presented in an accessible way, and allowing you keep abreast of changes as they happen rather than necessarily waiting for dissemination in school.

The Internet provides a rich resource for you in many ways, and you would be well advised at an early stage in your teaching career to identify those websites which contain information, advice and guidance to help you master the requirements on you and the sources of help available. Some are listed at the end of this chapter; you will come to see these as a starting point only, and will identify many more. Some time devoted to exploring these sites will help you identify those sources most helpful to you, and will no doubt lead you to links particularly relevant to yourself and your own teaching.

A thought

You should look carefully at the aims and purposes of the National Curriculum. Before you do, try the exercise yourself – if you were designing a school curriculum for the twenty-first century, what should its aims and purposes be?

Finding the time to read the wealth of information available will prove demanding! Once you are caught up in and swept along by the day-to-day pressures of teaching, the odd hour spent browsing websites of what seem remote, official bodies may seem a luxury. You will feel the need to attend to other, more pressing demands, such as the next day's lessons or marking. It is worthwhile, though, to continue to look at the bigger picture, and to keep abreast of how the system, of which you are a part, is developing.

GROUP EXERCISE

It can take a considerable amount of time to explore all the electronic resources available. As with many aspects of teaching, several heads are better than one, so devote some time to identifying a number of websites, say five or six, that you have found particularly useful in enhancing your understanding of your own area of teaching and its assessment. Share these with fellow trainees, and note any overlap. You will also discover resources that you may not have come across yourself.

National Curriculum subjects

Formal National Curriculum requirements begin when a child enters Year 1 at age 5, and a range of compulsory subjects should be taught throughout Key Stages 1 and 2, at the end of which pupils will be aged 11. Considerable emphasis will be placed on the core subjects of English (often referred to as literacy), mathematics (numeracy) and science, although it is important to remember that pupils also have an entitlement to learn art & design, design & technology, geography, history, information and communications technology, music and physical education. Schools have a duty to teach religious education, though parents are allowed to withdraw their children if they wish, therefore religious education stands outside the framework of the National Curriculum. Other subjects have a somewhat ambiguous status in primary education – modern languages, for example, are an 'entitlement' in primary schools from 2010, yet schools are only 'advised' to teach a language and it is not, as yet, statutory. Similarly, primary schools are advised to include personal, social and health education (PSHE) and citizenship in their provision, but also without statutory requirement.

Once children enter Key Stage 3, curriculum requirements change slightly. Often, but not always, this is marked by a change of school, but this depends on the system in place locally. Citizenship and modern languages now become part of the statutory curriculum, and schools must also provide sex and relationships education, usually as a component of personal, social, health and economic education (PSHEE), though parents have the same rights as for religious education.

The Key Stage 3/4 curriculum was reformed in 2007, for implementation from 2008, with the aims of

- cutting back on compulsory subject content;
- giving teachers more opportunity to personalise their pupils' learning;
- developing a greater emphasis on the development of personal attributes and practical life skills;
- helping teachers to make connections between subjects and to view the curriculum as a coherent whole.

The reform of the secondary curriculum introduced some changes to the programmes of study for subjects, but nevertheless retained the basic requirement for all to be retained at Key Stage 3 (ages 11–14). It is likely that schools will introduce a more flexible approach to the Key Stage 3 curriculum over the next few years, while taking care to retain statutory elements.

A thought

If you are working in secondary schools, find out how your schools responded to the 2007 changes in the National Curriculum and compare what you find out. How is the increased flexibility reflected in, for example, pupils' timetables? Is cross-curricular work more prominent than before? If you are working in primary schools, find out how the changes to the Year 7 curriculum will impact on Year 6 teaching.

Key Stage 4 (14–16) has been the focus of much debate, not only preceding the 2007 reform but throughout the lifetime of the National Curriculum. Gradually more flexibility has been introduced in response to a growing perception that the narrow academic focus which characterised early versions of Key Stage 4 provision were likely to be contributing to some pupils' disaffection.

The basic statutory requirement, therefore, looks minimal compared with the earlier key stages. The core subjects of English, mathematics and science remain, as do physical education, ICT, citizenship and PSHE. Religious education has the same status as in earlier key stages. What might be seen as other traditional academic subjects now become optional, for example history, geography, languages, though schools are obliged to offer pupils the chance to follow a course of study in each of four entitlement areas, namely the arts, design and technology, humanities and modern languages. There is of course scope at this point for schools to introduce subjects which do not appear anywhere as statutory, such as business studies or social sciences. Innovations in the 2007 reform include non-statutory programmes of study in personal well-being (including the requirements for sex and relationships and drugs education) and economic well-being and financial capability (including careers education).

National Curriculum assessment

Each subject of the National Curriculum has one or more attainment targets. These contain a description, expressed in levels, of the standard a pupils will reach to be deemed to have attained a certain level. There are eight levels, plus a description of 'exceptional performance'. It is important to remember that these level descriptors apply only up to the end of Key Stage 3, therefore describe attainment up to age 14. It can thus appear that many of the level descriptors seem very ambitious and so quite daunting for pupils and teachers. It is important that you do not rely simply on the language of the National Curriculum documents to understand how the levels work, but relate them as soon as possible to pupils' work. The QCA provides a helpful website with exemplification of work in all subjects at different levels at: www.ncaction.org.uk. Experienced teachers build up a knowledge of the levels at which work should be assessed, which can appear almost intuitive. You will need to draw on this experience as you begin to acquire the sure touch that comes with practice over time in the practicalities of National Curriculum assessment.

Application to teaching

Choose a number of pieces of pupils' work that you are assessing. Look at them in detail against the level descriptors in that subject area. Is it clear to you how they meet a certain level? Did the task you set allow the pupils to demonstrate their knowledge, skills and understanding? Build steps as to how you will help them to move on to a higher level into your current lesson planning.

14–19 education and the diplomas

Heralded by ministers as the most significant development in education since the National Curriculum itself, the 14–19 diplomas were announced with a scheduled start date of 2008. The report by Sir Mike Tomlinson in 2004 proposed a radical overhaul of 14–19 education. Although his proposals were not accepted wholesale by the government, the diploma programme which emerged owed much to his thinking.

The diplomas are conceived as an alternative to traditional GCSE or A Level qualifications, with an aspiration to offer a combination of classroom learning, creative thinking and experience in and directly related to the workplace. Employers are intended to play a key role in diploma provision – the emphasis is on practical learning based around an area of work rather than an academic subject.

The government announced an ambitious timescale for the diplomas – that a new national entitlement for 14 to 19 year olds would be in place for 2013. This would include a right for all young people to pursue any of the 14 new 'lines of learning' covered by the diplomas. These were announced as:

- Engineering
- Health and Social Care
- Information Technology
- Creative and Media
- Construction and the Built Environment
- Land-based and Environment
- Manufacturing
- Hair and Beauty
- Business Administration and Finance
- Hospitality and Catering
- Public Services
- Sport and Leisure
- Retail
- Travel and Tourism.

The distinctly vocational feel to these titles was tempered by the announcement in autumn 2007 of additional diplomas to complement the existing proposals. Areas of study added were:

- Science
- The Humanities
- Languages.

The intention behind the diplomas is that they should have the same rigour as GCSE and A Level courses, and not be perceived as a less challenging alternative. They should, therefore, prepare students for progression to further study, including at university degree level.

The assessment and examinations system

In whichever phase of education you teach, the role of assessment and examinations will have considerable importance. Schools are often judged by their communities, local authorities and Ofsted, to say nothing of the media, on public examination statistics. Indeed, these are often given so much weight that it can appear that other indicators of a school's quality are overlooked. Nevertheless, you will undoubtedly feel pressure to 'deliver' results, and one way in which you can prepare for this is to be as well informed as possible about the tests, examinations or other assessments that your pupils will undergo.

A thought

Talk to a selection of people 'involved' in education – parents, governors, teachers, administration staff. Ask them what they think a 'pass' is at GCSE and why. What conclusions can you draw from this?

One consideration is the location of your school – England and Wales have national curricula which differ in some respects, as do their testing regimes. For example, it was the Welsh Assembly which led the way in changing the nature of Key Stage 1 assessment, and it is in Wales that the most serious debates have been held about abolishing all formal end of key stage testing.

The Qualifications and Curriculum Authority updates and issues guidance on assessment and reporting arrangements for each key stage – this is known as the ARA, and it is important to check that you are consulting an up-to-date version, especially in a time of change and rethinking of statutory requirements.

Foundation Stage

Children who are nearing the end of the reception year will be assessed against the early learning goals and have their learning needs identified. This is termed foundation stage profile assessment. Assessment is made in the six areas of learning described in *Curriculum Guidance for the Foundation Stage* (QCA 2007). These areas are personal, social and emotional development; communication, language and literacy; mathematical development; knowledge and understanding of the world; physical development; creative development. Further information is available from the QCA, from the Department for Children, Schools and Families, and from Surestart.

Key Stage 1

Assessment of children at age 7 is carried out by teachers in the course of teaching and learning. Assessments take into consideration a child's progress and performance throughout Years 1 and 2 – teachers need to arrive at separate levels for each of the English attainment targets of reading, writing, speaking and listening, an overall level for mathematics, and a level for each attainment target in science. Schools are obliged to report these assessments for each child, but they are not passed on for integration into any local or national performance tables at this stage.

Key Stage 2

End of Key Stage 2 tests, often referred to by their original acronym of 'SATS', are given considerable importance by primary schools, mainly because these results figure in performance tables and are thus perceived as contributing greatly towards a school's reputation. This is despite concerns expressed by many observers about the skewing of the curriculum towards the core subjects, and the amount of time children spend on practice test activities. Optional test material is available for years 3, 4 and 5 also, so schools exercise the choice of having children in all year groups undergo formal assessment, often arguing that such tests give a reliable guide to progress and facilitate individual target setting.

Teacher assessment of each pupil is also made in the core subjects, and in Year 6 must be reported along with formal test results.

Key Stage 3

Pupils take statutory tests at the end of Year 9 in English, mathematics and science. Preparation for these is likely to have a high priority in your school, and you must ensure that you are familiar with not only the content of the programmes of study that are being tested but also the style of the tests and the requirements on pupils. Marked scripts are now returned to schools in the weeks following the tests and these can be used as a good development exercise – take the opportunity to look at where pupils demonstrated their understanding and also their misconceptions.

Teacher assessment of all National Curriculum subjects takes place throughout the key stage and schools are required to report to parents annually. There is variation between schools in exactly how and when this takes place, but it will be important for you to build up your familiarity with the levels of attainment in your own subject and your own school's requirements for reporting.

The piloting of on-screen tests in ICT has led to the development of a bank of formative assessment tasks covering the programme of study which are available to schools but are not a statutory requirement.

Key Stage 4

Formal assessment requirements following the National Curriculum levels of attainment end with Key Stage 3, although of course the programmes of study apply until the end of Key Stage 4. Teaching and assessment in years 10 and 11 are likely to be focused on the requirements of the General Certificate of Secondary Education (GCSE), which is taken by the vast majority of pupils. Although there are no formal 'pass' and 'fail' grades, pupils' and schools' achievements are often measured by their attainment of grade C and above. Performance tables published annually by the government focus on the percentage of pupils attaining this benchmark in five or more subjects, although it is important to bear in mind that the lower grades often represent a creditable level of attainment for many pupils. Nevertheless, schools often dedicate much effort to those pupils whose predicted achievement is at the C/D borderline.

Like the National Curriculum, GCSEs are in a process of reform. New science specifications became available in 2006. In most other subjects, pupils reaching Year 10 in 2009 follow revised specifications, with those for English, English Literature, Mathematics and ICT following in 2010.

Functional skills

The development of functional skills qualifications began from 2007. Functional skills are defined as practical skills in English, mathematics and ICT, with a focus on work and everyday life. These qualifications are planned to be either stand-alone qualifications or as components of the 14–19 diplomas described above. Functional skills standards will also be incorporated into the new GCSE specifications in English, mathematics and ICT.

Post-16 education

The majority of those who stay on in the school sector after the age of 16, or go to sixth form college, do so to pursue AS and A2 courses. The AS (Advanced Subsidiary) level was introduced to provide a stepping stone from GCSE to Advanced level, and also an exit qualification for those who decide during their course that they do not want to pursue a full A Level. Students are often encouraged to take four or even five subjects, and often drop one of them after Year 12. The AS examinations count for half of the full A Level grade.

A2 examinations contain an element of synoptic assessment, which tests the student's ability to make connections between different aspects of the subject. Full details of AS and A2 specifications are available from the examination groups which administer them, often with exemplar material, past papers and marking schemes.

Some changes to AS and A2 have come about in response to certain concerns about the rigour of the examinations, and about the difficulty of differentiating between the ever higher number of candidates achieving top grades. A wholesale review of the system, however, due to take place from 2008, was postponed until the future to allow the 14–19 diploma programme (see above) to become established.

Specifications taught from 2008 nevertheless reflect several changes to A Level, of which the main points are as follows:

- a reduction in the number of assessment units from six to four in the majority of subjects;
- the introduction of an A* grade to reward exceptional candidates who achieve an overall A grade plus 90 per cent or more across their A2 units;
- more challenging examinations at A2;
- more synoptic assessment to test holistic understanding;
- the possibility of an extended project to develop independent learning and research skills.

In addition to A Levels, schools may offer a range of vocational options, both in post-16 education and to complement GCSEs. These lead to qualifications which are approved by the Secretary of State and fit into the National Qualifications Framework. Qualifications for learners under 19 are governed by section 96 of the Learning and Skills Act of 2000, and more information is available at www.dfes.gov.uk/section96/.

The National Qualifications Framework

As a wider range of courses becomes available in schools as a result of the changes to the National Curriculum, the introduction of functional skills and the 14–19 diplomas, it will become increasingly important for you to be aware of the National Qualifications Framework (NQF). This specifies the levels at which a qualification is recognised in England, Wales and Northern Ireland. You will notice from the examples of qualifications in Table 14.1, taken from the government's website www.directgov.uk, that both academic and vocational courses feature, along with an attempt to describe the meaning of the different levels in the contexts of work and study. Examples of the first four (of eight) levels of the NQF are given as those most appropriate to you in a school or college context.

The content of the new 14–19 diplomas will be closely linked to the framework.

Table 14.1   Examples from the National Qualifications Framework

NQF level	Examples of qualifications	What they give you
Entry	Entry level certificates	Basic knowledge and skills
	Skills for Life at entry level	Ability to apply learning in everyday situations
		Not geared towards specific occupations
Level 1	GCSE grades D–G	Basic knowledge and skills
	BTEC Introductory diplomas and certificates	Ability to apply learning with guidance or supervision
	OCR Nationals	May be linked to job competence
	Key Skills Level 1	
	NVQs	
	Skills for Life	
Level 2	GCSE grades A*–C	Good knowledge and understanding of a subject
	BTEC First diplomas and certificates	Ability to perform a variety of tasks with some guidance and supervision
	OCR Nationals	
	Key Skills Level 2	Appropriate for many job roles
	NVQs	
	Skills for Life	
Level 3	A Levels	Ability to gain or apply a range of knowledge, skills and understanding at a detailed level
	Advanced Extension awards	
	GCE in applies subjects	Appropriate if you plan to go to university, work independently or, in some cases, supervise and train others in their field of work
	International Baccalaureate	
	Key Skills Level 3	
	NVQs	
	BTEC diplomas, certificates and awards	
	BTEC Nationals	
	OCR Nationals	
Level 4	Key Skills Level 4	Specialist learning involving detailed analysis of a high level of information and knowledge in an area of work or study
	NVQs	
	BTEC Professional diplomas and certificates	Appropriate for people in technical and professional jobs and/or managing and developing others

Conclusion

There is a considerable amount of information to be assimilated about the curriculum and its assessment. You will need to gain a working knowledge of statutory requirements and your own school's way of approaching these as well as new developments that are happening around you. At first, this task may seem bewildering, if not at times almost overwhelming. However, it is important to bear in mind that there are lots of sources of advice available, not least from the many websites set up to inform you and to illustrate practice. Above all, remember that much knowledge and experience in this area is acquired gradually and with the guidance of more experienced colleagues. Your professional knowledge of the curriculum and your confidence in assessment practices should grow considerably if you make full use of the sources of help available.

Summary

- The National Curriculum is relatively recent.
- It differs from previously in that parts of it became statutory.
- Recent reforms are meant to make the National Curriculum more flexible.
- 14–19 diplomas are heralded as an alternative to traditional examinations.
- Change is the norm – the curriculum and examination requirements are in constant flux.

Key reading

DfES (2004) *14–19 Curriculum and Qualifications Reform: Final Report of the Working Group on 14–19 reform* (The Tomlinson Report)
QCA (2007) *Curriculum Guidance for the Foundation Stage*

Also visit:
QCA National Curriculum in Action – exemplification of pupils' work in different subjects and at different levels of the National Curriculum at: www.ncaction.org.uk
SureStart – a government programme bringing together early education, childcare, health and family support for the benefit of young children at: www.surestart.gov.uk

References and bibliography

1988 Education Reform Act
2000 Learning and Skills Act
Assessment and Qualifications Alliance (AQA): http://www.aqa.org.uk
City and Guilds: http://www.cityandguilds.com
Edexcel: http://www·edexcel.org.uk
Oxford Cambridge and RSA examinations (OCR): http://www.ocr.org.uk
WJEC/CBAC (previously known as the Welsh Joint Education Committee): http://www.wjec.co.uk
Department for Children, Schools and Families: http://www.standards.dfes.gov.uk/locate
National Assessment Agency, responsible for National Curriculum assessment and testing at key stages 1, 2 and 3: www.naa.org.uk

National Curriculum online: www.nc.uk.net

Qualifications and Curriculum Authority www.qca.org.uk

Qualifications, Curriculum and Assessment Authority for Wales www.accac.org.uk

Teachernet, a government site for teachers and schools-related profession www.teachernet.gov.uk

Websites

Assessment and Qualifications Alliance (AQA): www.aqa.org.uk

City and Guilds: www.cityandguilds.com

Edexcel: www.edexcel.org.uk

Oxford, Cambridge and RSA examinations (OCR): www.ocr.org.uk

WJEC/CBAC (previously known as the Welsh Joint Education Committee): www.wjec.co.uk

Department for Children, Schools and Families: www.standards.dfes.gov.uk/locate

National Assessment Agency, responsible for National Curriculum assessment and testing at Key Stages 1, 2 and 3: www.naa.org.uk

National Curriculum online: www.nc.uk.net

Qualifications and Curriculum Authority: www.qca.org.uk

Qualifications, Curriculum and Assessment Authority for Wales: www.accac.org.uk

Teachernet, a government site for teachers and schools-related professionals: www.teachernet.gov.uk.

CHAPTER 15

EVERY CHILD MATTERS: CHANGE FOR CHILDREN

Jonathan Glazzard

Standard addressed

 Know and understand the relevant statutory and non-statutory curricula and frameworks, including those provided through the National Strategies, for their subjects/curriculum areas, and other relevant initiatives applicable to the age and ability range for which they are trained.

Introduction

Teaching is an ever-changing profession, continually facing and adapting to new government policies, initiatives and agendas. Every Child Matters is the latest major agenda with far-reaching implications for teachers and other members of the children's workforce. As a trainee teacher you will have the opportunity to observe how different schools are responding to this agenda. Every Child Matters focuses on schools being committed to enabling all children to succeed and breaking down barriers to participation and achievement. Inclusive education is therefore central to this aspect of government policy. Multi-agency collaboration and pupil and parent partnership are critical to improving educational outcomes for all learners. All members of the profession need to be aware of the implications of this new policy and be committed to the values and principles on which it is based, so that all learners have the maximum opportunity to achieve good educational outcomes.

Every Child Matters identifies five outcomes for children and young people:

- Being healthy
- Staying safe
- Enjoying and achieving
- Making a positive contribution
- Economic well-being.

All services in the children's workforce, including education services, need to be committed to helping children to achieve these outcomes. As a trainee teacher you will be expected to embed these outcomes into your practice and Ofsted inspections of schools now focus on the extent to which schools address these outcomes. Try to make your lessons creative and exciting so that your pupils enjoy learning. Give your pupils rich learning experiences so that learning experiences become deeply embedded. During school experience try to give your pupils specific targets for improvement to help them move forward in their learning. Think about creating opportunities for enabling pupils to make a contribution. Think about how you can consult pupils about aspects of classroom practice and learning.

Every Child Matters: rationale for policy development

The early death of Victoria Climbié in 2000 was the catalyst for change. Victoria was the victim of cruelty by those close to her. Lord Laming's inquiry into the case identified that fragmentation of the agencies involved with this case had played a part in allowing the child to be abused: information was not shared between agencies resulting in a delay in providing support, assessments were duplicated and there was no coordination of services. The Green Paper (2003) *Every Child Matters* was the government's response to the Laming Report. The aim of the agenda was to reduce the risk of incidents like this being repeated through more effectively coordinated inter-disciplinary methods of working and the introduction of efficient information-sharing systems. In addition the Green Paper identified the need to maximise opportunities for all children and young people.

Children Act 2004

The Children Act provides the legislative spine for the reforms. This legislation aims to improve multi-agency collaboration between different agencies and to improve outcomes for children, young people and their parents. The legislation emphasises the importance of early intervention to protect children and places statutory duties on all agencies to make arrangements to safeguard and promote children's welfare.

Promoting children's participation: giving children a voice

According to the United Nations Convention on the Rights of the Child children and young people have a right to express an opinion and to have their opinion taken into account (Article 12). The Ofsted framework for school inspections requires inspectors to make judgements on the extent to which schools involve pupils in the development of policies and practices and the extent to which schools seek, value and act upon children's views. Therefore schools have a duty to ensure that pupils' views are sought, heard, valued and acted upon. In healthy schools regular consultation with pupils is valued and pupils are agents of change.

The notion of pupil participation can affect the balance of power in schools and staff may feel threatened if pupils are given increased levels of power. Shier (2001) offers a model of participation which allows schools to develop pupil participation progressively through giving pupils increasing levels of empowerment and responsibility. In this model schools can initially develop participation by listening to children, encouraging them to express their views and taking them into account. Schools can then start to involve children in decision-making processes, eventually allowing pupils to share power and responsibility for decision-making. All children have a right to be heard and the real challenge for some schools will be the issue of how to provide opportunities for children with language impairments to have their voice heard.

Moves to increasing pupil participation will challenge the current value systems in some schools. Mutual respect between pupils, their peers and their teachers is central to this process. Pupil participation helps to foster awareness that children have rights as citizens to express their views.

Safeguarding children

Schools have a legal duty to safeguard and promote the welfare of children and young people. The DfES (2006) have made the statutory requirements clear in *Safeguarding children and safer recruitment in education*. All schools are required to have a child protection policy and to nominate a designated person from the leadership team responsible for child protection issues. Schools must operate safe recruitment practices and staff must receive refresher training once every three years. Schools must review policies and procedures annually. Each local authority must appoint a senior officer responsible for safeguarding children. It is vital that all staff working with children in schools are aware of the policies and procedures for safeguarding children. It is the responsibility of the leadership team to ensure this.

'Safeguarding' is not limited to child protection. Schools have a statutory responsibility to safeguard the health and safety of all children. Schools therefore need to ensure that they are addressing issues such as bullying and implementing policies and practices which help to safeguard pupils' health and safety. As a trainee teacher it is essential that you have read the child protection policy. It is also important that you are familiar with policies on physical contact and policies on speaking to pupils privately. As a teacher you will be expected to report any concerns you may have about children in your charge to the designated child protection officer.

Multi-agency working: integrated front-line delivery

Multi-agency working practices are central to the Every Child Matters agenda. Professionals from health, education and social services must work together effectively to improve outcomes for children and young people. Effective communication is of vital importance. Clearly there is a need for professionals to understand the roles and responsibilities of representatives from other agencies. The Common Assessment Framework and the Information Sharing (IS) Index facilitate effective communication between different agencies. The lead professional also plays a key role in information sharing between different agencies. As a teacher you will be expected to work with professionals from across a range of services. You will be expected to understand the roles and responsibilities of other professionals involved with children in your class and you will need to listen carefully and take account of any recommendations they make. Ultimately this will help to improve provision for children and raise levels of attainment.

GROUP EXERCISE

Discuss with your colleagues the challenges and issues associated with effective multi-agency working. Your task is to learn to share information with a different group of students in your university or college. For example, you might choose to present information to students in health, social work or youth work. You could also present to a different group of students working within the education sector, such as teaching assistants on Foundation Degree courses or other students on non-QTS education-related courses. Working as a group you will give a presentation on the implications of Every Child Matters for teachers, plus an overview of your own role. The aim is to give the students a clear understanding of your own role within education and an awareness of how you might address Every Child Matters. To follow this up, the group you have presented to will then present back to you.

The role of the lead professional

The lead professional acts as the single point of contact for the child and the family. In addition to this s/he will coordinate the service provision for the child in cases where there is multi-agency involvement. The role may be carried out by professionals in health, social services or education. Lead professionals coordinate multi-professional meetings and monitor the child's progress. The role will be carried out by a nominated professional who is most relevant to the child's needs.

The Common Assessment Framework

The Common Assessment Framework (CAF) provides a standardised assessment of a child's additional needs. The CAF provides a holistic assessment of a child's needs using non-technical vocabulary. Once a CAF has been completed by one agency, it can be accessed other agencies. This reduces the need for multiple assessments from different agencies and facilitates earlier identification of additional needs. The CAF is completed if a child or young person is in danger of failing to achieve the Every Child Matters outcomes.

A Common Assessment might be initiated if a child is making slower progress than expected or is being abused (including self-abuse). However, an assessment might be initiated for other reasons. Children who live in homes where they are exposed to alcohol abuse, drug abuse or domestic violence may be at risk of abuse or neglect. Children who are bullied or present aggressive behaviours may also need an assessment. Cheminais (2006: 27) states that 'Information from the Common Assessment assists in informing the provision of relevant services to meet the child's needs'. The assessment can be carried out at any time from birth to the age of 19 but parents/carers and the child (if appropriate) must be consulted prior to an assessment being undertaken. If children are at risk of harm or neglect then parents' refusal to cooperate will have no bearing on the assessment process.

Information Sharing Index

This is an electronic tool which holds information on all children. Authorised practitioners who have concerns about a child are able to access the electronic database to determine whether a Common Assessment has been made. The database enables frontline practitioners to indicate that there is information to share, that a Common Assessment has taken place and to detail appropriate action taken. The database enables information to be shared quickly among different agencies.

Common Core of Skills and Knowledge

The Common Core of Skills and Knowledge for the children's workforce identifies the basic skills and knowledge needed by all people who work with children, young people and their families. Staff must be able to:

- communicate effectively with children, young people and their families;
- have knowledge of child and young person development;
- safeguard and promote the welfare of the child;
- support transitions;
- work effectively with professionals from a range of different agencies;
- share information across different agencies.

Everyone working with children and young people needs to demonstrate competence in these six areas and qualifications frameworks will increasingly reflect the Common Core of Skills and Knowledge.

Removing barriers to achievement

The government's strategy for special educational needs is documented in *Removing barriers to achievement* (DfES 2004). This strategy focuses on four key areas:

- **Early intervention**. This ensures that children with learning difficulties receive the help and support they need to help them learn.
- **Removing barriers to learning**. Schools must operate inclusive policies and practices and find ways of ensuring that all children participate and achieve. Schools therefore need to work closely with a range of professionals from different agencies to find ways of enabling all children to access a broad and balanced curriculum.
- **Raising expectations and achievement**. Schools are required to track closely pupils' progress and achievement. Formative assessment is the key to ensuring progression. All teachers must have high expectations of all learners and use assessment to inform subsequent planning. This will ensure that learning activities are pitched at the correct level to secure progress.
- **Delivering improvements in partnership**. Schools of the future will offer integrated provision. Multi-agency support will be available on a single site. Many schools are already operating in this way. This will help to ensure that children receive the support they need quickly.

(Cheminais 2006)

Removing barriers to achievement focuses on personalised learning and takes account of recent disability legislation. The Special Educational Needs and Disability Act 2001 (SENDA) requires schools to make *reasonable adjustments* to ensure that disabled pupils are not disadvantaged. The Disability and Discrimination Act 2005 requires schools to improve educational outcomes for disabled children and promote equality of opportunity. In addition schools have a duty to have regard to the three principles of inclusion identified in the National Curriculum: setting suitable learning challenges; responding to pupils' diverse learning needs and overcoming potential barriers to learning and assessment. As a trainee teacher it is important that you differentiate your teaching to take the needs of your pupils into account. Give pupils small, achievable targets so that progress can be evidenced. Personalised learning is the key to unlocking potential and raising attainment, thus breaking cycles of poverty and disadvantage.

A thought

Every Child Matters emphasises the need for effective multi-agency working practices. Potentially this could be interpreted as only being of relevance when different agencies are involved in supporting a child. However, with a little thought it is possible to involve professionals from different services in educating children about the five outcomes. For example, the police force could be involved in educating children about road safety or members of staff from health care could teach children about issues such as sexual health. Think carefully about how you are going to integrate these outcomes into your practice on your next placement and when you qualify as a teacher.

INDIVIDUAL REFLECTION

Think about what the barriers might be in terms of inclusion and how these might be overcome. Now think about how you are going to address Every Child Matters in your placement. Obviously you will not be able to address all aspects of the agenda but you might want to focus on one part of it. For example, how might you develop pupil participation in terms of giving children a voice and allowing them to contribute to the development of policies and practices?

Try to identify the children who are not participating and achieving as well as they could. Then reflect on your own practice. Sometimes small changes to classroom practice can help to improve levels of participation and achievement. It is possible, for example, to motivate children with behavioural difficulties by providing them with stimulating, active learning experiences which relate to their interests. Rather than blaming the child for failure, think about how your practice may be a contributory factor.

Theory

According to Hirsch (2007: 3):

> Socio-economic circumstances in childhood which result in low qualifications in adulthood help transmit poverty across generations.

Therefore children who are born into poverty are more likely to be low achievers at school. Hirsch summarises research findings from a range of studies (Cassen and Kingdon 2007; Horgan 2007; Sutton *et al.* 2007; Frankham *et al.* 2007; Wikeley *et al.* 2007; Thomson and Russell 2007) which have indicated a correlation between poverty and low educational achievement. Research has indicated that uptake of free school meals is a strong predictor of low achievement and that boys are more at risk of poor educational outcomes than girls (Cassen and Kingdon 2007). This research highlights the importance of providing opportunities for parents and carers to gain the necessary knowledge and skills needed for employment. Opportunities for adult education are therefore critical. Parents and carers who re-engage with the education process act as powerful role models for disaffected children.

Research from the Effective Provision of Pre-school Education (EPPE) Project has indicated that quality home learning environments, which supplement learning in school, promote intellectual and social development in children (Sylva *et al.* 2003). Therefore it is important that parents and carers are able to support their children's learning outside of school. The EPPE research also found that staff with higher qualifications in early years settings had more of an impact on children's cognitive development than staff with lower qualifications. This highlights the need for a highly qualified and knowledgeable children's workforce. In addition to these findings, this project also highlighted that children from disadvantaged families benefited significantly from high-quality pre-school experiences. Thus high-quality early years provision is essential for improving educational outcomes for children. Significant capital investment in terms of training, resources and provision is paramount if these outcomes are to be achieved.

Traditional methods of educating children with special educational needs have focused on the medical model of disability (Oliver 1993). This model locates the source of the disablement within the body and Oliver therefore views this as a tragic model. The child is blamed for the problem. In the medical model, *impairment* within the body is the cause of *disability* and this places limits on expectations. In contrast, the social model of disability conceptualises disability as a social construct. This model examines the extent to which environments, curricula, pedagogies and assessment systems disable children. In this model the source of the disability is deemed to be external to the child. Individual limitations are not held responsible for creating disability but rather society's failure to provide appropriate services for people with impairments (Oliver 1996). This model does not make an automatic link between impairment and disability. Therefore it is possible that schools can be proactive in breaking down barriers to pupils' participation and achievement by making changes to policies and practices.

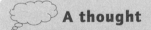 **A thought**

Your own values are extremely important as a trainee teacher and you will need to reflect on these in order to implement Every Child Matters. Do you demonstrate mutual respect to your friends, your family and the professionals you work with in school? Do you believe that everyone has a key role to play and do you value the contribution other people make? Do you respect difference and diversity? How inclusive is your classroom and how do you know?

Application to teaching

Early Years

Invite parents/carers of children you teach into school to take part in a workshop about helping their child to read. Introduce them to synthetic phonics and show them examples of good practice in the teaching of phonics. Make sure you talk about blending and segmentation. This could be though DVD material.

(Continued)

(Continued)

Then ask them to observe you working with a group of children and leading a phonics activity. Use multi-sensory methods of teaching to really embed the learning. Give the parents suggestions for ways of supporting their child's reading at home. Talk about the importance of having books in the home and reading with children. Give them suggestions for activities they could try with their children.

Key Stages 2 and 3

Ask the pupils for suggestions on ways in which the school playground could be developed. Set up a development group made up of pupils, staff and parent/carers. Ask the development group to consult the rest of the school for their ideas. The development group will then appeal to businesses in the local community to provide funding, equipment and labour necessary for the change to take place. The pupils will have made a positive contribution to the school.

In any phase

Think about the changes you can make to your practice to engage a disengaged learner. Small changes can increase motivation, participation and achievement. This is a social model stance. Rather than blaming the child for the problem you need to think about how your practice may in fact be contributing to it.

Summary

- *Every Child Matters: change for children* is a bold political agenda designed to raise educational outcomes for children, young people and their parents.
- It emphasises the importance of agencies working cooperatively.
- Schools have a duty to respond to the agenda by developing strong professional relationships with a range of partners from different services and with parents and carers.
- Schools also need to find ways of consulting with pupils.
- Effective partnerships are genuine partnerships where stakeholders have an influence on school improvement planning.

Key reading

Cheminais, R. (2006) *Every Child Matters: a practical guide for teachers*. London: David Fulton

Hirsch, D. (2007) *Experiences of poverty and educational disadvantage*. Joseph Rowntree Foundation. Online at: www.jrf.org.uk

There is a wealth of useful information on the *Every Child Matters* website. Go to www. everychildmatters.gov.uk to find key documents related to the policy.

References and bibliography

Cassen, R. and Kingon, G. (2007) 'Tackling low educational achievement'. Cited in Hirsch, D. (2007) *Experiences of poverty and educational disadvantage*. York: Joseph Rowntree Foundation. Available online at: www.jrf. org.uk

Cheminais, R. (2006) *Every Child Matters: a practical guide for teachers*. London: David Fulton

Department for Education and Employment (1999) *The National Curriculum: handbook for primary teachers in England*. London: DfEE/QCA

Department for Education and Skills (2004) *Removing barriers to achievement: the government's strategy for SEN*. London: DfES

Department for Education and Skills (2006) *Safeguarding children and safer recruitment in education*. Nottingham: DfES Publications

Frankham, J., Edwards-Kerr, D., Humphrey, N. and Roberts, L. (2007) 'School exclusions: learning partnerships outside mainstream education'. Cited in Hirsch, D. (2007) *Experiences of poverty and educational disadvantage*. York: Joseph Rowntree Foundation. Available online at: www.jrf.org.uk

Hirsch, D. (2007) *Experiences of poverty and educational disadvantage*. York: Joseph Rowntree Foundation. Available online at: www.jrf.org.uk

Horgan, G. (2007) 'The impact of poverty on young children's experience of school'. Cited in Hirsch, D. (2007) *Experiences of poverty and educational disadvantage*. York: Joseph Rowntree Foundation. Available online at: www. jrf.org.uk

Oliver, M. (1993) 'Redefining disability'. In Swain, J., Finkelstein, V., French, S. and Oliver, M. (eds), *Disabling barriers – enabling environments*. London: Open University/ Sage, pp. 60–67

Oliver, M. (1996) *Understanding disability: from theory to practice*. London: Macmillan

Shier, H. (2001) 'Pathways to participation: openings, opportunities and obligations'. *Children and Society*, 15 (2), 107–117

Sutton, L., Smith, N., Dearden, C. and Middleton, S. (2007) 'A child's-eye view of social difference'. Cited in Hirsch, D. (2007) *Experiences of poverty and educational disadvantage*. York: Joseph Rowntree Foundation. Available online at: www.jrf.org.uk

Sylva, K., Melhuish, E., Sammons, P., Siraj-Blachford, I., Taggart, B. and Elliot, K. (2003) *The Effective Provision of Pre-School Educaiton (EPPE) Project: findings from the pre-school period*. Institute of Education, University of London and University of Oxford

Thomson, P. and Russell, L. (2007) 'Mapping the alternatives to permanent exclusion'. Cited in Hirsch, D. (2007) *Experiences of poverty and educational disadvantage*. York: Joseph Rowntree Foundation. Available online at: www.jrf.org.uk

Wikeley, F., Bullock, K., Muschamp, Y. and Ridge, T. (2007) 'Educational relationships outside school: why access is important'. Cited in Hirsch, D. (2007) *Experiences of poverty and educational disadvantage*. York: Joseph Rowntree Foundation. Available online at: www. jrf.org.uk.

CHAPTER 16

CROSS-CURRICULAR ISSUES (INCLUDING CITIZENSHIP, DIVERSITY AND CROSS-CURRICULUM DIMENSIONS)

Neil Denby

Standards addressed

 Q15 Know and understand the relevant statutory and non-statutory curricula, frameworks, including those provided through the National Strategies, for their subjects/curriculum areas, and other relevant initiatives applicable to the age and ability range for which they are trained.

Q16 Have passed the professional skills tests in numeracy, literacy and information and communication technology (ICT).

Introduction

This short chapter is designed to put in one place the various key issues that are considered to be cross-curricular but that do not find a natural place elsewhere. Major cross-curricular skills such as literacy, numeracy and the use of ICT are either discussed in the chapters on teaching and learning or in separate chapters where it is felt that a particular focus is necessary. The new National Curriculum promotes 'cross-curriculum dimensions' as a useful vehicle for schools to plan a more integrated curriculum. These are not statutory, but building them into the curriculum will help to provide a richness and to ensure that schools meet obligations such as those for Personal, Social and Health Education (PSHE), Citizenship and community cohesion.

Cross-curriculum dimensions

These non-statutory dimensions should be embedded in your teaching wherever possible. You should not be attempting to teach them in isolation, as often they are inextricably bound up with each other. To understand the global dimension and sustainable development, for example, requires a clear understanding of identity and cultural diversity. Schools have found several ways to include these dimensions, in much the same way as Citizenship was introduced in different ways. Some examples are teaching dimensions as themes so that the themes are brought out in subjects, 'off timetable' teaching, i.e. putting the curriculum to one side for a day or week to focus on groups of dimensions, and using external speakers, community representatives or visits. Some schools have decided to integrate key areas of the curriculum so that both subject and dimension are given equal opportunities. Wombwell High School in Barnsley, South Yorkshire, is a long-standing partner of the University of Huddersfield School of Education. It is planning to integrate up to 50 per cent of the curriculum in a cross-curricular way. Integrated Humanities currently (2007) covers history, geography, literacy and thinking skills and is to have RE, PSHE, personal finance education, citizenship, drama and ICT added to it. You can see that any of these strategies presupposes teachers working across departments, integrating knowledge and sharing planning. The dimensions (QCA 2007) are as follows:

- **Identity and cultural diversity**. This promotes understanding of the diverse society of both the UK and the world. It includes ideas regarding tolerance, the origins of diversity and ethnicity and how and why, historically, different cultures, values and beliefs have developed. It encourages young people to think about who they are, where they have come from, and their contextual place in the society in which they live.

- **Healthy lifestyles**. This includes eating healthily, taking exercise and enjoying play. Pupils need to meet and be comfortable with a range of professionals who can offer advice and be educated to make informed and sensible choices regarding their lifestyles.
- **Community participation**. This is already built into the Citizenship curriculum, but is reiterated here as understanding the community in which they live and developing a positive role within it, acting as responsible citizens.
- **Enterprise education**. This encourages children and young people to 'be enterprising', i.e. to take risks, tackle problems and to innovate.
- **Global dimension and sustainable development**. Young people should be aware of global issues and their own responsibilities within this context. They should know what is meant by sustainability and aim to develop sustainable and environmentally friendly lifestyles as responsible and aware citizens.
- **Technology and the media**. Young people should be able to treat the media in a critical way. They should have the skills to take the advantages of new technology, but the awareness not to fall into any of the dangers.
- **Creativity and critical thinking.** Pupils should learn to use their imagination to develop ideas and to seek creative solutions to problems and issues. They should have the capacity to learn from others and to hold and support an opinion on their own or others' work or viewpoints.

A thought

Remember that none of these dimensions is a subject in its own right. Consider them more as part of the scaffolding or framework of all subjects.

GROUP EXERCISE

In your group, consider and share ways in which you could introduce a concept or idea in your subject that could be used in another subject. Suggest which other subject and how it could be taught. Some examples of cross-curricular links provided by the QCA include:

- Mathematics concepts are taught in art, geography, history, biology, business and science.
- Literacy is an integral part of all written and spoken learning.
- In art, learners need to understand the history of art.
- In history, learners need to have an understanding of the borders between different countries or the consequence of a geographical structure.
- In literature, history is integral.

PSHE

At some point in your teaching career, you are likely to be asked to teach some part of the PSHE curriculum. This is usually because, although there is an expert PSHE teacher or team of teachers who organise the PSHE curriculum, resources are stretched for its delivery. You therefore need to be familiar with the National Curriculum (NC) guidance on this subject relevant to your chosen age range. Personal, Social and Health Education is, in the existing National Curriculum (www.nc.uk.net), an entitlement governed by non-statutory guidance. In the new National Curriculum (www.qca.org.uk) it has become Personal, Social, Health and Economic Education. (PSHEE). It is taught, in a variety of different ways, alongside the subjects of the National Curriculum. It has, in common with the subjects of the NC, programmes of study for each of the key stages.

> Schools can therefore choose how they provide PSHE based on the national curriculum framework and guidance. A combination of different forms of provision is recommended. (QCA 2000)

Each key stage is marked by expectations that pupils will gain from specific understanding, experiences and interactions with others. There are no Attainment Targets but End of Key Stage statements have been set so that teachers can measure progress. Briefly, these are as follows:

- **End of Key Stage 1**. Children can identify some feelings and be able to manage them in themselves and others. They can make simple choices about some parts of their life and know, for example, how to keep clean, eat well and the importance of exercise and rest. They can tell right from wrong, especially in cases that could be specific to them such as bullying.
- **End of Key Stage 2**. Children have developed a sense of their own worth and that of others. They can begin to look to the future and the development of appropriate skills to manage change or for jobs. Healthy lifestyle understanding includes that related to emotional issues. Pupils have some understanding of drugs and the harm that they can do. They understand how actions have consequences and can recognise and challenge negative behaviour.

- **End of Key Stage 3**. Young people have developed the capacity to evaluate their own achievements. They can plan targets for the future and manage money competently. They know how to stay physically and mentally healthy and have the capacity to counter negative pressure. They recognise difference and diversity and develop the skill to challenge prejudice.
- **End of Key Stage 4**. Young people are self-aware, can set goals for the future and can respond positively to both praise and criticism. They are competent to manage their personal finances. In terms of health, they can judge the relative merits of different lifestyle choices, can assess risks and benefits and know where to go for professional advice on such issues. They understand and can discuss relationships. They are aware of diversity and challenge offensive behaviour in this context.

In secondary education (11–19) the new NC promotes a personal development (PD) curriculum. This lays down the subject matter that schools must teach, such as drug, sex and relationship education.

Citizenship

Citizenship became a compulsory subject in the secondary curriculum in 2002, following the recommendations of the Crick Report (Crick 1998). It is part of the PSHE curriculum at Key Stages 1 and 2 and becomes a NC subject in its own right at Key Stages 3 and 4. There are non-statutory guidelines for Key Stages 1 and 2 (www.nc.uk.net) and Programmes of Study for Key Stages 3 and 4. Crick fought for the content of the Citizenship orders to be minimal, and to allow schools to build their own frameworks for teaching it. The Citizenship NC document is the shortest of all the NC subjects, and the requirements for Citizenship at KS3 or KS4 fit onto a single page. The three central strands of Citizenship education are:

- **Social and moral responsibility**. Pupils learn, from the beginning, self-confidence and socially and morally responsible behaviour, both in and beyond the classroom, towards those in authority and each other.
- **Community involvement**. Pupils learn how to become helpfully involved in the life and concerns of their neighbourhood and communities, including learning through community involvement and service.
- **Political literacy**. Pupils learn about the institutions, issues, problems and practices of our democracy and how citizens can make themselves effective in public life, locally, regionally and nationally, through skills as well as knowledge.

(www.nc.net)

For each of these strands, a school could decide on its own method of delivery. In general, these are either as a discrete subject, through cross-curricular audit plus enhancement or by whole-school (or year group) events or activities – a citizenship 'week', for example. The reality was that, while some schools were very good at teaching citizenship, many were less than adequate. Of the three strands, the easiest to teach – involving institutions, processes and procedures – is political literacy. Community involvement is more difficult as it involves taking children and young people out of school confines and into the community (or organising visitors and speakers to come in). Of greatest difficulty is the teaching of social and moral responsibility. By 2005, Ofsted's initial inspections of Citizenship led them to conclude:

> Increasingly, schools are taking National Curriculum citizenship seriously and establishing comprehensive programmes. As yet, however, pupils' achievement and the quality of teaching compare unfavourably with established subjects and there is little that is graded very good. In one in four schools, provision is unsatisfactory. (HMI 2005)

In certain subject areas, you will find that you have a natural affinity to Citizenship. It is often taught by historians, or as part of the RE department's brief. Much of the NC content is native to Business and Economics Education. In whatever subject you teach, however, you will be expected to promote citizenship and its associated skills. Increasingly, schools are seeing it as an important subject in its own right and allocating resources appropriately. In the new NC, it is expanded to include a fourth strand as a result of the Ajegbo Report. This is 'Identity and Diversity: Living Together in the UK' and is part of the drive to promote community cohesion.

Keith Ajegbo's report (Ajegbo 2007), commissioned after the London terrorist attacks, has led to the establishment of a duty on all schools to promote community cohesion. The review was of how Citizenship was taught, and how it could contribute to a better understanding within and between communities. Good citizenship education – when it actually delivers the social and moral elements – could combat intolerance, bigotry and religious extremism.

A thought

Do you know which concepts that might be applicable to your subject or age range are taught in other subjects or ranges? You should make a point of observing lessons in other subjects, or in the age range before or after yours, with this question as a particular focus of the observation.

Key skills

The key skills are a set of six specifications of which, if you are training for secondary, you need to be aware so that you can plan for pupils to develop the appropriate skills. They are designed to help pupils succeed in education, work and further study. The central key skills are communication, application of number and ICT. Of course, you have to pass QTS Tests to demonstrate that you are competent in each of these areas (Standard Q16). What are commonly known as the 'wider' key skills are working with others, improving own learning and performance and problem-solving. They are available at Levels 1 to 4 of the National Qualifications Framework.

The future?

The RSA (Royal Society of Arts) Examinations Board has been a long-time champion and promoter of key skills. One of its innovations is the Opening Minds curriculum which has been developed as a way of making the curriculum more flexible and more responsive to the needs of individual learners. According to the RSA:

> The National Curriculum is information-driven and struggles to cope with the competing demands of subjects and the rapidly increasing volume of information. Meanwhile, it is neglecting the broad range of skills for life including skills for learning, the ability to manage people and situations well, and good citizenship.
>
> Opening Minds argues that these life-skills need to be taught directly and specifically. It starts from a competence framework that aims to meet the individual's needs in the personal, social and employment worlds. (RSA 2007)

This innovation has been the subject of a three-year pilot study, which has already shown some significant improvements:

> ... the schools involved have experienced some quite stunning improvements in both student and teacher motivation and solid gains in student performance. The benefits seen included:

- less low-level disruption in the classroom
- students are more mature and more motivated, ready to learn
- students and teachers enjoy the Opening Minds lessons. (RSA 2007)

Application to teaching

Opening Minds describes five competence categories. Each category contains a number of individual strands, expressed in terms of student progress and outcomes. They include:

(Continued)

(Continued)

» **Competences for Learning** – taking account of their own learning style and managing learning (see Chapter 9 and Chapter 12), being creative, being able to handle and use ICT.

» **Competences for Citizenship** – developing an understanding of ethics and values and their own place and role in society along with an understanding and respect for cultural diversity. Included in this competency are also personal financial management and the social implications of technology.

» **Competences for Relating to People** – understanding how to relate to other people in varying contexts, how to operate in teams, how to develop other people, how to communicate effectively and how to manage relationships, stress and conflict.

» **Competences for Managing Situations** – such as managing their own time, managing change, managing risk and uncertainty and being entrepreneurial and initiative-taking.

» **Competences for Managing Information** – developing techniques for accessing, evaluating, differentiating, analysing and synthesising information and developing reflection and critical judgement.

Consider these five areas and use them in planning a short series of lessons. How do they change the style or direction of your teaching? Do they improve learning?

Summary

■ There are numerous cross-curricular skills and aptitudes that pervade the curriculum.

■ These include literacy, numeracy and ICT skills

■ The new NC introduces non-statutory cross-curriculum dimensions

■ Other important elements include PSHE (PSHEE) and Citizenship.

■ All schools have a duty to promote community cohesion.

Key reading

National curriculum documents are available for the current NC at: www.nc.uk.net, and for the new NC at: curriculum.qca.org.uk and www.qca.org.uk/curriculum. Follow links to cross-curriculum dimensions, citizenship, PSHE etc.

The Ajegbo Report (2007) can be downloaded at: http://publications.teachernet.gov.uk/eOrdering Download/ DfES_Diversity_&_Citizenship.pdf

References and bibliography

Crick, B. (1998) *Education for citizenship and the teaching of democracy in schools.* London: QCA

DfES (2007) *Diversity and Citizenship curriculum review.* Available online at: www.teacher.gov. uk

HMI (2005) *Citizenship in secondary schools: evidence from Ofsted inspections (2003/04)*, HMI 2335. Available online at: www.dfes.gov.uk/keyskills/

QCA (2007) – see curriculum.qca.org.uk/cross-curriculum-dimensions/index.aspx

RSA (2007) – see www.rsa.org.uk/newcurriculum/ (accessed November 2007).

CHAPTER 17

USING STATISTICAL DATA TO EVALUATE AND IMPROVE THE EFFECTIVENESS OF TEACHING

Ian Quigley

Standard addressed

Q13   Know how to use local and national statistical information to evaluate the effectiveness of their teaching, to monitor the progress of those they teach and to raise levels of attainment.

Introduction

In the past, when schools largely followed their own curricula, the comparison of one school with another, or of one performance with another, was at best ad hoc and at worst biased and ill-informed. Now that clear statistics do exist, you are expected to know how schools make use of them and how you can use them to improve your own effectiveness.

The Education Reform Act of 1988 introduced a National Curriculum to the state schools of England, Wales and Northern Ireland. For the first time, the content of the curriculum in primary and secondary schools would be decided by central government and specified in detail. A central feature of the Act was the introduction of Standard Attainment Tests in the core subjects of English, Mathematics and Science. These SATs – as they became known – would be attempted by the vast majority of pupils at the ages of 7, 11 and 14.

Running concurrently with reform of the curriculum came rationalisation of the public examination system. The dozens of examination boards that existed in the early 1980s were eventually reduced to just three major boards by 1997 (AQA, OCR and Edexcel). These institutions were overseen by the Qualifications and Curriculum Authority (QCA) an 'executive non-departmental public body', whose core function was to ensure a consistency of standards between the qualifications offered.

With a common curriculum, standardised assessments at selected key stages and comparability between public examinations (especially GCSEs) the performance of individual schools could now be compared. The first *School and College Performance Tables for Secondary Schools* were published in 1994, with primary 'league tables' following two years later. They have been a source of information (and controversy) ever since.

A thought

Acronyms abound in the education sector. These apply to the discussion of statistical information contained in this chapter.

ALIS = Advanced level information system
CATs = cognitive ability tests

(Continued)

(Continued)

CEM	=	Centre for Education Management
CVA	=	contextual value added
DCFS	=	Department for Children, Families and Schools
FFT	=	Fischer Family Trust
MidYIS	=	Middle Years Information Management System
MTG	=	minimum target grade
NFER	=	National Foundation for Educational Research
SATs	=	Standard Attainment Tests
YELLIS	=	Year Eleven Information System

How the DCFS assesses the performance of a school – the measurement and comparison of attainment

Every year the performance of a school is measured by an analysis of its SAT scores and, in the case of secondary schools, its results at GCSE. Where appropriate, post-16 achievements are also scrutinised. The resulting document, currently known as 'RAISEonline', forms the basis of all Ofsted inspections. There is, therefore, an expectation that the governors and managers of a school will be able to interpret the data it contains and act on this information by formulating plans to improve the achievements of the school.

The first 'league tables' contained quite basic information regarding the performance of a school's students at Key Stage 2 in the case of primary schools, and at Key Stage 3 and public examination results for the secondary sector. Examples of these 'early' tables are shown in Tables 17.1(a) and 17.1(b).

Table 17.1(a)   Early examples of school performance tables – primary schools

	Primary School A	Primary School B
Percentage of students achieving level 4 plus in English	47%	89%
Percentage of students achieving level 4 plus in Mathematics	39%	87%
Percentage of students achieving level 4 plus in Science	49%	86%
Number of SEN students	16	4
Number of authorised absences	9.7%	4.9%
Number of unauthorised absences	3.5%	0.9%

Table 17.1(b) Early examples of school performance tables – secondary schools

	Secondary School C	Secondary School D
Percentage of students achieving 5 plus A* to C grades at GCSE	23%	82%
Percentage of students achieving 5 plus A* to G grades at GCSE	46%	98%
Percentage of students achieving 1 plus A* to G grades at GCSE	90%	99%
Percentage of students achieving level 5 plus in English	39%	87%
Percentage of students achieving level 5 plus in Mathematics	40%	86%
Percentage of students achieving level 5 plus in Science	36%	85%
Number of SEN students	24	2
Number of authorised absences	8.6%	5.1%
Number of unauthorised absences	2.3%	1.2%

A thought

Study the data shown in Tables 17.1(a) and (b). What does this information tell you about these schools? Is it possible to judge which is the most successful primary and secondary school? What factors may influence the results these schools achieve? As a parent, which schools would you choose?

Problems

Even a quick glance at these tables will alert you to the problems of these initial attempts to compare the performance of different schools. Raw data such as this measures only the output of an institution. It does not consider the ability of its intake or the social and economic circumstances of its students.

Analysis based only on results cannot assess the 'value' that a school adds. Pupils who attend a secondary school whose intake comprises a significant number of low-achieving children may in fact make greater progress than those in a neighbouring school who select the most able students in the district. Similarly, though many may assume that the children entering the reception classes of primary schools are 'blank canvases', those within the profession recognise that the early experiences of a child impact on their primary school years. Such experiences are influenced by home circumstances and the education of their parents (Douglas 1964).

Today's performance tables try to take account of differences in prior attainment and social demography. With over 15 years of statistical data to draw on, National Progression Lines have been created to predict the attainment of students as they pass

Table 17.2 Conversion of NC levels and GCSE grades into numerical equivalents

National Curriculum level	Points equivalent	GCSE grades	Points equivalent
8	51	A*	58
7	45	A	52
6	39	B	46
5	33	C	40
4	27	D	34
3	21	E	26
2	15	F	20
1	9	G	14
W	3	u	0

through a key stage. By converting National Curriculum levels and GCSE grades into numerical equivalents, a student's 'points score' at the end of one key stage can be used to predict their grades at the end of the next key stage (see Table 17.2 and Figure 17.1).

Consider Pupil A, who achieved English level 4, mathematics level 5 and science level 4 in their Key Stage 3 SATs. This equates to a total points score of 87 and, therefore, an average Key Stage 3 points score of 29. When plotted on the progression line this would generate a prediction of 250 points in her best eight GCSE grades (the median capped points score). In contrast, Pupil B achieved an average points score of 49 and, therefore, a prediction of 450 points at GCSE.

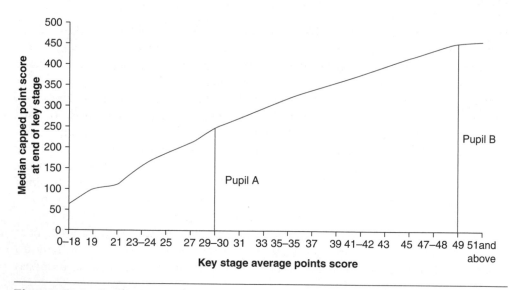

Figure 17.1 Predicting grades

Table 17.3   Adjustments to pupil points predictions

Characteristic	Rationale
Gender	Different rates of progress are made by boys and girls. Adjustments are made for all females in a cohort.
Special educational needs	SEN pupils, whether identified by the LA or the school, have different progression rates. Adjustments are made for all pupils identified as such within the cohort.
Ethnicity	Different ethnic groups have different rates of progress. Adjustments are made for 19 ethnic groups identified in the census data.
Eligible for free school meals (FSM)	FSM pupils often make less progress, but this is heavily influenced by ethnic group. Both factors are therefore used to make adjustments.
First language	Children whose first language is not English make different rates of progress. This is especially true for those with low levels of prior attainment. Thus both factors are used to adjust predictions.
Mobility	Pupils who move schools during a key stage have their predictions adjusted to take account of the differences in progress made by such students.
Age	The youngest pupils in a year group will not make the same progress as those born at the beginning of a school year. Adjustments are made according to a pupil's date of birth.
In care	Adjustments are made to each pupil's points prediction if they have been in care during the key stage.
IDACI	The Income Deprivation Affecting Children Index is a measure of deprivation based on a pupil's postcode. Adjustments are made according to the size of the IDACI indicator for each child in the school.

At the end of Year 11, if Pupil A gained results with a capped points equivalent of 300, she has exceeded her prediction. This would result in a *positive* score of 50. Pupil B, however, despite achieving considerably better grades only achieved a capped points total of 400, a *negative* score of 50.

This is known as *value added analysis*. By averaging the positive and negative scores of all pupils in a cohort, each school can be awarded a *value added score* for its results at the end of a key stage. Consequently, a school with a small percentage of pupils gaining five plus A* to C grades and a positive value added score could be regarded as outperforming a school with a large percentage of five plus A* to C grades and a negative value added score.

In recent years, this value added score has been further refined to take account of the social and economic context of the institution. The census data collected electronically from a school's computer management system contains details of every pupil on roll. Adjustments are made to pupil points predictions according to the characteristics shown in Table 17.3.

This complex statistical manipulation of the data is known as *contextual value added analysis* (CVA). Since 2005, all schools are awarded a CVA score for progression across different key stages.

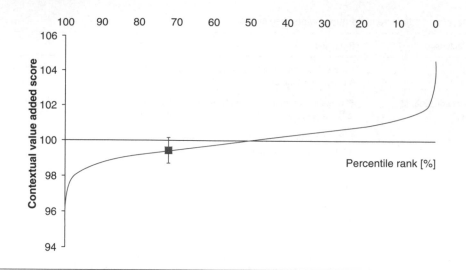

Figure 17.2(a)   Primary School A: KSI–2 overall CVA (Cohort = 15, CVA score = 99.4)

The averaging of positive and negative scores could lead to overall negative results, consequently, zero CVA scores are repositioned at 100 (Key Stage 2 and 3) or 1,000 (Key Stage 4). A school awarded a CVA score of 95 at Key Stage 3 would be considered as not achieving its predicted results, while a school with a CVA score of 105 would be regarded as exceeding predictions. Because this measure is 'contextualised' to take account of differences in both academic ability and social circumstances, the DCFS believe this form of analysis enables them to accurately judge the relative performance of a wide variety of different schools.

Thus the CVA score leads to schools being given a national percentile ranking for their achievements. These are represented on graphs similar to those shown in Figures 17.2 (a–c).

Primary School A achieved a CVA score of 99.4 for the Key Stage 2 SAT results of its 15 pupils. This gives it a national percentile ranking of 73 (see Figure 17.2(a)). Notice the bars that protrude above and below the square positional indicator. This is known as the *confidence interval* and is a measure of the statistical significance of the results. As the top bar intersects the 100 line this score would be considered satisfactory.

Primary School B has been awarded a CVA score of 100.4 for the SATs results of its 27 pupils. This merits a percentile ranking of 34 (see Figure 17.2(b)). While this appears to be a much better performance, because the bottom bar of the confidence interval intersects the 100 line, these results are not significantly better than School A and should also be regarded as satisfactory.

With such small cohorts, factors such as the long-term illness of one or two children could markedly affect a school's results. Consequently, as these two examples demonstrate, relatively small changes in a CVA score can have a disproportionate effect on the

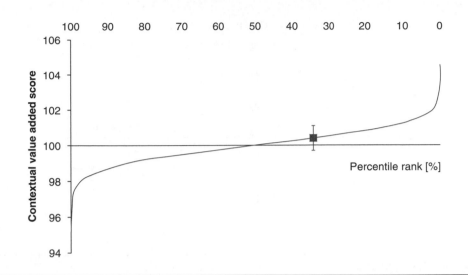

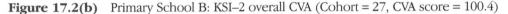

Figure 17.2(b)   Primary School B: KSI–2 overall CVA (Cohort = 27, CVA score = 100.4)

national percentile ranking and, therefore, illustrate the need to take account of the confidence interval when judging performance.

In contrast, the GCSE performance of the 192 pupils in Secondary School C generated a CVA score of 975 and a percentile ranking of 93 (see Figure 17.2(c)). As the confidence bars do not intersect the 1,000 line this would be regarded as significant under-achievement at Key Stage 4.

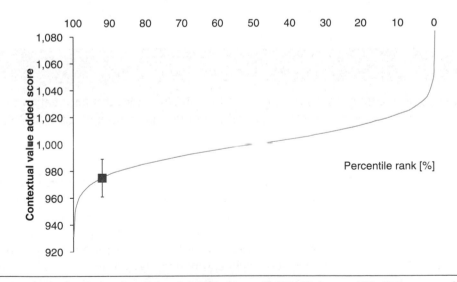

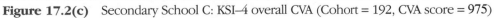

Figure 17.2(c)   Secondary School C: KSI–4 overall CVA (Cohort = 192, CVA score = 975)

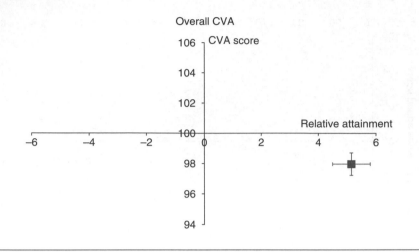

Figure 17.3   Quadrant graph

Relative performance is also illustrated on *quadrant graphs* as shown in Figure 17.3. Here the relative attainment of the cohort at the start of a key stage is compared with the CVA score achieved by the same students at the end of the key stage. So, for example, a positional indicator in the bottom right-hand quadrant as in Figure 17.3 would indicate that, while the school had an intake of above average ability, those pupils had not achieved their expected results. If the confidence bars did not intersect either axis this would be considered to be significant under-achievement.

INDIVIDUAL REFLECTION

Consider the three quadrant graphs in Figures 17.4 (a–c). What does this information tell you about each of the three schools? Where could you focus an improvement strategy?

Despite the continued attempts to refine the ways in which the performance of schools is measured, the initial 'headline' figures of the early league tables remain, in the minds of the public at large, the most significant measure of a school's effectiveness. Perhaps, with the complexity of CVA analysis, this is inevitable. Remember, however, judging a school only by its examination results shows you little about the progress its pupils are making or the quality of learning and teaching within its classrooms.

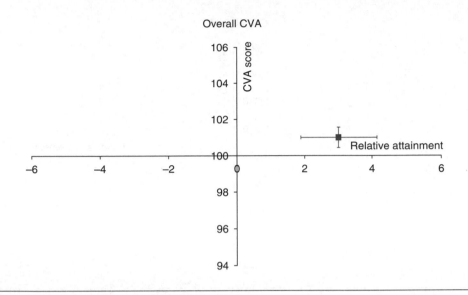

Figure 17.4(a)   Primary School A

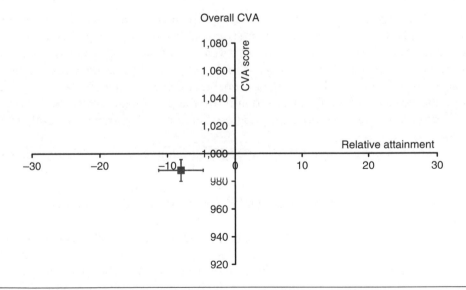

Figure 17.4(b)   Secondary School B

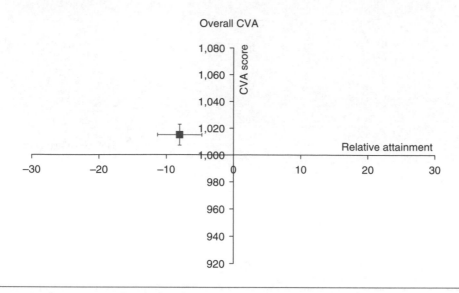

Figure 17.4(c)   Secondary School C

How schools assess their own performance – the measurement and comparison of progression

Today's performance data runs to many pages. Percentile rankings and quadrant analyses are applied not only to each key stage but to the core subjects of English, Mathematics and Science. Similarly, the achievements of the pupils you have taught are delineated by gender, ethnicity, free school meals and special educational needs. Detailed consideration of this information enables a school to identify areas of strength and weakness and to formulate plans to improve the performance of future cohorts. It tells them little, however, about the progress being made by pupils currently in the school.

In recent years, the majority of educational institutions have introduced further systems to monitor the academic progress each student makes as they pass through the school. By doing so potential under-achievement can be spotted early and interventions taken to ensure that individual pupils achieve or exceed the grades expected of them.

The Fischer Family Trust (FFT) is a registered charity undertaking and supporting projects addressing the development of education in the United Kingdom. The FFT Data Analysis Project provides statistical information to assist local authorities and schools in the monitoring of performance. Each year a school will receive FFT data about the children currently on roll. This data includes predictions about each pupil's performance in future key stages and the performance of the school.

National Curriculum Level	4	5	5	5	5	5	5	5	5	5	5	6
FFT fine grade	4.9	5.0	5.1	5.2	5.3	5.4	5.5	5.6	5.7	5.8	5.9	6.0
School sub-level	4a	5c	5c	5c	5c	5b	5b	5b	5a	5a	5a	6c

Figure 17.5   Presentation of FFT data

While still using national progression lines, the individual predictions are presented in a more 'user friendly' format. Instead of points scores the predictions are presented as National Curriculum levels or GCSE grades. These predictions are also broken down into 'fine grade' levels. This is often reinterpreted by schools as three 'sub-levels' using the suffix a, b or c after each level (see Figure 17.5). With the majority of pupils improving by less than one National Curriculum level in one academic year, the use of fine grading or sub-levels is popular, because they facilitate the measurement of progress.

These data are presented in four versions. Type A data comprises predictions based solely on the prior attainment and gender of each pupil. Type B data contextualises this data to take account of the social context of the school. Type C data adds to these predictions to create the grades that would be required to meet national and local targets. Type D data takes the contextualised predictions and adjusts them to match the results achieved by the top 25 per cent of schools.

The senior managers of a school will select the data type most appropriate to their institution and from those predictions formulate *performance targets* at different levels throughout the organisation (see Figure 17.6).

FFT data is used extensively at the primary and secondary level to set targets for the local authority, the school and individual pupils. As teachers you must remember, however, that these predictions are based on prior attainment. At the pupil level this could be problematic. A child who attended a successful primary school whose parents prepared her for the Key Stage 2 examinations may achieve excellent grades and, therefore, be predicted to achieve the highest levels at Key Stage 3. In contrast, however, she could have attended a school with a history of under-achievement and live in less supportive circumstances. Her attainment may be lower and, consequently, her FFT predictions reduced.

Many schools, therefore, also use mechanisms to generate pupil predictions based not on prior attainment but on a standardised measure of academic potential. The Centre for Education Management (CEM) based at the University of Durham provides predictive systems known as MidYIS, YELLIS and ALIS which can be used at different key stages. The most commonly used, however, are the cognitive ability tests (CATs) provided by the National Foundation for Education Research (NFER). These are usually attempted in the first few weeks of secondary school.

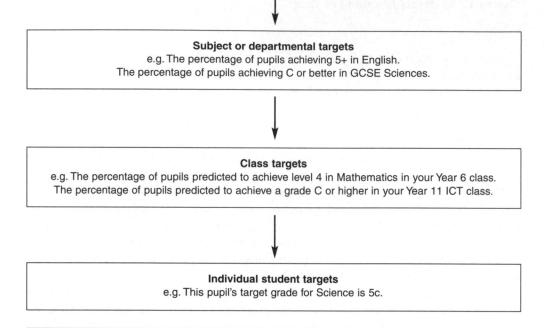

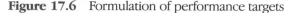

Figure 17.6   Formulation of performance targets

The CATs require pupils to sit three papers on three consecutive days: Paper 1, the Verbal Test, attempts to assess a child's linguistic ability; Paper 2, the Quantitative Test, is a measure of numerical ability, while Paper 3, the Non-Verbal Test, gauges spatial reasoning and sequential decision-making.

Each test is given a numerical score and all three tests are averaged to give an overall measure known as the Standard Age Score (SAS). In all cases, a score of 100 would be regarded as the result for a student of average ability.

Consider Figure 17.7. Pupil A has an SAS of 100 with a similar score in all areas; she could be regarded as a student of average ability. The results for Pupil B would be commensurate with a pupil of greater academic potential. Her score for the Quantitative paper, however, indicates that her numerical ability is only slightly above average. In contrast, Pupil C has achieved scores that suggest her academic potential is significantly lower. The Quantitative score is better than her other results, indicating that, for this pupil, numeracy is a strength.

Pupil	Verbal score	Quantitative score	Non-verbal score	Standard age score
A	99	101	100	100
B	118	108	120	115
C	79	95	78	84

Figure 17.7   Calculation of SAS

Pupil	FFT KS3 English	FFT KS3 Maths	FFT KS3 Science	CATs SAS	NFER KS3 English	NFER KS3 Maths	NFER KS3 Science
A	5a	5c	5b	102	5b	5b	5b
B	4a	4a	4b	120	6c	6b	6c
C	6b	6c	6b	92	4a	4a	5c

Figure 17.8   Predictive data

In addition to this raw statistical data, the NFER will convert individual scores into predicted grades for end of key stage SATs and GCSE examinations. Individual schools will use their own unique combination of FFT predictors, CAT scores and CAT predictors to generate targets for their pupils. As teachers it is important that you remember the essential distinction between the two sources of data. Predictions made from prior attainment are fundamentally different from those made from assessments of academic potential. When presented with predictive data for the pupils in your class, only by understanding how this information has been generated can you make appropriate judgements about their abilities.

> ### GROUP EXERCISE
>
> Consider the predictive data given in Figure 17.8. What does this information tell you about each pupil? Judge the information individually, and then share your judgements with members of your group. Do you all agree?

How teachers can use data to improve the performance of their pupils – ensuring progression

As Farmer Giles knows: 'Weighing pigs don't fatten them'. Prior attainment data and predictions of ability provide you with the information you require to make judgements about the potential of each individual pupil. This, however, is just the starting point. Using the data to ensure children meet or exceed their potential is one of the major tenets for effective teaching in today's schools.

As described above, the vast majority of schools now use predictive data to generate end of key stage targets for their pupils. These are often referred to as *minimum target grades* (MTGs). Sometimes these predictions will be used to set or stream pupils into different ability groups. Equally often, your class will be of 'mixed ability'. In either case, you can use the statistical data to assess the range of ability within your teaching groups and pitch the content of each lesson at a level appropriate to the students' abilities.

For example, when you are writing schemes of work and planning individual lessons it is useful to compare the statistical data with National Curriculum levels and subject specifications. By doing so it is easier to generate lesson objectives and learning outcomes that focus on the knowledge and skills required of the pupils if they are to meet or exceed their target grades. In this way, statistical data can facilitate more effective differentiation by generating different learning outcomes for different sets or individual children within a mixed ability group.

Application to teaching

Imagine you are teaching a similar topic to classes of different ability. In the first group the average MTG is 3c, in the second it is 5a. Use the National Curriculum level descriptors for your subject specialism to write lesson objectives and learning outcomes for a topic with which you are familiar. A more challenging task is to write differentiated outcomes for a mixed ability class with pupils whose targets range from 3c to 5a.

Recent government initiatives designed to improve the effectiveness of teaching stress the importance of lesson objectives and learning outcomes for ensuring pupil progression. The outcomes for each lesson can be viewed as the rungs on the ladder each child needs to climb as they move through a topic. At the end of each unit of work, you can measure the pupil's progress by a formal or informal assessment of the learning outcomes you have generated. In this way you can judge if individual pupils are on course to meet or exceed their targets. More importantly, however, by identifying those learning outcomes that have been forgotten or misunderstood, you can identify potential barriers to progress and apply intervention strategies to get the young person 'back on track'.

As teachers, therefore, you will be expected not only to be familiar with the levels of attainment each of your students is expected to achieve by the end of their current key stage, you will also be expected to accurately judge the progress your pupils are making towards achieving these targets and identify areas for improvement. An understanding of the ways in which statistical data are generated can help you to meet these expectations but it can also provide an important perspective on the whole process.

You must always remember that these statistically generated targets are just predictions. While they may have the validity of large numbers at the local authority or whole-school level, they can only be regarded as a rough guide when considering each individual pupil. Predictions made from a child's performance in a few hours of written testing over a limited period of time can never be more than a snapshot that could easily be affected by factors such as illness, bereavement, the misreading of a major question or even lucky guessing! Teachers who know their pupils well soon become aware of those children who are not being stretched because their targets are set too low or, conversely, are developing a sense of failure because their targets are unrealistically high. By understanding the limitations of the data, you should feel able to temper your expectations of these pupils accordingly. However useful statistical data have become, they can never replace the professional judgement of the effective classroom teacher.

Summary

- The performance of all public sector schools is assessed annually. The most important figure in assessing a school's effectiveness is its CVA score.

- Most schools set targets at all levels of the institution using predictions generated by the Fischer Family Trust or NFER CATs.

- As a teacher, you will almost certainly have performance targets for your classes and the individual pupils they contain. You will be expected to regularly assess your pupils to see if they are on course to achieve their predicted grades and identify the areas for improvement for those students who are not 'on target'.

Key reading

Ealing Grid for Learning (EGfL):

- *Understanding RAISEonline: Primary schools* (pdf)
- *Understanding RAISEonline: Secondary schools* (pdf)

Available at: www.egfl.org.uk/categories/admin/data/raise.html

Fischer Family Trust (2007) *Using the FFT database and online reports*. Available online at: www.fischertrust.org/downloads/dap/Training/A_school_guide_to_usingFFT_databases_and_online_reports.pdf

References and bibliography

Association of School and College Leaders (2007) *Understanding RAISEonline*. ASCL Publication

DCFS (2006) *Value added technical information*. Available online at: www.dcfs.gov.uk/performance tables/school_ 06/s8.shtml

Douglas, J.W.B. (1964) *The home and the school*. London: Panther

Fischer Family Trust (2007) *Using the FFT database and online reports*. Available online at: www.fischertrust.org/downloads/dap/Training/A_school_guide_to_using_FFT_databases_and_online_reports.pdf

Webber, R. and Butler, T. (2005) *Classifying pupils by where they live: how well does this predict variations in GCSE results?*. London: UCL Working Paper Series, Paper 99.

CHAPTER 18

SENSIBLE USE OF ICT IN TEACHING AND LEARNING

John McComish

Standards addressed

Q16 Have passed the professional skills tests in numeracy, literacy and information and communication technology (ICT).

Q17 Know how to use skills in literacy, numeracy and ICT to support their teaching and wider professional activities.

Q23 Design opportunities for learners to develop their literacy, numeracy and ICT skills.

Introduction

Most teachers are able to, and do, use ICT first and last as a tool, either in the preparation of lessons, in teaching or in learning exercises. For you as a trainee teacher, it is there to support and enhance your professional experience and should be an enabler for your students. The question most often asked is – when should I use ICT? The equally important question, and in many cases the more appropriate one, is – when should I not use ICT? All too often this question and its answers, which may be unpopular, are ignored, with the accompanying suspension of sound teaching and learning.

Promoting ICT

Some of the worst teaching and learning experiences can be those in which making use of ICT was the sole purpose of the lesson. If you are using ICT just to 'tick the box', then this is a misuse of resources. Most teachers try to use ICT for sound pedagogical reasons, and are often very inventive in its use, basing it on sound subject knowledge. They are able to bring new ideas to their pupils' classroom experience in both the subject and the pupils' experience of sensible application of ICT skills. In your placement school(s), and in your first teaching post, there will be an ICT coordinator, part of whose role will be to promote the use of ICT in lessons in all areas of the school curriculum. In some areas, this is easy. No one needs to tell teachers of science, mathematics and English the advantages of using ICT. All too often the only problem is finding sufficient available ICT equipment to enable its use in enough of these lessons. Demand in these subjects is always likely to outstrip supply. Other areas of the curriculum have, until recently, been more reluctant to engage with the new technology, preferring a more traditional pedagogical approach, with the notable exception of a few pioneers who were not afraid to take the plunge.

Recent changes

Any difficulties in enthusing teachers in the use of ICT in their subject have been mitigated by a number of factors in recent years. These include:

- the increased emphasis on teacher use of ICT in DfEE Circular 4/98 (Annexe B; Initial Teacher Training National Curriculum for the use of Information and Communications Technology in Subject Teaching);
- the substantial impact of initiatives such as New Opportunities Fund (NOF) training;

- the promotion of 'ICT Across the Curriculum' (ICTAC); and
- the requirements for all current teachers to be able to use ICT in their subject, and their wider professional experience, when qualifying to teach.

Most teachers, including all NQTs, are now aware of the advantages of using ICT. They are routinely looking for ways they can use it to enhance, expand and develop the learning experiences of children and young people and contribute to an improved learning environment for them.

Improved resources

With static ICT resources, such as purpose-built ICT rooms, it was often too much of a problem to relocate pupils to the other side of a building or campus, without adequate prior notice. This disruption often accounted for the loss of a substantial part of lessons. Much has changed with the arrival of relatively cheap laptops that can be networked to servers and other peripherals such as printers. Most school networks allow pupils the possibility of logging on at any non-admin computer on a site and continuing with their previous work. In addition, increasingly, schools are developing wireless systems. The possibility even exists for progressive schools to allow pupils access to their stored files off-campus, i.e. when children and young people are at home or, for that matter, anywhere with a suitable connection. This type of access – though possible – has drawbacks that some schools and colleges may not wish to consider until they have worked through the many pros and cons. Unfortunately, when you open up access to a site you have to control it. With the arrival of virtual learning environments (VLEs) such as Blackboard, WebCT and Moodle, many of these problems *may be* overcome.

Increased access

A portable 'suite' of laptops with printer can now be set up for between £10,000 and £20,000. This would purchase 20–25 computers of a suitable specification on a secure trolley with a printer. The price is dependent on the specification of laptop and printer, but would mean a secure lockable resource that can then be taken to the students or departments. The use of ICT will then take place in a familiar environment for the teacher and their students, with minimal disruption.

> **A thought**
>
> If you have portable departmental resources, who will make sure the laptops stay charged? Who will maintain them? These are key questions that need answering *before* the resources are purchased rather than as an afterthought.

The heart of the curriculum

ICT is at the heart of the curriculum in both ITE and in all subjects taught in schools and colleges. (The QTS skills tests, including ICT, must now be passed before you begin your first teaching post.) Its place is enshrined due to the positive impact it has on pupils'/students' work (Ofsted 2005). Children and young people now have access to data/information from a wide range of sources that were previously inaccessible outside of higher education. Prior to the routine use of ICT in schools and colleges and their connection to the Internet, such access was not possible other than by going to national or regional resource centres for materials.

ICT enhances presentation skills and enables pupils to access an enormous array of resources. This can be distracting. The emphasis must be on teaching students to discriminate between reliable and less trustworthy sources and to constantly challenge the validity of all materials that they access.

All too frequently the missing element in ICT is creativity! This is more often than not sacrificed in favour of the functional use of ICT for some mechanical objective. Pupils are thus denied a channel for their skills or abilities. Word processing is not just about using the application; it's also about preventing the slavish use of the application from impairing students' creative abilities. If they're worrying about how to use the package, then their efforts will be diverted away from their creative input. This can easily be corrected, early in a pupil's education, if they are taught to use important software such as word processors efficiently and correctly.

So why do we use ICT in lessons?

ICT is a teaching resource that is able to accommodate the needs of all types of learners. If you examine the classifications of those who seek to identify learners according to their learning styles (such as VAK or VARK, or Gardner's multiple intelligences) then the incorporation of ICT is easily achieved in most of the models. It is after all merely a tool, an enabler. How it is applied to a given situation is up to the individual teacher or learner. It's their choice.

Cox *et al.* (1999), in a paper to the British Education Research Association (BERA), looked at the reasons for using ICT in teaching in all phases from primary to tertiary. Her findings were that ICT is a positive influence for a number of reasons. Her studies have dealt with the complex psychology of using ICT in the classroom and asserted the advantages and value of the use of ICT at all key stages and in all subjects.

ICT should be used for a variety of reasons. For example, some topics can only be studied with any safety or efficiency by using ICT. Pupils would be unable to study dangerous chemical reactions or look at the effects of altering the variables in, say, a nuclear reactor in any other way. They can also propose 'what if' scenarios in several subject areas. In addition, ICT …

- is a National Curriculum requirement in terms of appropriate use in all subject areas;
- is a great motivator;
- gives teachers and pupils another method/approach for teaching traditional topic areas;
- can bring a new dynamic to the learning environment;
- can provide children with more control over their learning environment and empower them to become more independent learners;
- can enhance pupils' presentation skills and thus increase their self-esteem and therefore motivate them in other areas of their work.

GROUP EXERCISE

In your group, discuss ways you could use ICT in the different phases in a lesson. Consider the materials available on the web for obtaining starter materials for your subject.

Try www.teachers-direct.co.uk. On the left-hand pane select 'free resources' and then choose the 'Quizbusters' option. Select one of the existing quizzes and try it within your group.

Discuss how you would integrate it into a lesson plan. Discuss its best position in such a plan. List what you think are the possible advantages and disadvantages and then share these within the group.

Discuss ways in which this resource might contribute to teaching and learning in your lesson. Devise a quiz of your own using the design option. Once you've tried this in a lesson, reflect on it – did it work? did it add anything? was your lesson better with it?

It is vital that ICT is seen as a tool to be used as part of an array. It is not a panacea – it does not eliminate all known problems like some pedagogical bleach. Look at some of the hype that surrounds technology and its use in the media and the sort of claims that have constantly resurfaced since ICT was first promoted as a useful teaching aid/resource in the late 1980s. There were unfounded fears that teachers would be replaced by computers. As David Thornburg famously said: 'Any teacher that can be replaced by a computer, deserves to be.' His comment is just as true today. Despite the views of some zealots to the contrary, 'ICT is no more about computers and pro-grams, than astronomy is about telescopes', to paraphrase E.W. Dijkstra, a philosopher on computing.

Application to teaching

Consider lessons that you've taught involving ICT and also those where you haven't. How would you teach the lessons differently? Would you use ICT differ-ently in future? Look at some of the freely available word search packages on the web, for example: www.teachers-direct.co.uk/resources/wordsearches/index.aspx. Devise a word search for the lesson you're going to teach. Decide in what phase of the lesson you would use it. Would you use it interactively, online or as a printed exercise, perhaps as a homework task?

Look at your lesson plans and try to identify areas where you can use ICT. Ask members of your department and the ICT staff at your school or college for advice. Outline your plans. Consider:

» Is the topic suitable? Could you deliver this topic better in another way?
» Are there sufficient resources for the task(s)?
» Have you the necessary skills to deliver your plan?
» Will you have support if necessary?

When should I use ICT?

Think about why you want to use ICT. Have clear aims and clearly defined goals. If you make these achievable by both you and your pupils then you both win and the rein-forcement that takes place is positive. Don't let the ICT component of a lesson obstruct the learning objectives for the subject or for that matter cloud them or rank them of less importance. If you bolt the ICT onto the lesson for effect or for little reason other than to 'do something' with or on the computers your department has obtained (no doubt after much wrangling and submitting of bids), then you belittle their use and seek out opportunities to fail rather than promote your subject and its use of ICT. You also end up with an outcome where it's obvious to all that you contrived to use ICT for no good reason. The most important aspect of your teaching is subject – even if you are an ICT teacher!

Identify your aims, objectives and learning outcomes for the lesson. Establish how ICT will be used to help you to achieve the targets. Don't reinvent the wheel! Look for sites run by LAs and by those that promote subject use of ICT. Here, with a small amount of effort, you may save yourself a lot of work. Many of these subject sites are run as members-only sites. You gain access by registering, and in some cases downloads are totally free. Other sites may require you to send in work of your own in exchange. By sharing the load the burden becomes less for all. It also stops a lot of duplication of effort. Integrate the ICT into the lesson so that it fits neatly and logically like any of the other phases. It should flow seamlessly and with practice it will!

A thought

If, for example, you're a geography, history or business teacher and you want to do some work on data handling, there is a whole treasure trove of data available out there in census materials or in climate and demographic databanks. Go to your ICT department and ask them for advice *before* you take the plunge. They can advise you on strategy and tactics here as well as on the availability of suitable resources. One thing ICT will make easier is communication. Look for subject wikis and/or blogs. Start one of your own! There is a lot of help available out there. Don't be afraid to ask!

ICT in the classroom

ICT can be used by the teacher alone to demonstrate or present, or in a whole-class strategy to allow hands-on use by the pupils. The use of ICT is limited only by you. Any restrictions to your inventiveness are self-imposed. All too frequently the motivator for the teacher here is fear of making a mistake or of 'making a fool of themselves'. This is a powerful agent against innovation. Training or a little practice can pay dividends many times over here. A little practice on your own or with a supportive audience can mean the difference between success and catastrophe. It is not a good idea to try something out for the very first time with your worst class. That begs failure. You would not attempt to fly a plane without at least using a flight simulator first. While the outcome may not be as crucial, less ICT-savvy teachers might fear their lesson crashing just as much as they would the plane.

Children mostly have no fear. They will and do try things out. By a process of elimination they eventually find a way that works – a valid learning strategy. The only difference is that children will try things out in class. They have no face to lose. No one expects them to be perfect. Children will forgive teachers if they attempt something,

fail, then eventually get it right. It reveals not only their frailties, but also their human-
ity. It can be a way to build relationships. The traditional Confucian paradigm – with the
teacher as the master of all and the fount of all knowledge – is directly confronted by
ICT. ICT shifts the focus of their efforts and enables the pupils to direct their learning
and research. Your function is to help them do so productively, effectively and, with
your guidance, selectively.

INDIVIDUAL REFLECTION

Consider your ICT skills level.

- How comprehensive do you think your individual ICT skills are? Have you identified any skills gaps? How do you *know* what skills level you have? Can you identify your areas of strength and weakness?
- Could you apply these skills to enhance the teaching and learning of children and young people in your care?
- What do you need to do to develop your skills level to that needed, or become expert in the skills area(s) of choice?
- When are you going to arrange training to bring yourself up to the required level?
- Have you included these as targets in your action plans or CEDP?
- Use these questions to help you put together an action plan for the short, medium and long term.

What do I teach?

Children and young people need to be taught both how to use ICT applications and
when to use them. From frequent studies and the reports that they generate (Ofsted
2005) ICT has been shown to be most effectively taught and deployed by both teachers
and learners using a hybrid model where pupils are taught the skills required in specialist ICT lessons, skills that are then more effectively applied when they encounter
opportunities to do so in lessons.

Much government funding has gone into providing teachers with support materials
to use in their teaching. The websites which contain materials related to ICTAC are
numerous. There are excellent resources from government sites as well as local initiatives from the many local authorities (LAs) (the Standards and Kirklees sites listed at the
end of the chapter, for example). Most are freely available to order as hard copy or
download in a number of standard formats.

There are also websites containing lesson plans, exercises and a variety of other
teaching resources, freely shared by other professionals, for you to use and develop

which will enrich the learning experience of your pupils. You may need to register at some of these sites if you are to gain access. They are usually well worth it.

Summary

- ICT is a tool that should be used only when it is going to be effective.
- Avoid using ICT 'for its own sake'.
- Use ICT creatively.
- Teach both how to use applications and when.
- Don't be afraid to innovate.

Key reading

Cox, M.J. (1999) 'Motivating pupils through the use of ICT'. In Leask, M. and Pachler, N. (eds), *Learning to teach using ICT in the secondary school*. London: Routledge, pp. 19–35

Cox, M.J., Preston, C. and Cox, K. (1999) *What factors support or prevent teachers from using ICT in their classrooms*. Paper presented at the BERA 1999 Conference, Brighton

Ofsted (2005) *Embedding ICT in schools – a dual evaluation exercise*, HMI 2391. London: HMSO

References and bibliography

Cox, M.J. (1999) 'Motivating pupils through the use of ICT'. In Leask, M. and Pachler, N. (eds), *Learning to teach using ICT in the secondary school*. London: Routledge, pp. 19–35

Cox, M.J., Preston, C. and Cox, K. (1999) *What factors support or prevent teachers from using ICT in their classrooms*. Paper presented at the BERA 1999 Conference. Brighton

Ofsted (2005) *Embedding ICT in schools – a dual evaluation exercise*, HMI 2391. London: HMSO

Websites

www.icteachers.co.uk/resources/resources_re.htm#Buddhism (accessed 18 November 2007)
www.kirklees-ednet.org.uk/subjects/ictks3/ictac.htm (accessed 18 November 2007)
www.standards.dfes.gov.uk/secondary/keystage3/all/respub/ictac (accessed 18 November 2007)
www.teachers.tv/ (accessed 18 November 2007)

APPENDIX: LIST OF COMMON EDUCATIONAL ACRONYMS

AfL	Assessment for Learning
ALPS	Assessment and Learning in Practice Setting
APP	Assessing Pupils' Progress
AQA	Assessment and Qualifications Alliance
ASDAN	Award Scheme Development and Accreditation Network
ASK	Attitudes, Skills and Knowledge
AST	Advanced Skills Teacher
BSF	Building Schools for the Future
BTEC	Business and Technology Education Council
CARD	Choose a Real Deal
CAT	Cognitive Ability Test
CCEA	Council for Curriculum, Examinations and Assessment
CfLaT	Centre for Learning and Teaching
CIDA	Certificate in Digital Applications
CLAIT	Computer Literacy and Information Technology
CLASI	Capable, Listened to, Accepted, Safe and Included
COVE	Centre of Vocational Excellence
CPD	Continuing Professional Development
CTC	City Technology College
CUREE	Centre for the Use of Research and Evidence in Education
CVA	Contextual Value Added
DCSF	Department for Children, Schools and Families
DIDA	Diploma in Digital Applications
EAL	English as an Additional Language

EBP	Education Business Partnership
ELLI	Effective Lifelong Learning Inventory
GNVQ	General National Vocational Qualification
GTCE	General Teaching Council for England
GTP	Graduate Teacher Programme
HMI	Her Majesty's Inspector
IAG	Information Advice and Guidance
ICEDIP	Inspiration, Clarification, Evaluation, Distillation, Incubation, Perspiration
ICT	Information and Communication Technology
IEP	Individual Education Plan
ILP	Individual Learning Plan
KS	Key Stage
KTP	Knowledge Transfer Partnership
LiL	Leading in Learning
LSA	Learning Support Assistant
LSC	Learning and Skills Council
MFL	Modern Foreign Languages
MIS	Management Information System
MLD	Moderate Learning Difficulties
NCSL	National College for School Leadership
NFER	National Foundation for Educational Research
NQT	Newly Qualified Teacher
OCR	Oxford, Cambridge and RSA
P_4C	Philosophy for Children
PASS	Pupil Attitude to Self and School
PC	Personalised Curriculum
PLTS	Personal, Learning and Thinking Skills
PSHE	Personal, Social and Health Education
QCA	Qualifications and Curriculum Authority
RE	Religious Education
RSA	Royal Society for Encouragement of Arts, Manufactures and Commerce
SAPERE	Society for the Advancement of Philosophical Enquiry and Reflection in Education
SAT	Standard Assessment Task
SBEIP	South Brent Education Improvement Partnership
SEAL	Social and Emotional Aspects of Learning
SEELS	School Emotional Environment for Learning Survey
SEF	Self-Evaluation Form
SEN	Special Educational Needs
SLT	Senior Leadership Team
SMART	Specific, Measurable, Achievable, Realistic and Time-related
SMT	Senior Management Team

SPRinG	Social Pedagogic Research in Groupwork
SSAT	Specialist Schools and Academies Trust
T&L	Teaching and Learning
TDA	Training and Development Agency for Schools
TfL	Teaching for Learning
TLR	Teaching and Learning Responsibility
TLRP	Teaching and Learning Research Programme
TSPC	Thinking Skills and Personal Capabilities
VLE	Virtual Learning Environment
YST	Youth Sport Trust
ZPD	Zone of Proximal Development

BIBLIOGRAPHY AND FULL LIST OF REFERENCES

Assessment and Qualifications Alliance (AQA) see: www.aqa.org.uk

Assessment Reform Group (1999) *Assessment for learning: beyond the black box*. University of Cambridge, Faculty of Education.

Assessment Reform Group (2002) *Assessment for Learning: 10 principles to guide classroom practice*. Assessment Reform Group.

Association for School and College Leaders (2007) *Understanding RAISEonline*. ASCL Publication.

Berry, J. (2007) *Teachers' legal rights and responsibilities*. University of Hertfordshire Press.

Birkett, V. (2003) *How to support and teach children with special educational needs*. LDA McGraw-Hill Children's Publishing.

Black, P. and Wiliam, D. (1998, 2001) 'BERA Final Draft'. *Inside the black box. Raising standards through classroom assessment*. London: Kings College. Available online at: http://ditc.missouri.edu/docs/blackBox.pdf.

Blanden, J. and Machin, S. (2007) *Recent changes in intergenerational mobility in Britain*. London: Sutton Trust.

Blandford, S. (2000) *Managing professional development in schools*. London: Routledge.

Blandford, S. (2001) 'Professional development in schools'. In Banks, A. and Mayers, A.S. (eds), *Early professional development for teachers*. London: David Fulton.

Boston, K. (2006) *Tipping points in education and skills*. Speech to QCA Annual Review 2006. Available at: www.qca.org.uk/qca_11280.aspx.

Boud, D. (1995) *Enhancing learning through self assessment*. RoutledgeFalmer.

Bruner, J. (1960) *The process of education*. Cambridge, MA: Harvard University Press.

Bruner, J. (1996) *The culture of education*. Cambridge, MA: Harvard University Press.

Burton, D. and Bartless, S. (2005) *Practitioner research for teachers*. London: Paul Chapman.

Butroyd, R. (2007) 'Denial and distortion of instrumental and intrinsic value in the teaching of Science and English: its impact upon fifteen Year 10 teachers'. *Forum*, 49 (3), 313–329.

Butroyd, R. and Somekh, B. (1999) *Research into values in secondary education*, Report to the Gordon Cook Foundation. University of Huddersfield.

Buzan, T. (1995) *Use your head*. London: BBC Books.

Cairns, J. (2000) 'Schools, community and the developing values of young adults: towards an ecology of education in values'. In Cairns, J., Gardiner, R. and Lawton, D. (eds), *Values and the curriculum*. London. Woburn Press, pp. 52–73.

Caldwell, B. and Spinks, J. (1998) *Beyond the self-managing school*. London: Falmer Press.

Carr, D. (2003) *Making sense of education*. London: Routledge.

Cassen, R. and Kingon, G. (2007) 'Tackling low educational achievement'. Cited in Hirsch, D. (2007) *Experiences of poverty and educational disadvantage*. York: Joseph Rowntree Foundation. Available online at: www.jrf.org.uk.

City and Guilds: www.cityandguilds.com.

Cooper, H. and Hedges, L.V. (eds) (1994) *The handbook of research synthesis*. New York: Russell Sage Foundation.

Cox, M.J. (1999) 'Motivating pupils through the use of ICT'. In Leask, M. and Pachler, N. (eds), *Learning to teach using ICT in the secondary school*. London: Routledge, pp. 19–35.

Cox, M.J., Preston, C. and Cox, K. (1999) *What factors support or prevent teachers from using ICT in their classrooms*. Paper presented at the BERA 1999 Conference, Brighton.

Crick, B. (1998) *Education for citizenship and the teaching of democracy in schools*. London: QCA.

Crowley, S. (2006) *Getting the buggers to behave*, 3rd edition. London: Continuum.

Cullingford, C. (1990) *The nature of learning*. London: Cassell.

Cullingford, C. (1991) *The inner world of the school*. London: Cassell.

Cullingford, C. (2006) 'Children's own vision of schooling'. *Education 3–13*, 34 (3), 211–221.

Day, C. (2002) 'Revisiting the purposes of continuing professional development'. In Trorey, G. and Cullingford, C. (eds), *Professional development and institutional needs*. Aldershot: Ashgate.

Day, C. (2004) *A passion for teaching*. London: RoutledgeFalmer.

Day, C., Kington, A., Stobart, G. and Sammons, P. (2006) 'The personal and professional lives of teachers: stable and unstable identities'. *British Educational Research Journal*, 32 (4), 601–616.

DCFS (2006) *Value added technical information*. Available online at: www.dcfs.gov.uk/performancetables/school_06/s8.shtml.

Department for Children, Schools and Families (DCFS) – see: www.standards.dfes.gov.uk/locate.

Dewey, J. (1966) *Democracy in education*. New York: Free Press.

DfEE (1999) *The National Curriculum: handbook for primary teachers in England*. London: DfEE/QCA.

DfES (1999) *School teachers' pay and conditions 1999*. Available online at: www.dfes.gov.uk/publications/guidanceonthelaw/12_99/paycondoc99d9.doc.

DfES (2004) *Removing barriers to achievement: the government's strategy for SEN*. London: DfES.

DfES (2004) *Pedagogy and practice: teaching and learning in secondary schools*. London: HMSO (Unit 18: Improving the Climate for Learning, and Unit 20: Classroom Management).

DfES (2004) *Pedagogy and practice: Unit 12: Assessment for learning*. London: DfES.

DfES (2005) *Every Child Matters: common core of skills and knowledge for the children's workforce*. Available at: www.everychildmatters.gov.uk/.

DfES (2005) *Learning behaviour: the report of the practitioners' group on school behaviour and discipline*. London: HMSO.

DfES (2006) *Safeguarding children and safer recruitment in education*. Nottingham: DfES Publications.

DfES (2007) *Diversity and citizenship curriculum review.*

DfES (2007) *Pupil achievement tracker.* Available online at: www.standards.dfes.gov.uk/performance/pat/.

Dix, P. (2007) *Taking care of behaviour: practical skills for teachers.* Harlow: Pearson Education.

Douglas, J.W.B. (1964) *The home and the school.* London: Panther.

Edexcel – see: www.edexcel.org.uk.

Ertmer, P.A. and Newby, T.J. (1993) 'Behaviorism, cognitivism, constructivism: Comparing critical features from an instructional design perspective'. *Performance Improvement Quarterly*, 6 (4), 50–72.

Farell, T.S.C. (2004) *Reflective practice in action: 80 reflection breaks for busy teachers.* Thousand Oaks, CA and London: Corwin.

Fischer Family Trust (2006) *Using the FFT database and online reports.* Available online at: www.fischertrust.org/downloads/dap/Training/A_school_guide_to_using_FFT_databases_ and_ online_reports.pdf.

Frankham, J., Edwards-Kerr, D., Humphrey, N. and Roberts, L. (2007) 'School exclusions: learning partnerships outside mainstream education' Cited in Hirsch, D. (2007) *Experiences of poverty and educational disadvantage.* York: Joseph Rowntree Foundation. Available online at: www.jrf.org.uk.

Fuller, F. (1969) 'Concerns of teachers: a developmental conceptualization'. *American Educational Research Journal*, 6, 207–226.

Ghaye, T. and Ghaye, K. (1998) *Teaching and learning through critical reflective practice.* London: David Fulton.

Gilbert, C. (2006) *Report of the Teaching and Learning in 2020 Review Group.* DfES. Available to download from: *http://publications.teachernet.gov.uk.*

Goodson, I.F. and Hargreaves, A. (1996) *Teachers' professional lives.* London: Falmer Press.

Gray, J., Hopkins, D., Reynolds, D., Wilcox, B., Farrell, S. and Jesson, D. (1999) *Improving schools: performance and potential.* Buckingham: Open University Press.

GTC (2004) *Code of conduct and practice for registered teachers.* Available online at: www.gtce.org.uk.

GTC (2006) *The statement of professional values and practice for teachers.* Available online at: www.gtce.org.uk.

Hannam, A. (1998) Cited in Ruddock, J. and Flutter, J. (2000) 'Pupil participation and pupil perspective: "carving a new order of experience"'. *Cambridge Journal of Education*, 30 (1), 75–89.

Hargreaves, D. (1994) 'The new professionalism: the synthesis of professional and institutional development'. *Teaching and Teacher Educator*, 10 (4), 423–438.

Harrison, J. (2007) 'The assessment of ITT Standard One, Professional Values and Practice: measuring performance or what?' *Journal of Education for Teaching*, 33 (3), 323–340.

Hegarty, S. (2000) 'Teaching as a knowledge-based activity'. *Oxford Review of Education*, 26 (3 & 4), 451–465.

Helsby, G. (1996) 'Defining and developing professionalism in English secondary schools'. *Journal of Education for Teaching*, 22 (2), 135–148.

Hirsch, D. (2007) *Experiences of poverty and educational disadvantage.* York: Joseph Rowntree Foundation. Available online at: www.jrf.org.uk/knowledge/findings/socialpolicy/2123.asp.

HMI (2005) *Citizenship in secondary schools: evidence from Ofsted inspections (2003/04)*, HMI 2335.

Holt, J. (1982) *How children fail.* New York: Delacorte/Seymour Lawrence.

Horgan, G. (2007) 'The impact of poverty on young children's experience of school' Cited in Hirsch, D. (2007) *Experiences of poverty and educational disadvantage.* York: Joseph Rowntree Foundation. Available online at: www.jrf.org.uk.

Hoyle, E. (2001) 'Teaching: prestige, status and esteem'. *Educational Management and Administration*, 29 (2), 139–152.

Hoyle, E. and John, P. (1995) *Professional knowledge and professional practice*. London: Cassell. www.nc.uk.net/nc_resources/html/inclusion.shtml.

Humphreys, M. and Hyland, T. (2002) 'Theory, practice and performance in teaching: professionalism, intuition, and jazz'. *Educational Studies*, 28 (1), 5–15.

Hutchin, V. (2006) 'Meeting individual needs'. In Bruce, T. (ed.), *Early childhood: a guide for students*. London: Sage, chapter 4.

Joyce, B., Calhoun, E. and Hopkins, D. (1997) *Models of learning – tools for teaching*. Buckingham: Open University Press.

Kolb, D.A. (1984) *Experiential learning: experience as the source of learning and development*. Englewood Cliffs, NJ: Prentice-Hall.

Leask, M. (2002) 'The student teacher's role and responsibilities'. In Capel, S., Leask, M. and Turner, T. (eds), *Learning to teach in the secondary school*. London: RoutledgeFalmer, pp. 18–28.

Lee, B. (2002) *Teaching assistants in schools: the current state of play*. Windsor: NFER.

Lee, C. (2007) *Resolving behaviour problems in your school: a practical guide for teachers and support staff*. London: Paul Chapman, chapter 5.

Lewis, P. (2007) *How we think but not in school*. Sense Publishers.

Lonergan, B.J.F. (1957) *Insight: a study of human understanding*. London: Longman.

McEntee, G.H. (2003) *At the heart of teaching: a guide to reflective practice*. New York and London: Teachers College Press.

MacGilchrist, B., Myers, K. and Reed, J. (2005) *The intelligent school*, 2nd edition. London: Sage.

Mehrabian, A. (1971) *Silent messages*. Belmont, CA: Wadsworth.

Mehrabian, A. (1981). *Silent messages: implicit communication of emotions and attitudes*, 2nd edition. Belmont, CA: Wadsworth.

Miliband, D. (2004) *Personalised learning: building a new relationship with schools*. Speech delivered at the North of England Education Conference, 8 January.

Moylett, H. (2006) 'Supporting children's development and learning'. In Bruce, T. (ed.), *Early childhood*. Sage, pp. 106–126.

Nias, J. (1989) *Primary teachers talking*. London: Routledge & Kegan Paul.

Nias, J. (1996) 'Thinking about feeling: the emotions in teaching'. *Cambridge Journal of Education*, 26 (3), 293–306.

OCR – see: www.ocr.org.uk.

Ofsted (2005) *Embedding ICT in schools – a dual evaluation exercise*, HMI 2391. London: HMSO.

Oliver, M. (1993) 'Redefining disability'. In Swain, J., Finkelstein, V., French, S. and Oliver, M. (eds), *Disabling barriers – enabling environments*. London: Open University/Sage, pp. 60–67.

Oliver, M. (1996) *Understanding disability: from theory to practice*. London: Macmillan.

Oxford, Cambridge and RSA examinations (OCR) – see: www.ocr.org.uk.

Perkins, D. (1993) 'Teaching for understanding'. *Journal of the American Federation of Teachers*, 17 (3), 28–35.

Pickering, J., Daly, C. and Pachier, N. (2007) *New designs for teachers' professional learning*. London: Bedford Way Papers.

Platt, J.A. (2002) *Peer and self-assessment: some issues and problems*. School of Social Sciences, Sussex University. Available online at: www.c-sap.bham.ac.uk/resources/project_reports/findings/ShowFinding.htm?id=Platt/1

Powell, S. and Tod, J. (2004) 'A systematic review of how theories explain learning behaviour in school contexts'. In *Research Evidence in Education Library*. London: EPPI-Centre, Social Science Research Unit, Institute of Education.

QCA (2007) – see: http://curriculum.qca.org.uk/cross-curriculum-dimensions/ index.aspx.

Rees, C. and Shepherd, M. (2005) 'Students' and assessors' attitudes towards students' self-assessment of their personal and professional behaviours'. *Medical Education*, 39 (1), 30–39.

Reimer (1971) *Peanuts*. Quoted in 'School is dead, an essay on alternatives to education'. *Interchange*, 2 (1).

RSA (2007) – see: www.rsa.org.uk/newcurriculum/.

Sachs, J. and Smith, R. (1988) 'Constructing teacher culture'. *British Journal of Sociology of Education*, 9 (4), 423–436.

Schön, D.A. (1983) *The reflective practitioner*. London: Temple Smith.

Shier, H. (2001) 'Pathways to participation: openings, opportunities and obligations'. *Children and Society*, 15 (2), 107–117.

Smith, A., Lovett, M. and Wise, D. (2003) *Accelerated learning: a user's guide.* Stafford: Network Educational Press.

Stanley, N. (2007) *Assessment*. Available online at: http://www.ict-tutors.co.uk/.

Stenhouse, L. (1975) *An introduction to curriculum research and development*. London: Heinemann.

Sussex: School of Social Sciences, Sussex University (accessed 9 November 2007).

Sutton, L., Smith, N., Dearden, C. and Middleton, S. (2007) 'A child's-eye view of social difference', Cited in Hirsch, D. (2007) *Experiences of poverty and educational disadvantage*. York: Joseph Rowntree Foundation. Available online at: www.jrf. org.uk.

Sylva, K., Melhuish, E., Sammons, P., Siraj-Blachford, I., Taggart, B. and Elliot, K. (2003) *The Effective Provision of Pre-School Education (EPPE) Project: findings from the pre-school period*. London: Institute of Education, University of London and University of Oxford.

TDA (2003) *Raising standards and tackling workload: a national agreement*. Available online at: www.tda.gov.uk/upload/resources/na_standards_workload.pdf.

TDA (2007) – see: www.tda.gov.uk/teachers/continuing professionaldevelopment/cpd (accessed 2 November 2007).

The 2020 Group (2006) *A vision for teaching and learning in 2020*. London: HMSO.

Thomson, P. and Russell, L. (2007) 'Mapping the alternatives to permanent exclusion' Cited in Hirsch, D. (2007) *Experiences of poverty and educational disadvantage*. York: Joseph Rowntree Foundation. Available online at: www.jrf.org.uk.

Turner, C. (2006) 'Informal learning and its relevance to the early professional development of teachers in secondary schools in England and Wales'. *Journal of In-service Education*, 32 (3), 301–319.

Wallace, M. and Poulson, L. (eds) (2003) *Learning to read critically in teaching and learning*. London: Sage.

Waters, M. (2007) 'New curriculum, exciting learning'. Comment, *Guardian*, 5 February.

Watson, R. (2007) *Primary progress toolkit*. www.primaryprogresstoolkit.co.uk

Webber, R. and Butler, T. (2005) *Classifying pupils by where they live: how well does this predict variations in GCSE results?*. London: UCL Working Paper Series, Paper 99.

Welding, J. (1998) 'The identification of able children in a secondary school: a study of the issues involved and their practical implications'. *Educating Able Children*, 2.

Wikeley, F., Bullock, K., Muschamp, Y. and Ridge, T. (2007) 'Educational relationships outside school: why access is important' Cited in Hirsch, D. (2007) *Experiences of poverty and educational disadvantage*. York: Joseph Rowntree Foundation. Available online at: www.jrf.org.uk.

Winch, C. (2004) 'What do teachers need to know about teaching? A critical examination of the occupational knowledge of teachers'. *British Journal of Educational Studies*, 52 (2), 180–196.

WJEC/CBAC (previously known as the Welsh Joint Education Committee) – see: www.wjec.co.uk.

Woods, P. (1979) *The divided school*. London: Routledge & Kegan Paul.

Woods, P. (ed.) (1980) *Pupil strategies: explorations in the sociology of the school*. London: Croom Helm.

Woods, P. (1990) *The happiest days? How pupils cope with school*. London: Falmer Press.

Yarker, P. (2005) 'On not being a teacher: the professional and personal costs of workforce remodelling'. *Forum*, 47 (2 & 3), 169–174.

Websites

www.assessment-reform-group.org.uk

www.dfes.gov.uk/keyskills/

www.fischertrust.org/downloads/dap/Training/A_school_guide_to_using_FFT_databases_and_online_reports.pdf

www.gtce.org.uk/publications/pub_reg

www.naa.org.uk – National Assessment Agency, responsible for National Curriculum assessment and testing at Key Stages 1, 2 and 3

www.nc.uk.net – National Curriculum online

www.parentscentre.gov.uk – information on how to help parents and carers support learners in their homework and other out-of-class learning

www.primaryprogresstoolkit.co.uk/

www.qca.org.uk – Qualifications and Curriculum Authority

www.standards.dfes.gov.uk/secondary/keystage3/all/respub/ictac

www.tda.gov.uk/ – the Standards for Qualified Teacher Status

www.tda.gov.uk/teachers/professionalstandards.aspx – the professional standards for teachers

www.teachernet.gov.uk – a government site for teachers and schools-related professionals

www.teachers.tv/

INDEX

Standards as addressed by Chapters.

Index